African Heartbeat

And a Vulnerable Fool

A novel based on a true story.

Jim Harries

WIPF & STOCK · Eugene, Oregon

Wipf and Stock Publishers
199 W 8th Ave, Suite 3
Eugene, OR 97401

African Heartbeat and A Vulnerable Fool
A Novel Based on A True Story
By Harries, Jim
Copyright©2017 Apostolos
ISBN 13: 978-1-5326-6930-9

Publication date 1/3/2019
Previously published by Apostolos, 2017

Dedicated to my brother, Tim.

CONTENTS

CHAPTER 1: HOW TO JUMP IN 8

CHAPTER 2: MY HERO 16

CHAPTER 3: SHARING MY VISION BEFORE LEAVING FOR AFRICA 19

CHAPTER 4: GIRLS 23

CHAPTER 5: ABOVE THE CLOUDS 27

CHAPTER 6: I AM DAVE 35

CHAPTER 7: DANGEROUS PUBLIC TRANSPORT 40

CHAPTER 8: END OF THE PROFIT MOTIVE 53

CHAPTER 9: RENT IS ILLEGAL 59

CHAPTER 10: THE WAY OUT 68

CHAPTER 11: SURVEY NOT FROM HEART 72

CHAPTER 12: UNIVERSITY CHALLENGE 77

CHAPTER 13: MISSIONARY TRAINING COLLEGE 91

CHAPTER 14: CUTTING WEEDS 100

CHAPTER 15: TO WARMER CLIMES 107

CHAPTER 16: PROPER MISSIONARY 113

CHAPTER 17: START A SCHOOL 125

CHAPTER 18: A TRUE BUS ADVENTURE 137

CHAPTER 19: RAISING CHILDREN 145

CHAPTER 20: ARE MISSIONARIES A NEW KIND OF FOOL? 158

CHAPTER 21: ARE YOU POOR? 180

CHAPTER 22: FINDING GOD 190

CHAPTER 23: LIFE, MONEY, EXORCISM 212

CHAPTER 24: DRUMBEATS 216

CHAPTER 25: THE *ROHO* 227

CHAPTER 26: A TRIUMPHANT ARRIVAL! 236

CHAPTER 27: THE CULTURE OF FOOTBALL 250

CHAPTER 28: HEADS ON 271

CHAPTER 29: SMALL MIRACLES 281

CHAPTER 30: ON THE STANDARDS OF EDUCATION 299

CHAPTER 31: ELECTION VIOLENCE 310

Part I

To Leap

CHAPTER 1: HOW TO JUMP IN

My name is David Candomble. As I write, I am in the USA for a period during the elections that are going on in Holima. My organization evacuated through fear there might be violence around the time of the election. I am using this period to complete a writing project.

My objective is to relate a story in which I have been closely involved. Our world today is very different to the way it was when this story begins. Amazingly, although this is as yet little known, much that I observed in Africa has contributed to the global state of affairs we have today.

My story revolves around the life of a missionary from the UK who I first met in Zambia. Before going on to the heart of his story, I want to relay something of Philo's history from his own mouth. I asked him to write a short biography for me in 2016, 18 months ago. This is his account below:

* * *

Even more merry than a graduation party, is a good business deal. Richard and I had just completed our agricultural studies together. We had become good friends since we met at the college in 1983. Richard's face was long and thin, and black hair, bushy in those days, crowned it. I was always struck by his preferred dress style. It struck me as dated. He dressed like a country gentleman; smart but baggy. Richard was more of "one of the lads" than was I. But, unlike some, he was not dependent on the approval of a crowd. He could think independently. If the crowd he was in looked like they were going to take him where he did not want to go, he would abandon them. Richard not being interested in being "one of the lads" perhaps contributed to his being married a few months after completing his studies. Perhaps that same tendency, to want to be more than a pleaser of his peers, is what caused us to be friends?

It was the evening of our graduation party, but since neither of us were drinkers, the partying was less interesting to us. Outside, the sounds of revelry dimmed. We walked. We went past a line of outbuildings into the dairy unit, various pungent smells hitting our noses, reminding us we were at an agricultural college. Leaning on parallel rails, we stood looking at some cows.

It was one of those cool, summer, picture-book nights. A crescent moon was centre piece to a sky full of stars. There was a lot of feel-good factor from having completed undergraduate studies. It was good to be alive, and it was good to be young, and it was good to be successful.

"Philo, it's fool proof," Richard told me.

"Fool proof? Yes!" I agreed. Life was good. Richard had an excellent business head.

"You have to come on board," Richard said. "You will make an excellent communicator of this new idea," he added.

One of the cows was restlessly troubling her colleague. She stood. Her neighbour mounted her.

"She's on heat," I said. "We need to tell the cowman so that she can be inseminated."

I was at that time very agriculturally in tune! I wanted to complete teacher training, then to take up Richard's offer. He could wait for a year. I could easily make £100,000 annually, he told me. His idea was a simple one: to preserve grass quality. Cows' transponders, already used to determine how much they were fed at milking time, would be used to assess grazing density, resulting in the automatic shifting of an electric fence, thus minimizing the trampling of grass, resulting in optimum grazing conditions. This was an entirely new idea. Its details were still shrouded in secrecy. Richard was already successfully marketing it.

It was flattering to be wanted. It felt good to have promising prospects. The position Richard wanted to offer me fitted well with my skills. But I was going to run into a problem.

***

It was some months after my conversation with Richard. I had taken up a course at teacher training college, and found myself struggling with a profound problem. At least, it was a problem in the sense that it would prevent me taking up Richard's offer. Sure, the promise of business success was enticing, but I could not escape something quite different which was pulling at my heart-strings. I felt the call of God.

No matter how much I might have liked to join Richard in his business, I felt God calling me elsewhere. As a result, in October of that year, I committed myself to spending my life working for the poor in the majority world.

I recall meeting with the chaplain of the teacher training college. Rob, the chaplain of the teacher training college, was an older man. His grey hair was like a picture frame to the bald top to his head. His eyebrows seemed excessively bushy. He was a little too "high church" for me. His behavior, it seemed to me, contradicted his appearance. From his physical experience, especially given his age, probably approaching sixty, one might have expected someone slow and cumbersome. He was lithe, agile, and refreshingly thoughtful. His voice was gentle, rather than chiding, as one might have expected judging from appearances.

We met mid-morning. The teacher-training college was very urban, not a quiet rural location as had been the agricultural college. I could hear the hum of traffic, apparently from all directions, coming through the window. Footsteps and scraping chairs indicated that a class was beginning below us.

"Tell me about your calling," Rob said to me after we had completed the polite conversation at the start of our time together. I felt very privileged to have this audience with him. His office, on the first floor above some of the classrooms in which I was being taught, seemed exactly how one would expect a chaplain's office to be. The old oak furnishings were a dark brown. More than one cross adorned the walls. One sensed something ancient in the very feel of the room. Rob was wearing his dog collar. All that though did not represent the way I saw myself going. I was breaking new ground. I was going to fulfil Old Testament prophecies perhaps, but in action. Certainly, I was a believer—but that did not mean I would ever have a serious interest in theology. I certainly was not interested in anything that smacked of stuffy churchiness.

I looked at Rob, his head situated, according to my vantage point, alongside the cross behind him. Looking at him and thinking of his career had me reflect on my own anticipated trajectory. I have an ego. Someone sitting quietly ready to listen in a place like that was certain to feed it. I appreciated such an opportunity to talk about myself. I shifted my rear-end trying to make it more comfortable on the flat hard surface that was the chaplain's office chair. Where to begin?

"I was saved at aged twelve," I told him. "I loved reading my Bible, especially the New Testament letters, and I was enthralled by the words of Paul. They spoke directly into my life, even at that age."

"I loved farming, so I went to agricultural college," I went on. I could have said much more. Like that I used to rear my own chickens and rabbits. How much I had loved working with the shepherd tending sheep. How I had reared orphan lambs on the bottle, and one had been called Tanya! I did not tell him about my family ancestry—of my parents' upbringing as Anabaptists. Although by the time I was around as a child my parents had very little contact with Anabaptists, the memory and impact of their upbringing very much affected the way we children were brought up. At the same time, my childhood period was filled with their comments on the irrelevancy of the church. To some, Rob's role was antiquated. Why should we still have chaplains in the secular UK! But then—why was I there with him? Rob smiled. He did not seem to realize that he was antiquated. He seemed very much alive. And he was available to students. I guess he'd heard many sad and happy stories in this office.

"I preferred agricultural college to university because I wanted to do real practical farming," I told Rob. "While at agricultural college, I had been an active member of the Christian Union. Our Christian Union would invite speakers. Sometimes they would come from far away. They presented us with a variety of challenges. Many Christians with an agricultural background seemed to have overseas experience, and we had many people come and relate of their experiences beyond British shores. They were people who had been involved with tropical agriculture. That sounded challenging to me.

One particular challenge was left to us, it seemed to me, time and time again. That is, 'Why not use your agricultural knowledge and skills in poor parts of the world where people are hungry, instead of in Europe where we already have mountains of food?'"

It had once been thought that a direct export of European agricultural methods would be the best to cut the mustard. By this time, one did not have to read very widely to discover that these methods had not worked. A new approach was needed. That was, by trial and error in practice in the majority world, to develop more appropriate means of assisting people to build on their pre-existing agricultural knowledge. I was asking myself; was there a role here for me?

"That challenge, to use our agricultural knowledge where it seemed to be really needed, had troubled my mind on and off for a number of years. 'Did God want me to devote myself to service overseas?' I would ask myself. I felt far from adequate. Who was I to be given an assignment like that? No—surely such a challenge should be to other more capable people. I was not particularly intelligent—as demonstrated by my A-level grades, having been C, C, E (E was for maths) whereas both my brother and sister were around A, A, B! They might have chosen to go to Oxbridge. I went to agricultural college. I was far less bright than many of my friends," I said to Rob.

Rob listened as I articulated my conundrum. "Do what God has called you to do," Rob told me. I could see a glint in Rob's eye. His position as chaplain was probably not well paid. For all I knew he was a volunteer. I got the impression that he did it for moments like this—when he could be a positive formative influence on young people—especially when he could encourage them to seek God. Rob reminded me of biblical characters who felt the call of God. Paul saw the light on the road to Damascus. He changed his whole life orientation, never again to look back. Paul certainly did not have an easy life. The difficulties he faced never seemed to have him regret or change his mind. Is that what God was asking of me? Peter the apostle, when he was condemned to crucifixion, apparently preferred to be crucified upside down. He did not consider himself worthy of the same death as Christ, his Lord. Moses had led God's people through thick and thin based on his belief that God had called him. As Rob spoke, more inspiring biblical characters flowed into my mind. I made a mental note that a list of such examples of faith was to be found in Hebrews 11, thinking that I should read through it later. One of my favorites is Gideon, called a "mighty hero," just when he was hiding. These were heroes who did incredible things by faith! They were challenging examples. But that was in Bible times, and despite what Rob said, the question still niggled in my heart: did God call people like me in my day?

"Let's go for a cup of tea," Rob suggested. After closing his office door behind us, we walked down an extremely noisy set of stairs, below which was a rustic kitchen. Rob cobbled together two cups of tea, and we sat on stools around a rough wooden table. I didn't know these kinds of places existed anymore. Rob pointed me to another Scripture: "He who saves his life will lose it, but he who loses his life for my sake will save it," he related. That gave me more food for thought. Unexpectedly, like a rush from a forgotten paradise, a memory of Richard flooded my mind! Richard, a top businessman already proving his mettle from reports I was hearing, had a job waiting for me. I was to earn £100,000 annually. Was I ready to lose that? The tea was strong yet tasteless. That may seem to be a strange combination of qualities. It is not so strange for Brits like me who did not know that one could drink tea without milk. I had not yet finished with Rob though. One big question remained in my mind. I wanted someone to whom I could ask that question. This seemed to be just the right moment to do so, whether the cobbled-together tea was good or not.

"A lot of people these days like to try out their calling," I said to Rob, the chaplain. "Hence they accept a short-term of service. That's how they find out whether God really called them. I guess that depends on the value of their experience as they perceive it. If they have a good experience, then they'll go back again and do some more. If they have a bad experience and don't like it, then they'll stop." I wanted Rob to help me with this dilemma. But I had more to explain before I gave him a chance to answer.

"Doesn't that mean, though," I asked him, "that we are choosing to serve God only if we like it? Is serving God about being fulfilled, contented, and happy or is it about devoting oneself regardless? After all—perhaps God would want one to have had a bad first year. Does the fact that you have a bad experience at the beginning mean that God does not want you in the field?" That did seem a crazy logic to me. Are we Christians seeking fun and joy, or are we wanting to be used in sacrificial service?

A vision swam in front of my eyes. I saw myself driving a Range Rover with a beautiful woman sitting beside me, and two children in the back. There was a pamphlet on the dashboard that included a prominent picture of Richard and some business contact information. I was driving to a spacious house at the end of a tree-lined lane surrounded by paddocks grazed by cattle and horses. It was a vision that, the more I talked, I was killing.

I was not yet done. Rob's eyes widened as he listened. Was it in shock, perplexion or joy; I am not quite sure. He clearly heard testimonies from many students. Widening his eyes might have been no more than his regular strategy for encouraging someone to continue. It worked for me.

I asked, "But what if I commit myself to serve for life, and then other people do not accept the legitimacy of my calling? Do I carry on anyway? Or do I stop? Do other people have a veto on how God calls me? If yes, then what is the point in seeking a calling from God? One might as well just try to keep people happy. If no, then do I just go on regardless of any opposition that might arise to what I am doing?" In my mind were plentiful examples of biblical characters who are recorded as having met major opposition to their exploits, but who carried on serving God in the way they felt called. Not least Jesus himself. Had the legitimacy of his task been based on his success, would he have been encouraged to continue? What of John Mark? What of Jeremiah whom many people seemed to hate!

"Good questions," Rob responded. He was a college chaplain, and probably less accustomed to questions of missionary strategy. He paused. Had he a pipe, I guess he would have puffed on it. "Use wisdom," he said simply, but he seemed to be speaking mostly through his eyes.

I had to gasp at myself. What was I letting myself in for? Was this what I wanted out of life? I don't think I was having any premonitions, but it was a little worrying. The biblical characters, I knew, did not have an easy ride. John Mark was martyred. Jeremiah went through all kinds of misery. Jesus was crucified. What was I letting myself in for? Did we need religious lunatics in modern times? I suspected not.

Yet much thought and prayerful consideration were taking me towards this option. Was God calling me to serve him in the majority world? If he was, then who was I to refuse? If he is calling me—then what should I allow to block the calling? Even marriage. When God called Jonah, would it have been better had he decided to get married, instead of taking a ship to Tarshish? Had his fellow sailors discussed his plight with him, would that have changed things? Had they listened to him, and agreed with him that it was not right for him to go to Nineveh, would that have calmed the stormy sea? Was he not obliged to heed the call that only he had received and only he knew of? For Jonah, the success of his mission eventually made him depressed! What was I letting myself in for? Perhaps a shipwreck.

I reiterated the same question to Rob aloud: "What am I letting myself in for?" I asked Rob, albeit rhetorically. Rob responded by telling me a little of his own life. He even read the Magnificat to me, pointing out that later Mary would have to watch Jesus being crucified. That's as much, really, of an answer that Rob gave me. My commitment was my decision, and Rob could not make that decision for me.

I said nothing to Rob about Richard, although thoughts about his proposal lingered deeply in my mind. Sometimes I wished I'd never had such a bright and successful friend as Richard. God's ways are higher than our ways! God's ways are not always the most pleasant, but that does not mean that they are not true. Was I ready to go through unpleasantness for God's sake? A negative answer hardly seemed to demonstrate any faith at all! How could I refuse passing through valleys in order to subsequently reach some hilltops? If I did end up succumbing in a valley—might that not be a part of God's plan anyway? Are we to avoid suffering or to anticipate it and seek to thrive through it? I reflected wryly on a comment I had heard people make, that Christianity was a crutch. For me it seemed my faith was more like a rocket about to launch me into a great unknown.

For a few days after our conversation, I continued to reflect much on the above issues, (more often than not, between classes, daydreaming during a class, or while walking to and from the campus). A few days later I came to the conclusion that my excuse, that I was too weak and incompetent and therefore the wrong man for the task, just would not do. I wasn't going to rely on my strength and intelligence anyway. I made up my mind right then and there, and committed myself to lifelong service to God in the majority world (those days known as the Third World), come what may, that was how he was calling me. To me—no other call made any sense. No one else knew at the time that I had made that commitment. It was between God and me. Even Richard was, at this point, still hanging. When I told him a few weeks later, of my decision to become a missionary, he was so shocked that he put the phone down mid-sentence.

CHAPTER 2: MY HERO

Everyone wants to meet their hero, and my hero was Max. Advising Tearfund about rural development, he was the expert I needed to speak to if I was to use my agricultural knowledge to make a difference in the lives of ordinary Africans. Max had an office at Reading University. He had agreed to meet me at lunchtime at a pub near the university.

Tearfund was, to me, a heroic organization. Anyone advising them had to be a giant of a man. That was Max. When, years before, he had accepted our invitation to speak to us at my agricultural college, we were thrilled. Slides were a part of his presentation. One particular slide stuck in my mind. The image was of a light aircraft. Around the aircraft were hordes of mostly poorly-dressed black people, especially children. Max, my hero at that point, stood in the midst of the crowd in the picture. "They had no money economy," he told us, "but inevitably it was going to come, so we felt no guilt in introducing them to it." There he was in the middle of a jungle or bush area surrounded by people whose way of life seemed to me to be an utter mystery. Then he reflected on as profound a thing as the consequentiality of having a money economy! My mind boggled at his words. "How can people not have money," my twenty-three-year-old "agricultural" brain asked itself? To think that the man standing in front of me had part-responsibility for introducing money to that community of black people was more than incredible.

Max was a few minutes late for lunch. As I waited for him, I felt myself almost quiver with excitement. It was as if nothing could faze this awestruck young man who was about to receive advice from the one who was, on his own reckoning, by far the most qualified to give it.

Max was a little taller than I, slim, greying and modestly dressed. His facial expression, while seeming to be one of empathy, also carried hints that he was not a stranger to difficult relational circumstances. I could, of course, not know the battles that may have worn him down. He survived them, perhaps, as it appeared to me, by bowing his head and grimacing in the light of onslaught.

To me, this made him no less prestigious. Now, this prestigious man, with an office in what to me was a high-ranking institution, a world expert in tropical agriculture (and what could be more exciting?) was taking the time to sit with me for lunch.

Max sat with a gentlemanly composure. Perhaps his mind was like a thousand stallions, racing to give inspiring counsel, but not quite sure how to do it, given my overall ignorance? Or perhaps he had seen enthusiastic young men like myself all too often, and had a standard spiel? I do not know. Sitting at the corner table in the pub might have been an everyday event for Max. It felt, to me, a little like the most important meeting I had ever had, a first step into a great adventure. Of course, it wasn't actually a first step; but it was one of many steps. In a sense, it was simply a part of an uphill slope into adulthood and into the prospect of responsibility.

Farming had been the love of my life; perhaps that was by default. My father had had no career other than farm working. Why shouldn't I get infected with the same urge? Farming was a way, perhaps, of setting me apart. My secondary school and A-level college had been in a small town. My fellow students were townies. They weren't like me. I spent my spare time roaming in forests and wide-open spaces, at times riding around in Land Rovers. It made me feel different but not uncomfortable. I felt a real freedom when I was in the countryside even at an early age. I was set apart; it seems "destined to be different!" It seems strange to ponder on that now. Especially as I reflect on the importance of the terms *set apart* in the new way of life for which I had been elected at aged twelve, the life, that is, of a Christian. A Christian is one who, in my understanding, follows Jesus. As he follows Jesus, he is filled by the Holy Spirit. The meaning of "holy" in that phrase "Holy Spirit," is *set apart,* hence from aged twelve, I had been a follower of Jesus filled by that spirit of "set apart."

I had three more conversations with Max in the months leading up to my departure for Africa. Although the very thrill of being with such an important person somewhat compensated for it, I was also disappointed. Max's gentle, affirming voice perhaps lacked the flesh and bones, the heavy content I was searching for, the kinds of insights that I could take a hold of to make a difference in people's lives. There was something wishy-washy in what he said, something lacking. I was about to embark on a course that would rock the foundations of the known world! There was something he didn't seem to be telling me. His story was complete, but in the telling of it, fell flat. The fizz on my glass of lemonade sparkled playfully to the surface, as I meditated on one occasion on the content and underlying presuppositions behind what he said. His eyes were at the same time revealing and concealing something deep. I had by that stage in life not realized how many people went through painful experiences. I think he had been through some of those. Disappointments had moderated his once youthful enthusiasm. He walked with a slight stoop, and he talked with a slight stoop. He was very ready to help, for which I was grateful, but he was not about to reveal all. Certainly, I came away the more intrigued.

"Goodbye, and see you again, Philo," he told me as he walked off, the sun sprinkling through the grey streaks in his black hair. He had some confidence in his step even as he stooped. He had made it. I was just a boy.

Max was not connected to my churches, the college I was at, or to the mission who were to provide my ticket to Africa. He had become a personal friend who I had grown to respect. Through Max, I had had an expert introduction. Max played no formal role in my selection, preparation or sending to the field. In effect, I had experienced some pre-field training. This was not entirely confined to meetings with him; I also had a week of residential training with the mission before setting out for Africa. How did pre-field training help me? It helped me to expect more than I was familiar with, might be in my answer to that question. It broadened but did not threaten my pre-understanding. Max seemed to have been careful not to threaten it. This would come later when I was on the field. From the West, from the UK, it is hard to teach someone a world they do not know. Instead of allowing explanations of the foreign to challenge and threaten prior knowledge, people tend to absorb it into what they already understand.

There were some forewarnings in Max's words. Why was he not more articulate? Why was he not more specific? Why was he not more encouraging regarding what I would go on to do? At the time, though, I could not know much more. Max was the expert, but he did not give me answers. Between the lines, Max seemed to be saying "there is much you cannot yet know."

CHAPTER 3: SHARING MY VISION BEFORE LEAVING FOR AFRICA

It was pouring with rain. My windscreen wipers ripped back and forth like the clappers. Torrents of water vanished down both sides of the gradual slope into a partly-blocked drain outside. Searching for a house number was rendered all the more difficult by the rain. I wanted number 54. That was 42. Then I got to 62. Backing the car the wrong way up the street was tricky, but necessary. I ignored the occasional gasps and grunts that emerged from my passenger. I did not have any rear windscreen wipers, and the house number was obscured by a dense bush. Then finally it emerged, 54 it was!

"We should wait," John Mix, my passenger, told me. John had been a farmer-cum-gardener all his life. He identified with my own rural orientation. My home church had asked him to be my personal "link" person. John eventually became like a second father to me. For many, frankly, to be out on the mission field meant to be "out of sight, out of mind," but not for John—who had an enormous compassionate heart.

I have never liked waiting. The rain pounded on the roof and flowed down all windows of the now stationary car. Was it worth breaking out of one's comfort zone? Or was it better to wait in the hope that conditions might improve? I did what seemed the right thing. I respected the advice given me by John. I glanced across. John was twenty-eight years my senior. That put him at aged fifty-two at the time. A father figure already to me even then. His red face and coarse hands gave away his favorite pastimes—farming and gardening. Over the years John occasionally told me that he was learning from my example. I find that hard to believe. John had a massive heart of compassion and care. His whole life was one big exercise of concern for people. Often he cared for the lost—ex-drug addicts, the sick, and so on. I was also to benefit from a constant reaching out of his heart to mine, for well over twenty years. John was to continue to care about me thousands of miles away in Africa, when others seemed to forget.

The rain eased. We rushed to the house door. Well, I would have rushed to the house door, if I had not fumbled and dropped the car key. I banged my head on the car as I searched. There it was. I turned the key in the lock. Kerplunk—the mechanism latched. Stooped as if to dodge raindrops, I dashed to follow John. By the time I got there, Kerry, the lady of the house, stood beside her open door with a wide smile, ushering me into a warm, carpeted space where the house-group meeting was to be held. I was the guest speaker.

I talked. I based my message on Isaiah 58.

> ⁶ "Is not this the kind of fasting I have chosen: to loose the chains of injustice and untie the cords of the yoke, to set the oppressed free and break every yoke? ⁷ Is it not to share your food with the hungry and to provide the poor wanderer with shelter—when you see the naked, to clothe them, and not to turn away from your own flesh and blood? ⁸ Then your light will break forth like the dawn, and your healing will quickly appear; then your righteousness will go before you, and the glory of the LORD will be your rear guard. ⁹ Then you will call, and the LORD will answer; you will cry for help, and he will say: Here am I. "If you do away with the yoke of oppression, with the pointing finger and malicious talk, ¹⁰ and if you spend yourselves in behalf of the hungry and satisfy the needs of the oppressed, then your light will rise in the darkness, and your night will become like the noonday. ¹¹ The LORD will guide you always; he will satisfy your needs in a sun-scorched land and will strengthen your frame. You will be like a well-watered garden, like a spring whose waters never fail. ¹² Your people will rebuild the ancient ruins and will raise up the age-old foundations; you will be called Repairer of Broken Walls, Restorer of Streets with Dwellings. (Isaiah 58:6–12 New International Version (NIV))

I felt that this passage of Isaiah well defined what I was setting out to do. I was to "loose … chains … untie … yokes … set [people] free … share … food … provide shelter … clothe [the naked] … [so that] … [God's] light will break forth like dawn." I was going to "spend [myself] on behalf of the hungry," and be a, "repairer of broken walls." The fasting spoken of in Isaiah seemed to refer to an excessive religiosity. I was going to be the practical person who brought Isaiah's predictions to productive fruition!

The critical time in such a meeting is often that when formal discussion has ended. The cakes put on the display table often troubled me; should I eat or not? My rule was—either eat nothing or make a meal of it. Just one biscuit would give me a sweet taste but certainly would not fill me up. Eating too many cakes and biscuits, however, could have people either comment, or look at me wide-eyed. I did ask myself why, when paying someone a visit in their home, one was put into a situation of temptation to gluttony? All too often I failed the test. How could I then possibly stand up to more profound or involved tests? Hence I never wanted to touch alcohol. Were I to do so, how did I know I was not going to get addicted? That night I went for the desserts on the table, and gorged myself. Meanwhile, "Your mother must be proud of you," Kerry said. That's the kind of comment that is difficult to respond to.

"Yes," I said, or did I mumble? Was she trying to feed my ego? Was that a real heart-felt conviction? Was it intended merely to encourage me? Should I be drawing on that kind of praise as encouragement, or to refute it? In theory at least, I wasn't looking for praise of man. Why was I setting out to serve God in Africa? Self-gratification, pride, to make a name, or in humble service? God knows!

One of the older men in the meeting identified with my experience. He had a somewhat bulging stomach, which was evident as he sat. His manner was warm and sincere. He began to lay out his own life-story. It was an impressive story. He had served as a VSO (Voluntary Service Overseas) volunteer, initially in Fiji in the Pacific, and then in Mali. He had met his wife in Mali. Both of them had been committed to further service in Mali. They spent a year after they married at missionary training college. But they never got back to Mali until twenty-nine years later for a two-week holiday! Did he look on himself as a failure?

"Do you regret not having gone back to serve in Mali?" I asked him.

"I love my wife very much," he responded.

His wife, sat resting her hand on a large cushion beside him, chipped in, "Once you have children of your own, everything looks different." "She must have been a very beautiful woman in her younger years," I thought to myself. Her black hair continued to frame an attractive if slightly aging face.

At that point, I succumbed to the urge to visit the bathroom. Our conversation had reminded me of other people who seemed to live with regret. People that is, who had been at one point or another in their lives strongly committed to long-term missionary service in the majority world. But they had not seen it through. "Would I be one of them?" I continued to ask myself, as I reached for the towel. "Did such people live the rest of their lives regretting? If marriage prevented them from doing mission, did they ever forgive their wives, really?" Richard also came to mind at that point. Regret can work both ways, I realized! I might regret not having given myself in service to God. Might I also regret not having taken the opportunity to make some money first? If I could make £100,000 a year, then a year's work would give me a foundation from which to continue to serve God. When I got back, I sat in the same circle, but in a different chair so I was no longer alongside the same couple. I admired them. I admired Christians who were sincere and came across as genuine. They knew a lot that I had yet to learn.

It was my turn to drive that day. Very often John drove me. We had to cross some rural areas. I am a relatively careful driver, I think. By this time, it was pretty dark. "What does someone mean when they say, 'Your mother will be proud of you'?" I asked John. He saw through my question straight away. "If you want to serve God, you just have to do so," he told me. Those words echoed in my head. Should I work for a year or two first? Not if God wanted me to serve him overseas! I dropped John off and drove home. I did want God to use me to fulfil some of the prophecies in Isaiah 58. Even in the smallest way. If it was not going to happen, then at least it shouldn't be my fault, I reaffirmed to myself. Surely that is the least that I could do for my Lord Jesus. Strangely, the words I had heard in conversation in that house-group were encouraging me in the same direction.

CHAPTER 4: GIRLS

Men don't like to be alone. They are aware that others agree with them on that. There are usually plenty of volunteers to help you do away with that loneliness. Women don't appreciate being alone either. I can only guess that women's minds might be like mine, except kind of in reverse. It's not easy for me to go very far in life without thinking of a girl.

No end of girls slipped through my hands. The opportunities were there. They were willing. At least they seemed to be waiting, and at least potentially willing for a friendship. Girls are not always so quick to tell you their intentions. At least not with their voice. They may just sit or stand in front of you, making it clear that they want to be the difference in your life between joy and misery. They seem to offer almost everything.

Christian men are looking for the right girl. Christian girls are wanting to be that right girl. Where then does God enter into the matter? God of course has a lot to do with it, as the basis for self-restraint. The thought of what might be unbridled fulfilment of sexual lusts is not non-existent, despite its being horrifying! It is not beyond imagination. Not at all. The sexual drive is powerful and absorbing. In order not to be an animal, life had to be a process of constant self-denial.

Doreen was seventeen when her path crossed with mine. We were both committed to leading the youth group in the church. She was quiet, meticulous, but not good at keeping time. She was an incredibly beautiful girl. Amazingly, when I asked her for a relationship she agreed. Her beauty was satiating. I could not believe that such a beautiful girl should be willing and keen to keep my company.

I was not one to rush to bed with a girl. My Christian upbringing had taught me enough cautions on that one. But then what to do? Perhaps girls were made for marrying rather than for courting? Courting produces a difficult limbo. One is neither here nor there. One might walk with someone beautiful. Yet the same beautiful person is out of bounds. One can hardly relate "normally," because there is no normal place at which to relate. As a young man courting, I had no home of my own. That was probably just as well, but it meant that courting activity was always on someone else's territory. My time with Doreen was bittersweet: she wanted one way of life but I was determined to follow my call. I knew we had to part. Having been in such a relationship, I knew it was something that I could never forget.

I have sat beside such a beautiful girl in raptured awe. Just having her hand to stroke in desirous admiration was captivating. At the same time, something troubled me. "Was this beautiful girl going to hold me back?" I asked myself. Had I found a girl who would understand my call, then maybe I would have been a married man by now. That understanding-one never crossed my path; at least not for me to know her! Maybe I missed her along the way? Maybe I should have been married long ago. Then, who knows the turns that life might have taken. Then again—I don't suppose it was a design-fault on God's part that made so many women I met seem unable to understand or have the same desire to serve God as I did.

Contrary to a man's dreams and lusts, women have a mind and will of their own. This is the case, even if they themselves do not know what that mind and will are. Marriage can be a brake. A single woman may not be a brake. She may be incredibly adventurous. A relationship with a woman with marriage in view becomes, at least potentially, a brake. She looks ahead and imagines babies, kitchens, needs for food, protection, security, and all that is entailed by them. Women very often fill the churches. Sure, they aspire to serve God, yet relating with them through marriage brings many responsibilities. What was my priority going to be?

One thing, I suppose, was for sure: in my own mind, I was going somewhere. I could not afford to have anyone hold me back from what I took to be God's will. This was usually uppermost in my mind, and made me wary of even contemplating a relationship. I knew I had to be set on what I believed was God's course for my life. I felt sure it was possible to avoid having a relationship with women. Even if it is difficult, surely it is possible, I assured myself.

Some men may struggle to understand how one can put aside living with a woman so as to remain free to serve God. (This is not to deny that a relationship with a woman can be, and often is, a means to serve God.) I just had difficulty imagining myself trying to meet the needs of a woman while trying to give myself to God's work. It did not seem straightforward to me. Unions are demanding. That is how they are made; to include emotional mismatch, joys but pressures of child-rearing, requirements of in-laws, differences of opinion, and so on.

The prospect of being childless tends to go hand-in-hand with singleness. It is another issue. The state of not having my own biological children induced in me not exactly a sadness, but at least a variety of regret. I could also add: that had God given me the variety of challenge that enabled living in a "normal" UK environment, then I may well have been married. Many careers are 9 to 5. At least, they are compatible with paying attention to a wife in evenings and over weekends. They allow a choice of living location that can be considered "normal." Such careers do not clash with women's desires for domestic stability. Instead, God has ensured for mutual complementarity in this respect, if a marriage works. My calling to serve God overseas, I was to discover increasingly, brought much more of a clash.

I found a solution to this dilemma. A group of us visited a village Baptist Church. Non-conformist churches in villages were generally rare in those parts. Those that were to be found were a sad affair. Various efforts were being made to save this church from extinction. Our visit was part of such an effort. Rural populations in the UK lost much of their community character with the advent of the motor car. Emerging chatting from a back door to this church, my general oblivion regarding my immediate context was abruptly brought to a halt. Gravestones at modern Baptist churches were a rarity. Not so here. There they were, and there I was standing in their midst. I was alive, they were all dead. Was that by my doing? Not really—my life came from God and not from me. I had not been responsible even for my own birth, after all. "Passed away aged twenty-one," said a gravestone. "That was young to die," I thought. I was older than that at the time. How come I was still alive beyond the age of twenty-one, but he, whoever he was, had long ago been composted back into the earth? He lasted only twenty-one years, and that was it.

I found my solution in death! Human desire clamored at my heart. Fear of regret was a part of that. Regret, that is, that I should marry and marry early and have children, maybe many, the rearing of whom would be joy and pleasure. I discovered that the medicine for worldly allurement is death. It was a matter of perspective. Dead men don't lust! Okay, so I wasn't dead. Instead, I was alive, and healthy, and even a little intelligent. But, was that my own doing? No. Could I ever be certain that it could continue even for another day? No. The solution was to die. That is—to take myself as already having died. Perhaps I could be hit by a bus. My situation of *not being dead* was sheer miracle. It was only God who saved me from being swept away by any old bus while riding my bicycle. I therefore had no more rights to life. I could make no demands. Dead men make no demands. All I am is by God's grace alone. Had I been killed by a bus, years before, then there was no way I could have procreated. So then—why should a potential failure to procreate trouble me now?

The problem with this *greater sacrifice* was perhaps that in its wake came a *greater expectation*. That is to say—the danger of trying to force God's hand! Does sacrifice enable God or not? Does it even push him to act?

Having a difficult task ahead required being able to hold one's head high. Not that I am perfect, and I was, in those days, a bit naive, but not a total fool. I knew enough about God's work to realize that relationships were frequently the cause of taking a man off course. I could not afford to be taken off course. I felt that I had to stay focused on what lay ahead.

CHAPTER 5: ABOVE THE CLOUDS

I had just finished teacher training college. I had been offered a contract to go to Africa to teach at a girls' boarding school in Zambia. For a recent graduate, aged twenty-four, few questioned that such was a great thing to do. Having a year out was a very respected move. Short-term missions were already all the rage at the time. If my parents and siblings were sad to see me go, they avoided turning their sadness into a guilt-trap for me.

"Philo, what's up?" asked Richard. I settled down in my chair. I thought—this could be a long phone conversation. It was.

"Hey, what do you mean?" I responded.

"You serious about that Africa stuff?"

"Shouldn't I be?" I could picture Richard standing at the phone in the hallway of his house, finely dressed. I had decided not to care much about that kind of thing. Richard did care. Why we should have become friends sometimes amazed me. He did tell me one time, he was impressed by my straightforwardness. "You'll ruin your prospects," was probably the crux of his message. He beat away at me with it.

"Those people don't need your help," he said. "There are many good Christians around, they don't do stupid things like throw away their lives," he added. I felt like I was being ground into a hole. Then Richard did the strangest of things. He did an about turn in mid-conversation, after an hour of talking! "Can't convince you can I, Philo?" he said. "In that case, go for it, but don't do half a job, as I know you won't." I was almost in depression at that point!

"What?" I asked.

"I believe in you, Philo," Richard said. I was confused. "If you are going to do a crazy thing, then do it well," he added.

I was more serious than people knew. I was also more serious than I would say. Yes, I did tell some people that mine was a life commitment. I am not sure just how they took that. Not as seriously as I did! I had not signed up for life to any institution. There was no institution I was aware of that would allow such a sign up. Now Richard was picking up on that. Somewhere along the line, he had understood me. That night I eventually got to feel better.

There was one thing for which I appreciated Richard. He once told me something of his own past. His parents' marital struggles were in his face throughout his childhood. His mother ended up committing suicide. She had taken an overdose. Richard found her. He rushed her to hospital, and he watched her die there. He had told me that story a few times. His approach to me, one of telling me his mind, was one he had learned to use in his own efforts at arbitrating in his parents' disputes. Richard was often harsh on me. Yes, in a sense I asked for it; I continued to stoke our friendship. I continued to encourage him to correspond, no matter what! I appreciated him for his gross honesty. I don't doubt others were thinking many of the things that Richard was saying, but they were too polite to speak out. By keeping Richard as a friend, I could know how the other half lived. In our ongoing communication over the years, I often received good advice from Richard. That, however, was much less consequential and pivotal in my life than the times when he attacked.

A great thing about short-term mission is that it is a way of getting to the field without years of preparation. Otherwise, five years of preparation time for long-term service did not seem unusual for other missionaries. I hardly wanted to delay my departure to Africa for another five years! If the door was already open before me, then why not go for it? Within three weeks of arrival in Zambia, I asked for an extension. There were no red flags in my case, and the school needed teachers, so that was agreed upon. Hence, I was granted a three-year posting on the basis of a minimal interview and one week of orientation.

To describe myself as a short-term missionary would be somewhat misleading. I had no doubt in my mind that, short of calamity, I was in it for the long haul. Yet everyone has to start somewhere. Everything has a beginning. Every long journey begins with a first step.

There seemed little point in trying to explain my long-term intentions to people. I got shrugged off when I tried. In due course, I learned at least one reason why. Many expressed an interest in long-term service. Of those many, few were serious. Partly that's because Africa "got" people. It got them emotionally. Once people had hit Africa, they acquired visions of changing the place by service over the long haul. There, I was different. I had made my long-term commitment before ever taking the first step, in October of the previous year.

I was to start teaching in September. Better to be there early to learn some ropes before my responsibilities formally began, I thought. The plan was for me to leave for Zambia in July. That was the theory. But folks on the ground in Lusaka could not get my work permit in time. "Wait!" came the word. There I was, ready to save Africa, and all they could say was "wait!" The traffic light got stuck on amber. Of course, when one is going to be a missionary, every hiccup is a message from God, so this was happening to help me to learn patience. That is one of the toughest lessons to learn. It was not practical to get a job when any day I could be told at short notice to get on a plane and fly into the sunset! It would have been hard to stick at a job if I had one anyway, given that prospect.

Given the delay, I had time on my hands. "I will go hitch-hiking," I decided. If I couldn't go to Africa, then at least I could get closer. Portugal was in my sights. I was going to explore how farming was done in warmer climes. I took a ferry to France, and started hitch-hiking south. I managed to get to Spain. Then, a phone call back to the UK revealed that my date for departure for Zambia was the following Monday. That night I slept under a hedge in Spain. Two or three days later I was back in the UK, telling the story of how I got closer to Africa than I had ever been before. A few days later it was time to fly to Zambia.

On August 28th I set out on my flight to Zambia, accompanied by an experienced long-term missionary, a lady by then about sixty years old. She did not have much to say. Once in Zambia, our ways parted. As in my previous experience, especially with Max, when she could have given me an oral introduction to Africa and what it means to work amongst the poor, I was met with largely silence. She did not seem to want to engage my plethora of questions. I would have to find out for myself.

Her prior years of experience meant that she knew vastly more than I did. Why couldn't she, with her wealth of experience, answer my issues? Having been with me on the start of my adventure, one might have expected this lady to become a bosom friend to me. Instead, after our arrival in Lusaka she simply disappeared from the scene. I heard no more of her, and I cannot even remember her name.

Yes, certainly, I was nervous. Yes, certainly saying goodbye to family and friends was extremely difficult. It was made a bit easier by the fact that at the time it was to be for just a year. It was difficult enough to say goodbye for a one-year trip, so it actually helped that my extension to serve for three years only came after I had already left and got to Zambia. The best strategy for saying goodbye was to avoid meeting Mum's tear-glazed eyes.

That was the first time I ever flew. I did not like the idea of being up in the air. I coped. The following morning was my first time ever to be able to wake up and realize that the dawn had broken, only to find myself up above the clouds. I know such is common fare for seasoned travellers. It was mind blowing to me, however. The start of my experience in Africa was to be marked by the phenomenal experience of floating in heavenly places! I was well and truly awe-struck.

A few hours later we touched down on African soil. Had I made it? Me, the farm worker's son, now in Africa? A missionary representative came to the airport on the wrong side of security. Missionaries were clearly well known at the airport. I soon became familiar with an American approach to the corrupt African systems. (In my experience, many mission-efforts in Africa have in recent decades been more American than British dominated.) Confident, assertive, our missionary hosts had their man behind enemy lines! Well, at least "behind the counter at Arrivals," to ensure that we would not become victims of corruption or be asked for some mega-bribe before we had even technically stepped onto Zambian soil. I was bundled into a truck, and off to the mission station in the city.

The first day in one's new life is quite a significant event. On the airport side of town, at the bottom of a dip, lay our destination. We crossed open spaces on dirt tracks. There were black boys playing with a homemade football. Dust flew as they ran back and forth. Although no doubt used to the spectacle, staring at this 4x4 filled with white people still seemed to be the normal ritual. A ten-foot wall surrounded the whole missionary compound. We entered through massive iron gates. The watchman ran quickly and opened them for us on our arrival.

My mind went back to prior years of having had missionaries come to my church to show slides of the kinds of things I was now witnessing with my own eyes. The trees, the bare dirt, the variety of bird life, were all amazing. The enclosed compound stretched a few hundred yards in all directions, as we removed our bags in the heat of the mid-morning sun. A missionary wife with a strong American accent welcomed us. I was only to stay there the one night, I was told, as I was shown to my bunk bed in a guest-house. This was the stuff of heroes, I thought to myself. These were no ordinary people. Everyone there had received a calling from God. They had all, no doubt, prayed and searched their hearts. Most had gone through a preparation time of around five years before coming to the field. I was meeting extraordinarily faithful Christians; some of the most dedicated people known to the Western world.

The woman who welcomed us was Daisy, the wife to the mission administrator Lever. At the time, she could not have known the trauma that was shortly to befall her. Months later her husband engaged in a gunfight with marauders onto the missionary compound. He survived that, but not long after, he succumbed to a heart attack. Daisy continued to serve faithfully after that, as a widow, for many years.

Those who have gone through this kind of radical transformation, enabled by a trip in an airplane, will understand some of the shock and disorientation that I felt. The experience reminded me of that of the children entering Narnia in *The Lion, the Witch and the Wardrobe* in C.S. Lewis' novel. I was in great awe. There I was in this place of legend! My travel companion and I dropped our bags. I recall that the same vehicle picked up others at the airport. We must have had a refreshing soft-drink and some kind of brief orientation to our new context, thanks to Daisy. I had already observed the bookshelf in our small guest apartment, and noted that it was crammed with missionaries' biographies. I would have a further glance through these books later.

For the time being, however, what really intrigued me was the compound in which we were staying. We were well south of the equator, although still well within the tropics. I was intrigued by what was growing out there. I was, after all, an agriculturalist. My identity as an agriculturalist was my ticket to Africa. I had been busy reading books on tropical agriculture.

Suddenly, all around me, within the mission compound, was tropical agriculture in practice. I wandered around, admiring banana plants, mango trees, cassava crops, planted apparently haphazardly around the compound, plus other tropical fruits and bushes. The books I had been reading and the pictures I had looked at came alive. It was now my task to transform all that, as I helped people to emerge from the binding chains of poverty.

Whether I slept much in that strange place that night, I cannot remember. I do know that the prospect for what we had to do the following day had me a little concerned. The following day was the onward flight to the mission station at which I was to be based. That would have been ten hours by road, but just an hour or two by air. This time though, no commercial airliner was in prospect. Instead a six-seater prop plane owned and operated by the mission itself, was to be piloted by a swaggering American. As we set off for the airport the next day, it was clear to him that the coming of this young British teacher at the girls' secondary school was nothing extraordinary. In the same way, neither was the flight from Lusaka to the mission in Mubantu, that he had made countless times. Having fresh-faced, naive adventure-seekers like me to take care of was, for him, run-of-the-mill. Our pilot had done this job for years. Within months he was retired and went back to the USA.

He got us strapped into our seats. Onto the runway, then forward went the throttle. The small plane spluttered, trembled, and shook as we rushed at an increasingly alarming pace down this African runway. A miracle as always, it seemed, and we were up in the air. The shaking didn't cease. I tried not to think too much about the flimsy little thing that had us perched precariously high in the sky. "Well, if I die now that's not a bad way to go I suppose," I thought to myself. Soon we were crossing miles and miles of bush. "No convenient nearby runway should our engine break down on us," I thought to myself. On and on we went, enshrouded by the ceaseless noise.

My stomach leapt into my mouth. We began our descent. There were a few low hills close to our destination. The hills rushed up to us. This was incredible! This seemed to be truly the "real Africa." If I wanted to be way out in the bush—then that is what I was achieving. The runway this time was not tarmac, but grass. Carefully, we touched the ground. A group of people were waiting for us at the end of the runway. There might have been 150 African people standing there. Most of the crowd was made up of children. We taxied along to the far end of the runway. The black people gawped in incredulity at the six of us emerging from this strange flying machine. The picture shown to us years before by Max, while I was at agricultural college, rushed back into my mind. Crowds of scraggily-dressed black people gathered around a small plane. Our baggage was removed from the pod that extended the belly of the plane. A truck was there waiting to take us white folks where we needed to go.

Some discussion broke out amongst my almost universally American white colleagues. I found myself to be the object of their discussion. "Where do we put Philo?" The other visitors were evidently to be stationed at the hospital. The latter was a much more prestigious institution. It was run by the Americans and received a lot of important visitors. The school was a mile or so down the road, and by that time even the head of the school was an African.

"We can't have a white man living in a house with an African," I heard someone say.

"We have nowhere else for him to stay," came a response. It seems I was only half-expected that day. And there I was coming to transform Africa. Little did they know! Someone obviously made a decision. I was told to sit in the back of a truck, and was taken a mile down the road. We arrived at a set of slightly dishevelled white homes lined up on both sides of a dirt road, on a slope facing up a hill. As I got out, a very short African man, emerging from one of the houses on the left, came towards us. I later discovered that people called him Tichi.

"This missionary is staying with you," he was told in an American accent. He evidently had not had a clue about my coming. That turned out not to be a problem for African hospitality. My bags were carried in. My short Zambian housemate raised a cloud of dust sweeping out an empty bedroom. My "temporary home" was to be my residence for a year. When the cloud of dust settled, I heard a swarm of mosquitoes whining noisily above my head.

My host was the very man who a few days later asked me a question. We were walking around the secondary school at the time, at his indomitably slow pace. Tichi knew how to walk slowly. He talked quietly and contemplatively. He had not chosen to have someone from Europe to stay with him. He found himself in that "predicament!" That made him, in my view, a particularly valuable person to learn from.

"So why are you here?" he asked me as we walked. I looked at him. I had thought for a long time about why I was coming there.

"To help you," I responded. His eyes surprised me and challenged me. Telling folks in the UK that I was going to "help" Africans was one thing. Now that I had arrived, to tell my African colleague the same suddenly took on a different meaning, and left me with a shallow feeling. "Not another self-righteous superior do-gooder from the West?"—his eyes seemed to ask. I realized that I had some more thinking to do.

* * *

That is the end of the biographical account given to me, Dave, by Philo—which recounts his life up to the time I met him in Zambia. From here onwards, I am the one narrating this story.

CHAPTER 6: I AM DAVE

My grandmother was a Cherokee Indian. Her story is almost as amazing as the one I tell in this book. Born on a reserve in Arkansas, she was raised tending rice plantations. Meanwhile my grandfather, fleeing the Dutch government where he was wanted on charges of manslaughter, had made his way to the USA. These charges I take as having been false; several visits to Holland in recent years have still not provided conclusive evidence one way or the other.

Somehow he met my grandmother. She was, at the time, an unschooled sixteen-year-old plantation labourer. She agreed to join forces with a fugitive from Holland. He might have thought the last place the Dutch government would search for him would be on an Indian reserve. He was probably right. He needed help to conceal himself and become incognito. That is the help my grandmother gave him. In return, he made her pregnant. When war broke out in Europe, he received notification of a pardon, plus an invitation from the exiled Dutch government to do undercover work in-country to undermine Nazi Germany. After getting to Holland he disappeared without trace, never to be seen again.

My father, born on a Cherokee reserve to a woman whose life was little better than that of a slave, had his own amazing story. That will have to be an account for another day. Let me say, in brief, that his antics took him as far as Brazil, where he married an American woman, at the time a missionary with the Quakers. I am not at all sure of the name he used to get into Brazil, but when he left Brazil to settle in the USA, he had adopted the name Candomble, a surname which I retain today.

* * *

Cindy and I married in 1986. She and I both anticipated a long married life. Unlike my globally-gallivanting predecessor, at that time I had few ambitions for travel. All was well, until eleven months into our marriage. Cindy might have been carrying our first child. I came home one day to find her collapsed just outside our kitchen, sprawled across, of all things, a child's bicycle that we were keeping for the neighbors. Tests performed were inconclusive, but Cindy had some kind of rare nervous disorder. It had been dormant for all these years. The shock of pregnancy to the system was what activated it. She collapsed on that Thursday. I found her at around 5.30 p.m. At 3 a.m. on the following Sunday morning, she left this world for another.

Cindy's demise struck a horrific blow to my hopes for the future. I was given two weeks off work. My work had been assisting a large car-hire company to improve its systems of operation. Two weeks later, I could not face the prospect of going back to sit behind a desk like that. I did not go back to work. The company gave me a generous handshake of $5,000 to help me seek a new way in my life.

Family efforts did not do enough for me. A month after Cindy's death I hit rock bottom, and hit the bottle. I can add that thankfully it was the only night that I did so. Drink was new to me. That day, however, I was desperate for solace. I could see no way forward for my life. Instead, I went to our local drinking house, for the first time ever. Could drink save people? I had seen rowdy, jolly folk frolic outside on summer evenings. I hankered after some jolly merriment myself. I did not even know which drink I ought to order. While standing at the bar a man in his fifties bought a drink for himself and one for his wife, before he went back to sit down. I noticed the bar attendant asking him; "Do you want a strong one for yourself?" He nodded. He went off with his drink, and sat alongside his wife. "A strong one for me too," I told the bar attendant. He brought it. I made a beeline for a table that I recall as being alongside a hat-rack with a pink hat on it. I sat, and sipped. I don't know how many glasses I had consumed by the time the evening was over.

I crawled out of that bar, people scowling at me. I reached a nearby hedge in time to vomit into it. That helped a little. I hadn't eaten since late morning. I felt that I walked away, but in reality I am sure that I staggered. The thought that I might want to walk home did not really cross my mind. I staggered further. Fortunately, that night was not too cold. A deep impulse was, by that time, driving me to stagger from place to place. I vomited again. No one cared a hoot about me, I assured myself. There was a bush at the edge of a small green clearing, perhaps large enough that it could have made a badminton court. I collapsed under the bush. Then, or at least at some point after that, an angel arrived.

The voice was that of a young man. He was carrying a brown bag over his shoulder. The bag had a long strap. I do not know what was in it. Papers I guess. The young man came alongside me. He read some words. Even in my stupor as he read, the words registered in my mind and touched my heart! I discovered later that they were the words of Paul's letter to the

Ephesians, chapter 2 verses 1–10. Here are these words, from the NIV version of the Bible:

> [1] As for you, you were dead in your transgressions and sins, [2] in which you used to live when you followed the ways of this world and of the ruler of the kingdom of the air, the spirit who is now at work in those who are disobedient. [3] All of us also lived among them at one time, gratifying the cravings of our flesh and following its desires and thoughts. Like the rest, we were by nature deserving of wrath. [4] But because of his great love for us, God, who is rich in mercy, [5] made us alive with Christ even when we were dead in transgressions—it is by grace you have been saved. [6] And God raised us up with Christ and seated us with him in the heavenly realms in Christ Jesus, [7] in order that in the coming ages he might show the incomparable riches of his grace, expressed in his kindness to us in Christ Jesus. [8] For it is by grace you have been saved, through faith—and this is not from yourselves, it is the gift of God—[9] not by works, so that no one can boast. [10] For we are God's handiwork, created in Christ Jesus to do good works, which God prepared in advance for us to do.

I was woken by a dog sniffing my face. I was frozen. I felt miserable. It was so cold. I lay for a while before I mustered the courage to try moving my right leg. It moved. I lifted my arm a little. Up it went. That was somehow reassuring. The dog backed away. I waved him off with the back of my hand. He didn't seem to care, but went, sauntering nonchalantly. At night, I had not cared where I went. Now I did not know where I was. I had to find my way home. I hardly noticed the crumpled paper in my shirt pocket. I had wandered about four miles from the bar where I had those drinks. How to get home?

A black man appeared, walking a hairy-looking collie, much like the collies used by shepherds to manage their flocks. "You alright?" he asked.

"Well, kind of," I responded.

"Need a lift?" he added.

"Yes," I answered.

"Where are you going?" I told him my estate.

"Wait for me in ten minutes under that tree," he told me, pointing to a tree alongside a road that was about 120 yards away.

"Thanks," I said. Fifteen minutes later a pickup truck pulled up under the tree. By this time the collie dog was tied by the neck to the back of the truck. That looked a little precarious—like turning a corner suddenly might throttle it. I was offered the seat next to my driver, obviously the seat regularly occupied by the dog. I only hoped the dog didn't mind me making his seat dirty. I thanked my savior profusely for his incredibly generous act. My "savior" told me about himself as he drove. Unfortunately, my state at the time prevented me from remembering very much. My key was in my pocket. I let myself into my house. Somehow, I got cleaned and collapsed in bed, waking up the following morning.

The clothes I had worn the previous day were still where I had thrown them in the corner of my room. I gathered them up, and was just about to tip them into my flowery (thanks to Cindy) wash basket, when I recalled something having been in my shirt pocket. I unravelled the bundle of clothes I was carrying. After a careful search, I found the pocket of my shirt. In it was a crumpled letter-size piece of slightly browned typing paper. On it, a little faded but still perfectly readable, in large print was a stencilled typed paragraph. "Ephesians 2:1–10," was the heading. The previous night's visit by that young man, whoever he was, came back to mind. So, he had left me with a paper. I placed the paper on my desk. The chair scraped against the floor as I dragged it up to the table. I sat. I read. I wept.

My experience was more than that of someone reading. It was as if a wind blew into me. Not a cold wind, but a warm, humid wind, as I read. "You were dead," the Bible said, "gratifying the … sinful nature … objects of wrath [but] God … made us alive with Christ … the gift of God [not] to boast." A gift of God! Life, health, knowledge, joy, everything, was a gift from God, I repeated the words to myself in my heart. It was not the words. That is—it was not *just* the words. Someone was speaking to me. Someone cared about this wretched fellow, who had fallen apart after the death of his wife.

I need to cut my story short. That is the core of how I came to be who I am now. While the throbbing recollection of Cindy's smile continued to be there, it no longer troubled me as it had. I had not been totally ignorant of these words before. After that night though, they hit me with a new punch.

God himself cared for me! He knew what he was doing, even when he allowed Cindy to leave me.

The following months were a whirlwind. The next day I went to visit my pastor. I recall that as I spoke to him, he rapped the table-top with his finger-tips. Whether he did so for all visitors, or whether he reserved this action only for me that day, I did not know. I noticed that the pace of his fingers accelerated whenever I said something that challenged his thinking. They were going the fastest, or so it seemed, as I explained to him that I was determined to serve God, no matter what.

"Just a month after you have been bereaved!" he exclaimed, his fingers belting their speedy course on the table. Yes, that was quick.

"It is what Cindy would have wanted herself," I said, without really having thought about whether she would have wanted that or not.

The upshot of all the above events is that in November of the same year, I was on a flight to Zambia. My project was to look critically at appropriate means of aid systems delivery. I did that in partnership with World Vision, but while immediately accountable to a small, evangelical mission agency. My remit was to explore the local and specific, as a means of helping others to understand how to operate on a large scale.

In this account I do not want to tell much of my own story. That I will have to reserve for another day. Except, that is, as it overlaps with the story of a certain guy named Philo whom I first met when I reached Zambia in that year. I did not have a clue at the time, how our lives would become intertwined. I became attracted by his honesty, radical thinking, and sincerity. Philo conceded to me, that times when we were together were the times when he felt most relaxed! We were soon to form a deep friendship that would last many decades.

CHAPTER 7: DANGEROUS PUBLIC TRANSPORT

I can clearly remember how I first came to meet Philo. A message came over the mission radio, "There's a secondary-school teachers' seminar happening. Please attend." Three-times-per-day radio was our staple for communication in those days. Short messages came and were sent out to recipients by various means. I received the message from the hospital administrator who was coming to visit us to inquire about the availability of vegetables. To be honest, I think his real reason for coming out was that he wanted to get away from the mission. Passing on the message to me gave him an excuse to do so. Within the confines of the mission, especially the hospital, life tended to lurch from crisis to crisis. I couldn't blame folks for wanting times to get away. I was staying ten miles from the mission at the farm of a certain Mr. Edgington. Having formerly worked for government, he married a local woman, and decided to stay in Zambia and set up his own farming business in his wife's home area. One thing that never ceased to amaze me about Mr. Edgington—was his lack of knowledge of the local tongue, despite having been married to a Bantu wife for fifteen years.

I had been posted to a rural location, staying with this white farmer about ten miles from a certain mission station. Right out in the sticks, surrounded only by *miombo* woodlands and local African subsistence farmers, this was far from the middle-class US suburb I had previously been used to. After about ten days, I was still in a daze, slowly getting used to a very different way of life.

Because my motorbike was under repair at the mission, I hitched a lift back there with Nick, the hospital administrator. I asked him about the new teacher. "Philo, you mean?" he responded.

"Yes," I said. The dust bellowed up in clouds as we went. The rain had not yet begun in earnest. The hospital administrator had a lot to say about the hospital. He might have had too much on his chest to worry about a school-teacher from England who was staying down the road. I had, however, already been intrigued by what I had learned about Philo, and wanted to know more.

"You will find him sharing a house with a Zambian," he explained eventually, when I probed him about Philo.

"What, really!" I was surprised. I knew that mission policy was to not have missionaries and nationals share the same accommodation. "How come?" I asked.

"No choice really. Two single ladies and him at the school. The single ladies each have their own houses. There was no spare house for Philo. Not that he'd want to stay alone anyway."

"They wouldn't have him stay with one of the ladies," I exclaimed. The hospital administrator laughed. "How's he coping?" I asked.

"Lots of gossip," I was assured.

"Gossip. Why?" I asked.

"Because Tichi stays there with his niece. When Tichi leaves, his sixteen-year-old niece stays with Philo," the administrator explained.

"Wow!" I exclaimed.

"You can't blame Philo. He didn't choose the situation. The old missionaries don't like it though. Their old rule is, 'never, never boy and girl together,'" I was told.

The road reached the end of the runway and turned. It was an amazing time of year. Until recently bare earth, was getting covered by every imaginable shade of green shoot! The long dry season was finally coming to an end. Some plants, the quickest to emerge, were already flowering, ready to produce and shed their seed, before the tall elephant grass came to smother them.

When I first met Nick at the hospital, I was beset by the thought that he would have fitted better in a college for business in the West. His composure, habits, and disposition always made me think—he should be teaching business at a business school! His presence at the mission hospital was always incongruous to me.

After parking at the hospital, Nick invited me in to greet others in the office. I had not expected quite such a lively conversation to be going on.

"Slam him in jail!" said one missionary to another. The one speaking was a rather large fat man. He turned to me, and greeted me politely before continuing, "That's the only way to teach them."

"Hospital folks will be upset," his colleague, an older thin man with a noticeable lack of hair, retorted.

"It's the only way to teach them," repeated the fat missionary.

"The accountant has been eating money," Nick explained to me as he pointed to a seat. I sat down.

"Almost the same as the last one," said the fat missionary. "But he lasted for five years before going down. This accountant has only been in office for two years, and he has already been caught with his fingers in the till."

"Maybe he wasn't so good at hiding," said the older thin man, cynically. It did not seem to be a laughing matter.

"When is this going to end?" repeated the first missionary. "We try to help them. They steal," he added. I had not expected to find such lively discussion. Neither had I expected to find such a massive chasm between missionary and national staff at a mission station. Practice was different. In practice, tensions between African people and foreign missionaries often ran high, and certainly constantly simmered.

"I'll go," I said.

"No, I'll take you," Nick retorted.

"No need," I explained. "Just ten minutes. I'll walk," I said. "I know the way well enough, and it's not raining yet." That was another unexpected move as far as European missionaries were concerned. For a white man to walk, why? Has his car broken down? Someone should give him a lift. I set out. I hadn't come to interfere with their program. I knew they were busy. Saving lives, the practice of the hospital, was no joke. The mortuary filled too quickly as it was! I had realized that people used the hospital as a last resort. They would come with the dying, once having exhausted all their own traditional remedies.

The dirt road between the school and the hospital was hardly busy, but there was a regular stream of walkers. Zambians, of course. An occasional mission vehicle would go by. I was not sure how aware drivers were of the amount of dust they kicked into people's nostrils every time they went by. As I walked, an old man crouched down on one side of the road, while facing an apparently equally old woman doing the same on the other side. They clapped rhythmically and in unison, their hands in a vertical motion. "*Ee mwane, ee mwane, ee mwane,*" they said to each other. Such clapping, while squatting looking at each other always amazed me. The two people doing so were in-laws. A man and a sister to his wife, or a woman and a brother to her husband. (It should be remembered that there are always many brothers and sisters, as fellow clan members of the same generation are considered to be siblings.)

"*Hodi,*" I said, as I walked into Philo and Tichi's home.

Tichi's niece greeted me, "*Muji byepi mwane,*" as I walked past.

"*Bulongotu,*" I responded as I raised an arm to greet her. This must be Direnes, I thought to myself.

"*Mwaiai mwane,*" said the younger of the two white men sitting talking.

"Welcome Dave," said the elder of the two men. I had previously met this man in Lusaka; his name was Lever (a most unusual name) and he was evidently visiting the mission station. An American, he handled a lot of administrative matters for the mission. He had decided to call on Philo. Both men stood up to greet and welcome me. Philo was about 5'10" tall, slim, in his mid-twenties.

"So, you are Dave. Welcome, take a seat," he told me. I obliged. We all sat.

"It is okay for a while," Lever said to Philo. Lever was probably forty or so, and thick set although by no means fat. "But you will have to get your own place so as to get some proper work done." Philo seemed to be more intrigued than in agreement, but he nodded.

"So tell me, Dave," Lever asked, "should Efik be put in prison, or not?" It was not hard to guess who they were talking about.

"Is the evidence clear?" I asked.

"As far as I know, clear as a bell," Lever responded.

"So how much did he take?" I queried.

"Millions of kwacha, it appears," was the response. I took a deep breath. Working in an accounts office as an African seemed to be a dangerous job! The previous accountant ended up in jail. Maybe the one before that as well. (I later discovered that "the-one-before-that" was a missionary from Canada, who had left to retire.)

"How else will they learn?" I stated, but I was really trying to ask a question rather than declare a truth.

"What do you think, Philo?" Lever asked, turning to him.

"Hey, I've only been here a few months. Sounds pretty bad to me," Philo responded, thoughtfully.

"Look, truth is he's going to prison," Lever said. "We can't have someone steal millions of kwacha and get away with it."

Lever needed to be on his way. Moments later his car engine roared into life. The tyres skidded and scraped on the sand and gravel as he pulled off the drive. I gave Philo some background about myself. It was around 4 p.m. and the sun was gradually dipping in the sky. Direnes, Tichi's niece, seemed to be happy working in the kitchen. She was good enough to bring me a cup of tea. It was black—milk was expensive and hard to come by in those parts. I was also struck by the house. This, I gather, is where Philo was living. But the house might as well have been an African house. Direnes worked sitting on the floor as in an African home, not standing, as maids tended to do in a missionary home. The sparse furniture seemed to be that which belonged to the house, rather than any which Philo had acquired or added. The kitchen had a fridge/freezer, but apart from that was not at all modern, shiny, or sophisticated. That felt a bit strange. One would hardly expect much different from a bachelor. Yet it was a strange paradox—to see a white bachelor and his African housemate being cared for by a sixteen-year-old African village girl. Philo did not seem to care. It was like my heart twitched! This was a little incongruous … but I was impressed. I took a liking to Philo from the beginning.

"I hope you don't mind black tea?" Philo asked. A simple question can reveal someone's identity. An American is unlikely to ask such a question. He would never think of adding any milk to a cup of tea. Philo was clearly a Brit. Of course, his accent revealed the same. I said I didn't mind.

"What about you?" I asked him.

"A cup of tea without milk is not a cup of tea," Philo responded. This was evidently a battle that Philo was engrossed in. He explained, in that somewhat halting voice that he used when he wasn't sure about something, that he very much liked milk in tea, but a tin of powdered milk seemed to cost a fortune. The figure he gave was to me not a fortune. It wouldn't be considered "a fortune" by the female missionaries who were Philo's colleagues at the school. Was Philo frugal or what?

"It certainly doesn't seem right," Philo confided in me, "to knowingly employ an African person in an office in which the level of temptation to corruption is likely to defeat him."

"But the Zambians want to take over from the white people," I responded. The tea was very sweet. I kept drinking.

"So?" Philo said back to me. I did not respond. "If they do nothing, we dominate them. If they do something about our domination, then we imprison them," Philo continued.

"So what should we do then?" I asked him.

"Dunno," he said.

"What do you think about Lever's suggestion that I need to get my own place so as to be productive?" Philo asked.

"Sounds right to me," I responded. Philo's face tightened a fraction. He gave a dry laugh. It seems he wasn't totally on board with me.

"So it's wrong to live as an African because it means one cannot be productive enough?" Philo responded. Our exchange was starting to be fun. This fellow was turning over some conventional wisdom. What he said made sense. Well, sort of, but I had never thought of that before.

"So what are you going to do, Philo?" I asked.

"What do you mean?" he responded.

"Well, if you live like this, you don't even have a motorbike, what on earth are you going to achieve?"

"Good question," was his response. Maybe Philo was suffering from missionary blues! It was not unusual for missionaries to get disorientated, but that usually took more than just a few months.

"I've come to see you for a purpose," I told Philo.

"Oh?" Philo replied.

"About the trip," I said.

"You mean for teachers?" Philo asked.

"Yes."

"Okay. What are you thinking?" he said.

"Are you planning to go?" I asked.

"Yes," said Philo "but I don't know how yet." I wondered what he meant.

"What do you mean 'I don't know how?'" I asked Philo.

"I mean how to get there," he responded.

"Oh right, you don't have a car?" I realized. It was hard to imagine a white missionary not having a car.

"No, I don't."

"So how are the other teachers going to get there?" I asked.

"The white teachers aren't going," he replied.

"Okay," I said. "So how to get there? Is there no lift?" I asked Philo.

"Yes, I can go with them on the school truck, and then get back as best I can. That's the plan," Philo shared with me. "But," he went on, "have you ever heard of a white missionary riding on the back of an open truck like that?" Probably I had never thought about it.

"I don't suppose I have," I responded.

"So then—should I?" he asked me.

"What do the other missionaries say?" was my next question.

"Up to me," he responded. "To show them up by travelling in a way they never would. Is that good?" Philo added.

"Uho," I responded, "You don't want to shame people."

"Right," said Philo, "But I don't have a car. To hire one would cost a fortune, if there was one for hire. Then I'd be taking everyone. But—can't a white man do what an African does? Are we so special?" Philo enquired.

That issue was obviously troubling Philo. He could quite understand why European missionaries used their own transport. African means of travel were frankly dangerous. News of accidents on Zambia's roads were a common occurrence. Deaths on the road per vehicle was a very high statistic. I could also understand Philo's view that individual missionaries shouldn't be trying to earn "brownie points" on their colleagues. In that sense, all missionaries should do the same. If an existing missionary only ever travels in a private car, then new missionaries should follow the same guideline. After all, if Philo or one of his colleagues experienced an accident through their recklessness, they would be a burden to the other missionaries. Doing that depended on one having a certain level of income. Did that mean now that it is not permitted for a missionary to do things in an African way. That would seem to be trying to maintain two separate communities—perhaps for eternity!

"I have not told you the reason I came to talk to you about the trip," I told Philo.

"Okay," Philo responded, "tell me."

"I am planning to join you," I answered.

"Really? I am surprised. The trip is for teachers," Philo responded.

"I have an invitation, and I am planning to be there," I said.

"That's excellent," Philo said. He was silent for a moment. Then he asked, "How do you plan to get there?"

I told him, "With you, in the back of the truck."

"Hooray!" Philo rejoiced. "And back?" he added.

"I won't be coming back with you as I'll go on to town," I told him. "So coming back you will be on your own," I continued. (I did not actually mean "on your own," but "only with Zambians.")

"Oh. Okay," Philo answered.

When the time came for me to go, Philo walked me part of the way, back to the services department of the mission where my motorbike, which had been repaired, was waiting for me. I thought of another question to ask Philo. "Why are you here?" I asked.

He paused for some while. "To help the Zambian people," he told me, "especially when it comes to agriculture, to do their agriculture better." He paused again. "In case you are wondering why I am a bit hesitant. It is hard!" Philo added, "I keep running into barriers that I did not know existed, but I'm not going to be deterred easily." Philo turned back.

"See you shortly," I said.

"*Twavavona*," he responded with his back to me—"See you again" in the local dialect.

As I was leaving, one of the hospital missionaries waved me down. "Dave! Glad we've seen you. Please come tomorrow if you can. We have a new visitor. I am sure he will be very glad to see you. We're giving him a welcome meal at Mildred's home at 6 p.m. You're welcome to sleep over."

"Look, Doc, I can't sleep over," I told the doctor. "But tell you what—I will come by and say hello before I leave for home tomorrow." This doctor had somehow achieved the privilege of being known as "Doc" instead of by his name. He was an American called Robert. He was very devoted to his healing craft. Unlike some doctors, he thought contextually as well as biomedically. I got to like to visit him. Sometimes when I visited him I would find Philo there. Incredibly, Doc's wife once knew Cindy. Sometimes I would go and talk to her about Cindy.

The next day I arrived at Mildred's home (Mildred is the hospital matron) at 5.30 p.m. Mildred was a single lady with a round face, and a pleasant demeanor, which she combined with a no-nonsense approach to life. I did not plan to stay for long. Just long enough to greet the new visitor. The contrast between the Matron's home and Philo's struck me as I walked in. She lived alone, was by that time in her early fifties, and her home was immaculate. I enjoyed the pleasure of caressing my toes against a woolly rug, while looking at carefully-positioned African ornaments and pictures on the walls.

"Cup of coffee?" asked a pleasant voice from the kitchen.

"I expected to find more people here already," I said.

"He's not coming," she responded.

"Huh?" I questioned.

"Mechanical problems. Trip postponed," she informed me.

"Hmm. Where's he from anyway?" I asked.

"England." I fell into that comfortable chair and glanced at the *Time* magazine lying on the table in front of me. Mildred came towards me, where I was sitting.

"Are you fully recovered?" I asked. She had been bitten by a snake a couple of weeks before.

"Thankfully, yes," she responded.

Later in our conversation I heard that an urgent delivery of goods from the local town was delayed. The reason it was delayed, Mildred told me, was so that the truck could be used to transport teachers to a seminar.

"I gather, Philo—the new teacher at the secondary school—is going to go," she added. "Sounds crazy to me! Dave, is that the only transport they can find? Does he have to go? We do not have missionaries travel on the back of trucks. Then—how is he going to get back? Ride on top of someone else's truck? …The trucks riding up and down our rough roads are death-traps. Many have bald tyres and no brakes at all." I did not tell her that I too was to go to the seminar on the back of the mission truck, but that I was not going to come back with Philo! I did realize that coming alongside African folks could be, for a missionary, a complicated procedure.

The day came. Ten of us were sat on the back of the open truck. There were no seats, just some tarpaulins thrown into the back. Then horror of horrors, and unexpectedly, it started raining. That rain was cold. Wind-chill added to the cold as we shifted down the road. The road was far from even. We were wet, cold, getting colder, and jolted back and fore, attempting to sit on a tarpaulin on a corrugated floor with almost nothing to hold on to. "If this is local transport, then it is miserable," I said to myself. About 9 p.m. that evening we were finally feeling a little less cold.

"How do you feel about 'local transport'?" Philo asked me.

"To be honest Philo, that wasn't even 'local transport', that was the mission truck. That truck is properly maintained." (I was remembering Mildred's comment about trucks without brakes.) "It was just that we were carried in the way local people are carried—just climb aboard and hang on somehow!"

"I am a bit stuck," Philo conceded. "Understandably, I think the African people are not entirely happy with the fact that missionaries ride in 4x4 whereas they must walk, or catch a lift on the back of a truck. But—if that's 'local transport' I am not sure I would want to go anywhere!" Philo went on to tell me of a trip he made a few weeks previously with some missionaries. He had made some peanut butter sandwiches, and shoved them into his pocket. When they stopped for a lunch break, however, the female missionaries set up a picnic spread more than equivalent to a three-course meal on the tailgate of the 4x4. The whole spread was put on a clean tablecloth that was laid out neatly like it was in a dining room. "There doesn't seem to be a middle road," said Philo.

"Yes, it's either full missionary luxury, or just sit on the back of a truck in the rain," I commented.

"Not sure I fancy any more teachers' seminars though," Philo responded.

I could understand both Philo's point and his dilemma! One wants to encourage people to do what they can do. That is, have a missionary work alongside rather than separately from locals. But where is the half-way house? It seems that one must be ready for any misery that comes. Including death itself. Some people in Zambia would, from a scientific point of view, die for things that could in the West so easily have been prevented or cured. But then, what of one's sending one's fellow missionaries to do things in a Zambian way? Should one say if something goes wrong, "these missionaries have acted irresponsibly therefore we should let them die?" Should they instead have a policy: "a missionary can take as many risks as he wants in his endeavors at building relationships with locals, and come what may, we (the mission) will jump in when life is at risk, and pull out all stops to save him?" I am not sure that a missionary like that would be much appreciated by their colleagues. From a European point of view, he could easily be considered to be irresponsible and not looking after himself.

Ironically, it was a government 4x4 that picked me up from the seminar the day before it finished. It was some days later that I discovered what happened to Philo. I've copied an account here that I found in his newsletter a few months later:

> I had a very interesting time recently coming back from a seminar. It was a distance of about 120 miles from the mission. Although transport had been provided to the seminar, we were left at a junction 100 miles from the mission to make our own way home. I was with two Zambian teacher-colleagues. We waited for about an hour before a truck turned up loaded with bags of maize meal. There were already ten to fifteen people on top. "Climb on to go to Mubantu," we were told. I looked at my colleagues. They looked at me! "Will this white man climb with us onto the top of a load of *mealy-meal* (ground-maize) bags?" I am sure they were asking themselves. I climbed on. So did they. Off we went, by now perhaps twenty-five or more people, a mixture of genders and ages, perched on top of those bags. At least this time around, there was no rain!

For quite a few miles, all was well. The ride was actually quite pleasant. A high vantage point gave quite a view, although those familiar with the area will know that the *miombo* woodlands can be rather monotonous. Occasional termite hills, perhaps ten metres tall, were found between the short trees. As I was admiring the scenery, suddenly the truck began to lurch and shake. People on the truck who had been silent, except for a few voices of men talking, murmured loudly. We ground to a halt, on the right-hand side of the road. (The road sloped sharply down on both sides.) We had a flat tyre on the front right wheel. I looked at the tyre. It was as bald as the neck of a turkey! I was thankful that nothing worse happened. Somehow, after we had all disembarked, they got the corner of the truck jacked up, and replaced the wheel. Soon we were away again. That was a great relief.

A few miles later the truck again began to lurch and to shake. This time the lurching was prolonged and got worse rather than better. Women and children, probably men as well, started screaming, and kept on screaming. I didn't scream, but perhaps I should have done. We were already on the left side of the road. The steep incline drew closer, the truck started tipping sideways to the left. I calculated my strategy. I perceived that there was a risk that we would not only fall onto our side, but roll and land upside down. Then there was a clear danger that passengers would be crushed under heavy bags of maize-meal, with an upturned truck on top. That perception of the risk prompted me to leap head first over the cab of the lorry, so as to land on my hands, clear of any danger that the truck might roll onto me.

Fortunately, the truck only rolled onto its side and did not roll right over. It came to rest with a massive thud, people screaming like crazy, bags tipping out over the side. Once having landed on my hands, I sprang up, and evaluated the damage. A few people were partially covered by bags that had fallen onto them. I went and dragged bags off victims with both hands. Unfortunately, it seems that in doing so, I strained a wrist bone that unknown to me had already acquired a hair-line crack in the course of my flying leap. Someone got a message through to the mission. A few hours later a rescue truck came from the hospital. One man there had a dislocated shoulder. It seems that I was the only one more seriously injured, with a fractured wrist bone. This was almost certainly because of my leap "for freedom" over the cab of the truck!

I guess this story largely speaks for itself. Philo's folly, thinking that he could live like a Zambian, had already got him admitted into casualty care to be attended by American missionaries.

CHAPTER 8: END OF THE PROFIT MOTIVE

Rickson had told me that I should visit the secondary school. He had been appointed headmaster some months before. The previous headmaster had been killed in a road accident. It had been an horrific accident—a head-on crash. The missionary who was driving was also killed. His wife was permanently disabled. In Zambia, people drive on the left. The missionary was American. One can only suppose that when a car appeared charging towards him around a blind corner, his instinct took him the wrong way. The late Zambian head had been a great friend of, and beloved by, the missionaries. The new head, Rickson, was less popular with missionaries. He was more of a rebel against Europeans, as were the secondary school teachers in general.

When I showed up at Rickson's home, I found him rather busy. He was about to leave for a meeting of head-teachers of local schools. His house was just a hundred yards or so from Philo's place. He asked his wife, Annette, to give Philo a call—in case he should be free to show me around the school. The internal phone system was very useful. Before long I heard a faint, crackled voice with an English accent. "Fifteen minutes, and he'll be here," she told me. Annette was also a teacher at the school. She was a devoted wife and mother. She and Rickson were both university graduates. They were both quite tall, and originated from the south of the country.

"I knew Philo was around. I was with him in the office for a couple of hours yesterday," Rickson told me.

"Oh," I responded.

"You need to ask Philo what we talked about," he added. I made a mental note of that. Before long we heard the roar of his motorbike as Rickson set off.

"He didn't sleep much last night," Annette told me as she re-emerged from the kitchen.

"No?" I asked.

"Very noisy," she said, "from about 2 a.m."

"What was noisy?"

"Girls!" she went on to explain. The teachers' houses were not far from the girls' dormitories. I had seen as much from Mubantu hill nearby, so I knew where they were. "From 2 a.m. the girls were screaming," she said.

"What happened to make them scream?" I asked.

"Usually it starts with one girl, thinking she has seen something," Annette explained, "or maybe she's heard a sound. That girl is startled, so she screams. Then when other girls hear her scream, they also scream. Then all the girls are screaming," she said. "At that point, the girls wake us up. The teacher on duty should go and sort the matter. Rickson also went."

"So, did they find anything or anyone?" I asked.

"No, nothing," she told me. "Neither could they determine who started the screaming."

At that moment, I heard a "*hodi,*" and Philo walked in.

"No, I didn't sleep well," he said. He knew what we were talking about.

"How many girls are at the school?" I asked.

"About five hundred," Annette explained.

"There's a depth to these girls that you wouldn't think," Philo told me. "The curriculum they are learning is pretty much a British one. The girls are obliged to speak English. But there is something else going on," he explained. A chicken walked into the sitting room. Annette stood up to chase it away. She went out, then came back.

"What is going on?" I asked. Philo looked at Annette.

"No, you tell him," she said.

"But you understand these things better!" Philo said to Annette. "You are a Zambian girl after all."

"You tell," she responded. Annette's English was good. She was a teacher of English.

"I'll tell you using an example," Philo said. "We had a weekend crusade recently. We invited a pastor from a Pentecostal church to preach to the girls. I listened in. When the preacher said, 'some of you have demons,' I expected the girls to laugh. Nobody laughed. Instead, minutes later girls started falling down and writhing on the ground. They did not deny, but seemed to accept everything that the preacher told them. Before long the whole school was engulfed in a major crisis. That crisis did not die down quickly. A significant group of girls did not go to class for a few weeks thereafter. They were convinced that the Holy Spirit told them not to go. They were criticizing teachers for not heeding the Holy Spirit. Isn't that so Annette?"

"Yes," she said.

Philo and I excused ourselves. We went walking towards the school. "So how is agricultural development developing?" I asked Philo.

"In the light of the things I've just told you," Philo responded, "there's more going on than meets the eye." He showed me the location of what had been the proposed chicken house. The project had been vetoed by the school board. There were to have been two hundred layers. We looked at maize, peanuts, beans, vegetables, orange trees and bananas. Philo had recently planted a new area of the school land with bananas. They looked to be prospering. Philo was doing good work, but something was troubling him.

Up the slope behind the bananas was a building that had recently been renovated. I had thought there were people screaming. Now I discovered that this was the piggery. It was not people I had heard, but hungry pigs.

"I think Rickson told you that I recently spent one and a half hours in his office," Philo said. "Well, I can explain that." We walked into the building. Mr. Shibanda was busy dishing out slosh to the pigs. Shibanda was Philo's great friend on the school farm. A local man, with a slightly crotchety beard, he was able to do jobs on the farm that girls couldn't do because of their class commitments. The slosh was left over food from the school dining room. There was a sow with six piglets. There was another one who was evidently pregnant. Then there were five or so young pigs, presumably being fattened for slaughter. They were all confined by four-foot walls, all under one roof. The walls were made of blocks, and there were walkways between the pens.

"I got some money, and we renovated this piggery," Philo explained. "At the time, we only had the small black and white local pigs. I was going to town. We found a farm that had modern pigs. I bought three, two female and one male, and we brought them here. They grow very fast and very big on the leftovers from the school — free food in effect. A month or so ago we slaughtered our first big white boar!"

"A good sale?" I asked Philo.

"Went like a dream," he told me. "I also got a good price," Philo added. "I managed to sell the meat for 65 kwacha per kg."

I thought about that price. "That price does not seem particularly high," I said.

"No, but it was higher than what had been the going price of 35 per kg," Philo explained.

"Okay. Yes I see. Good price then," I acknowledged.

"And I believe we could have pulled it off again and again and again."

"So why don't you?" I asked Philo.

"Well, that, you see, is what is interesting," Philo replied. "It is about the meeting with Rickson, the head of the school."

"Okay. Tell me about it," I responded. By that time we were walking amongst the school classrooms.

Philo explained what was what. "Let's just finish this part of the tour, then I'll fill you in," he said.

"What do you mean?" I asked him again later referring to the meeting with Rickson.

"We make a lot of use of corporal punishment," Philo said. "When girls break school rules, we beat them."

"You mean, you teachers cane the students?" I asked a little incredulously.

"Yes, well, the headmaster, whom you met, canes the girls on the hand. At times after some crime, we can have twenty or so girls lying out there bawling." I was somewhat bowled over, learning about Zambians saw as the "normal" practices of school discipline.

We sat down in the classroom. "Is it a requirement for all teachers to be Christian?" I asked Philo.

"Yes," he said. Philo explained the workings of the staffroom. He told me which was his seat. He explained the role of the big central table.

Then I asked him, "Okay, so tell me about your time talking with the headmaster."

"Okay," he said, "I had come from the piggery. Heading back to school, there outside the offices was Rickson. He was carrying a piece of chalk, so I guess he had just come from class."

"'We can kill another pig next week,' I told him, 'and I'm sure we can get the same price as the last one, 65 kwacha per kg.' I said to him." To me this meant that things were moving. That price could bring in significant income. That income could help us to further develop the piggery and advance the rest of the school farm, without having to look for donor funds.

"The price should be 35 per kg," Rickson said.

"Why?" I asked him.

"Because that's the price we teachers can afford. We don't earn much, and we can't afford to pay 65 per kg," he stated.

Philo continued, "Rickson ushered me into his office. Now I had just got to make him see sense, I was telling myself. No way can we refuse the benefits of a higher price. Even at the school, my teacher colleagues often bemoaned the dependency of our school on outside donations. We sat down. 'Don't you see,' I said, 'that if we make more money from the school farm, that will benefit the school, it will enable us to expand the school farm and increase production, then everyone will be happy.' I even went as far as to say, 'If we sell pork at a higher price, then certainly when the market at that price is saturated, we may have to bring the price down. But in the meantime—let us sell as much as we can at as high a price as possible which will provide us with funds to re-invest. In addition—those funds will not be coming from foreign white donors!' Rickson correctly identified that many who had purchased our pork were my fellow missionaries. He did not see why foreign missionaries should be eating pork, while he and his fellow teachers could not afford it, yet the pigs were being reared at the school. I told him that such a free-market mechanism was a good way of getting money for the school. Better than having to ask for donations from America. 'We will not raise the price of pork above 35 kwacha,' Rickson insisted."

"So that all contributes a major blow," I said. I was following what he was saying. The headmaster's stand was killing the prospects of the school farm ever getting anywhere. "You have come, Philo, in order to help Zambian people to develop their agriculture. You know how to do that, and you could succeed. But now one of the Zambian people, your boss, has put a block on your progress. Your whole project, in running the school farm, at least as you see it, is at stake. But despite one and a half hours of discussion, the head has refused to budge. Your great ideas, and those you had picked up in your training before coming here, are now all for nothing," I shared. Philo nodded.

We sat in silence. All the clever agricultural knowledge in the world was not going to help us, if the local people refused to let prices move with the market. If that was going to be the policy, it was long-live to scraping by and subsistence farming! Commercial farming didn't have a chance. Scarcity would be the order of the day. The only solution seemed to be to take the school back over again from the Zambians. There had been a white headmistress until a couple of years previously.

"The missionaries have to take back the running of the school from the Zambians!" I declared.

"Hmmm!" Philo responded.

"Re-colonization!" I said, laughing.

"That would go down well I'm sure." Philo responded, sarcastically.

I left Philo in a puzzled stupor, his dreams of saving Africa, if not in tatters, at least seriously threatened. I wondered, as I rode home, the reason for Rickson's response to have been what it was. Something was niggling me. Can a piece of European capitalism function in a place where people do not do capitalism? In other words, if Philo had been given authority to sell pork at the highest price he could find, how sustainable would that have been? Say Philo had made money by selling food to his missionary colleagues and a few wealthy people around, what would have happened when he left? Would someone else have been able to continue the same policy? Quite likely not. Rickson knew that. No point in taking the school down an unsustainable road. Could one guarantee that money made would be invested into the school? Even if it was—what benefit would there actually have been to local people, including Philo's Zambian teacher colleagues, if home-grown money displaced foreign donor funds? More sweat for them that way, but no net gain. The school, after all, operated in English, and taught essentially a British curriculum. Could the Zambian people's hearts be in something so foreign? Or were they only in it for the money?

CHAPTER 9: RENT IS ILLEGAL

Philo certainly took his agricultural role seriously. He did not only want to be able to wax lyrical in class. He wanted to link what he was teaching in class to what was going on in the community around the mission. That was to prevent him from making stupid mistakes. "Plant on south-facing slopes," Philo told me he once advised his students! That might have been good advice in the UK, but it made no sense in Zambia, that was well south of the equator. Philo had to try to make sure that what he taught was fully appropriate to the context in which he was teaching.

A trip of Philo's to visit us at Edgington's Farm was memorable. It was the first time I had known a missionary to make the ten-mile trip on a bicycle. I think Philo was pretty chuffed himself. He was daring enough to have a go. I told him to join us in scaring birds from the sorghum fields. Apart from a few subsistence farmers' plots, the farm was surrounded by bush. There were lots of breeding grounds for birds and there was usually a shortage of food for them. Edgington's sorghum fields became a prime target for marauding birds. The only way of keeping the birds away seemed to be the old-fashioned one of running up and down shouting at them! Throwing sticks at them was good too. Except that one would run out of sticks.

That afternoon I volunteered Philo to help me chase birds. We were little boys again, running excitedly up and down trying to deter flying, hungry creatures that had a clear sighting of their lunch. It was no easy task. If I remember correctly, this was a Sunday afternoon. It was more difficult to get local people to do this on a Sunday, as they preferred to be at church. Philo's having already cycled ten miles seemed to add to his available energy rather than to deplete it!

"Talking about bicycles, I had a fascinating experience a few days back," Philo told me. I was aware that Philo was volunteering to help his teacher colleagues in village evangelism. They would prepare a program a few months ahead of time, then go out two by two, ideally every couple of weeks, to hold a weekend of teaching for people in the churches. Usually teaching was oriented to youth. Philo had told me that he was to attend the meeting at which the next three months' program would be arranged. Now he was going to tell me about it as we were walking from the sorghum field (another name for sorghum is guinea corn) back to the farm.

"We were a bit late starting, but eventually our meeting got underway," said Philo. "Amazingly though, amazing to me at least, we never managed to get to what should have been the main agenda—planning of the program."

"Why on earth not?" I interjected.

"Because of a gift," he said.

"A gift?" I asked.

"Yes a gift!"

"From whom?" I asked again.

"I'm not sure from whom, but from a white missionary," Philo told me.

"What was the gift for?" I responded.

"To help the program," Philo explained.

"So then, what was the gift?"

"Two bicycles," he said.

"Okay. Tell me more."

"At the meeting, we started asking about the bicycles," Philo explained. "The questions went on and on. No resolution came into view! Questions like: Who will keep the bicycles at their home? Who will repair them? Who will pay for repairs? Who is to use them? What may they be used for, and what should they not be used for? Should the chairman of our group have one of the bicycles for his personal use? That hardly seemed fair. If someone took a bicycle home—how free would they be to use it? Could they use it for other church business, or only for activities connected to the program of visits over weekends? If we did stipulate certain limits on use—how could we be sure that the person wouldn't contravene the conditions and go beyond those limits? How can someone even begin to prevent someone else from taking the bicycle without asking? Didn't senior family members consider themselves to have a right to property of their children that was portable and could be used by them? Wouldn't they take the bicycles and use them for whatever they wanted without even asking? What if the missionary concerned saw someone use a bicycle that he had given specifically for one thing being used by someone else for something else? What conditions had to be put into the use of the bicycles? These questions went on" Philo said, "for six hours without resolution."

As a result of these endless questions, no program was planned. It looked as if the intended outreach simply would not happen.

"It is strange," said Philo. "Such a conversation has me wondering how we cope with gifts in the UK! How does it work in the USA if someone gives a bicycle or car as a gift to a church?"

"Good question," I thought, but I did not feel that I had the available processing power to sort that one out. I shrugged my shoulders, and that was about the time we were walking into the house to find tea and bread waiting for us.

After a few minutes of tucking into our bread, Edgington himself came to join us. "Hi Dave! Hi Philo!" he said, before sitting down. Many people from the mission enjoyed coming to visit Edgington. It was a pleasant place to go to in order to get away from the mission, but still to find a resemblance to European life. Edgington and his wife seemed a very contented couple, despite the vast cultural gap that their relationship bridged. Edgington's easy-going style was a favorite with many. I noticed that Philo was always especially animated by his engagement with Edgington. With all that agricultural background, Edgington had become Philo's hero.

"I have a plan, but I want you to advise me on it," Philo stated.

"Okay. Tell me more," Edgington said.

"I have often heard people say that the school should be self-sufficient in vegetable production?" Philo said, looking quizzically at Edgington.

"That sounds right," came the reply.

"Has it ever happened before?" Philo asked Edgington.

"Not in my time," he responded.

"I've got a fool proof plan," said Philo. Then he added, "I think!"

"Okay," we said, pretty much in unison.

"But I want to tell you about it in context."

"When?" Edgington asked.

"Tomorrow morning, if that will work?" Philo responded.

"That will work," Edgington replied. "I'll see you at the school in the morning."

That night it was getting late when I said to Philo, "Have you ever noticed anything about the way people here think about things?"

"What do you mean?" Philo asked in return.

"The way European missionaries reason in a way which is so different from Africans," I said.

"You're right, Dave. It is a wonder that we can agree on anything! It's something I am always thinking about, but that no one else seems to notice. I guess we could say, that Europeans think of processes whereas African people think relationally."

"Something to ponder on," I said. Then I added, "Really looking forward to the great idea you have to show to us tomorrow. I hope it lives up to expectations."

"I think it will, but I am not sure," Philo responded.

The next morning Philo set off early back to the mission on his bicycle, leaving me to follow with Edgington. Edgington didn't usually have the time for pet projects like this. He had considerable interest in the school though, and was supporting some students in it.

"Do you think Philo might have a workable plan?" I enquired, as we bumped along the road heading for the mission. Edgington did, anyway, have to take some produce to the hospital and to the school. This was not an extra trip for him. It took a while to do the deliveries. The mission was clearly an important market for Edgington. He was good at striking up rapport with his fellow Europeans.

"Projects don't work," was Edgington's response. "Either, it seems to me, something is started and run by Europeans or something is started and run by Zambians. For a Zambian to do something then hand it over to a European is very difficult. For a European to start something and then for an African to take it over is also very difficult," he added.

When we met, Philo had an air of anticipation about him. He was in the school staffroom. He began his explanation. "The school needs vegetables. Vegetables can be very expensive. A resource that the school has is schoolgirls, many of whom already know a great deal about vegetable growing. We have land, which is decently fertile. We have water." (Tapped water was available all year around, sourced from a spring on the nearby hill.) "We even have money. We have girls who have many needs for money. So now, let's use money to create a real incentive for girls to work hard on vegetable production." Now we were hearing about the plan Philo had been hatching!

"A problem with mass production by schoolgirls would be that of supervision," Philo added. "Workers who are paid by the hour are not very concerned for the quality of their work. We need to devise a system that pays for production and not by time. A problem with small-scale production is difficulty in obtaining the necessary inputs. In our case, that would be things like seeds and perhaps fertilizer. Yet the school has logistical capabilities, it is able to supply these things. It is important, if we introduce mass levels of production, that the risk be borne by the producer. That is to say — we must pay for a finished product. If there is no finished product of sufficient quality, then we do not pay."

"The answer to all the above," Philo continued, "I am calling Farm Business Venture, from here on, FBV. Participants in this scheme are to be school students. They must show a commitment to the scheme by pledging themselves to pay rent for a small piece of ground. Their production on that piece of ground will be considered their personal property. A 'loan' will cover the cost of the rent and cost of inputs to the scheme. When the products are ready, the school will guarantee a good price. In fact, for those who are early takers of the scheme, we can pay very well. That way we give a super-incentive for others to participate as well. Later the rate we pay can be reduced a little. Either way though — it is better to supplement a child's fees or pocket money in return for their innovation, initiative and hard work, than just to give them a gift."

"Wonderful plan," said Edgington.

"Great ideas," I said, adding "I have a question for you, Philo."

"Hmm?" Philo said.

I intentionally left a long pregnant pause. My delay in presenting this question to Philo wasn't an indication of any low opinion I had of his ideas. I guess I spoke for myself. I don't know what Edgington was thinking. For me, when I thought about Philo's "fool proof plan," and indeed it did seem so in many ways, a certain question came to mind. I asked Philo "Did you come up with this plan by yourself, or in consultation with your Zambian colleagues?" Now Philo was as slow to answer as I had been to ask that question!

At that moment Annette charged into the room appearing very flustered. "A girl has collapsed," she said. "I can't even feel a pulse." We all rushed out. For some reason, no other teacher was around. Philo felt the girl's neck. Thankfully, he found a pulse. The school nurse was one of the two single white ladies I have mentioned previously. People loved the idea that the school had a European nurse. I had more than a few times heard people say that European nurses and doctors were much preferred to their African colleagues. It was Edgington who performed the heroic act. He picked the thankfully rather small girl up in his arms, and carried her the two hundred yards to the nurse's station, where the nurse was ready and waiting to perform her craft. Thankfully, the girl soon recovered.

By the time we were back to continue our conversation, half an hour had passed. We sat back into our original locations. "So Philo, where is your answer?" I asked after a pause.

Philo responded, "The Zambian folk want us. Just look at how they value having a European school nurse. But there are only certain ways in which they want us," Philo paused, then carried on. "Your suspicions are correct," he added, "FBV is my idea. I did not feel that I could really have hatched it together with any of my Zambian colleagues. They don't think the way I do. I felt I had no choice but to present it to them, as I have to you, as a complete package. They wouldn't have come up with such a package. If they support it, as someone might support something that they do not understand, then it might work. If it works, then presumably they will believe in it. That seems to be my only practical hope." Saying all that was obviously sobering for Philo.

"Well said, Philo," Edgington added. "I agree with you. That is why I make the decisions on my farm. I have a farm manager who helps me. He is Zambian. But he knows that it is his job to agree with my decisions. If it were his farm, things would certainly be very different."

"Do your best, Philo," I told him.

Philo had to excuse himself at that point. He had a biology class to teach. He kept thinking, no doubt, about our conversation. As for me, my brain felt like it had been dragged up a rugged mountain slope. I needed something brain dead to occupy me! Our conversations had been intense. Philo had invested heavily into his thinking. Even querying him was hard work. I think I might have slept as Edgington drove me back to his farm. We were up against hard cultural realities.

A few weeks later Edgington asked me to deliver vegetables to the mission. A nephew of Edgington (on his wife's side) was having a wedding. I agreed to do the run to the mission for him. In the course of doing so, I ran into Nick, the hospital administrator.

"You a friend of Philo?" he asked me.

"Yes," I told him.

"Sounds like quite a remarkable plan he has there at the school," Nick added. Matters of FBV were well at the back of my mind at the time. "He is trying to get students to grow vegetables. I was at the school the other day. I read the document he produced. Do you know anything about it?"

"Yes, we've talked about it with him," I replied.

"Very clever incentive scheme," said Nick.

"So will it work?" I asked.

"Now there's another question. Full marks for trying. But whether it will work. I think …" Nick started saying, when a frustrated looking Zambian nurse appeared at the door. He went out with her to solve some crisis. We never did complete that conversation. One thing that aborted conversation told me—was that what Philo was doing at the school was getting wider attention, including amongst hospital staff.

The next time I met Philo he said nothing about FBV, so neither did I. I did get a report though from a schoolgirl. That was when Edgington's niece came home for a weekend. She was one of the students who got involved in FBV. It transpired that other teachers were opposing Philo's idea. One part of his plan was that a student should pay a rent for the land she used on which to grow vegetables.

"Rent is illegal in Zambia," Edgington's niece announced.

"What do you mean?" I asked her to clarify.

"Land is freely available" she said. "No one who wants land should be charged for it." She was right. Land in Zambia was not bought or sold. Those who wanted to invest in land over a long term were given a lease for up to ninety-nine years. That would be people like Edgington, and perhaps land for building a school. Local farmers would not anyway erect permanent structures. That system of land distribution, by which land was free, had many good points. Land was given according to need. If a family had many children, then they would be given more land than a family without children or with few children. Philo's plan depended on there being a price to pay for the rent of land. That could have him brush up against the authorities.

What that schoolgirl's report indicated even more strongly though, was that Philo's fellow teachers were not standing behind him. The girls were unlikely to pay attention to Philo the foreigner, if the native Zambian teachers were at the same time trying to undermine him. It seemed unlikely that his project was going to succeed. Indeed, next time I spoke to Philo, he did not conceal the same. He showed me the plots of ground involved in the project. Uptake had been very low. Perhaps ten girls had taken plots. Four hundred and ninety had not. Those ten were not very serious. The whole project fizzled out. Like so many great white men's ideas, it was a failure. One thing I did agree with Philo about though, was that the scale of the failure was small! That is to say, other people at other times have invested in much larger "fool proof" projects than FBV. Their projects have come with massive outside funding. Failure in such cases has led to much greater financial loss and much greater embarrassment. Philo's trying things out at the scale of a secondary school farm was much more economical. It allowed failures to be endured. Amazingly in a way — what Philo was able to learn at school-farm level echoed closely what, from my observations, others were learning at national-massive-project level.

The intensity of Philo's disillusionment should not be under-estimated. Edgington had a soil-testing kit which he allowed Philo to borrow. He needed it back unexpectedly, so he asked me (I was already planning a trip to the mission and the school) to get it for him. I gave my usual *'hodi'* at the door to Philo's house. "*Mwaiai mwane,*" said the occupant of the house (come in) with an English accent. I went in to find Philo in conversation with an older American man. It turned out to be the American director of the mission for the whole of Zambia.

"Welcome, Dave," Philo said. Before asking for the soil-testing kit and leaving, I got a snippet of the conversation.

"No amount of money will help things if the teachers do not change," Philo was telling the director. "You have to get the teachers to change, or we will get nowhere," he re-emphasized. The conversation had already been long.

"I can't just tell the teachers to change," the director responded to Philo.

"Well, if they won't change we are going nowhere," Philo said. In due course, the topic changed a little. "They always want things," Philo said. "When a fellow teacher comes to the door, they don't want to chat. They are not being sociable. They are wanting something—typically food. If not, then money." The director nodded in agreement. He did not argue with that.

"The people are as they are," he said. Philo started explaining about FBV. At that point though, I felt I had outstayed my "eavesdropping." I asked Philo for the soil-testing kit. He gave it to me, and I left.

A few days later Philo explained. He saw no other way to go forward, but for the Zambian teachers to change and agree with him on some key issues. Rightly, the director said, he could not enforce that. This meant that Philo had some tough thinking to do. He had come to Zambia to help the poor. In the early days, his task seemed to be easy. As he went on, he met more difficulties. Valiantly, let's say, he attempted to overcome the difficulties he faced. The difficulties were proving insurmountable. What should he do now?

CHAPTER 10: THE WAY OUT

What I often heard from Philo were words like "This is hopeless, it is never going to work." What I never heard from him is, "I am giving up and going home." He did tell me he was committed for life, no matter what—unless the commitment became impossible for some reason, like deterioration in his health. That was an admirable stand, I felt, but was still to be tried and tested. His contract in Zambia was for just three years. There were many short-term missionaries coming through Mubantu who were there at the same time as Philo. But they did not speak the way Philo did.

Mildred, the hospital matron, and I were to lead a Bible study with those short-term missionaries who wanted to join us. We needed to plan it. "Can I come out to see you at the farm instead of your coming here?" she asked.

"Sounds great," I told her, "providing it will be Thursday afternoon, as other days I am pretty occupied." When she checked her diary Thursday was free, so over she came. When she arrived, I did think she looked a bit out of place at the farm. Mildred was a perfectionist—she liked things to be right. Instead of sitting in a chair, she perched on it. The dust on the road was a serious source of irritation to her. Fortunately, the occasional shower of rain had reduced dust to a lower level than in the peak of the dry season. She brought out a wipe from her handbag and mopped her face.

"You look tense," I said to her. I thought I might as well be open. I did not expect what happened next though. I did not expect to see a senior staff member at the hospital burst into tears in front of me. But that is what happened. A little alarmed, I tried to offer some words of encouragement. Thankfully, Edgington's wife was in earshot. When she heard the sobbing, she came and put her arm around poor Mildred. I left the ladies to it for five minutes. When I got back, Mildred was sitting in her chair instead of perching on it. Mrs. Edgington had gone to make some tea.

"Sorry about that," I said to Mildred. She looked notably relieved at this point.

"No problem, Dave. Sorry for exploding on you. I guess I was carrying a lot of built-up tensions."

"Sure," I said, "it happens."

"The student nurses have been stealing medicines," she said. "I can hardly believe it. We are there to help people and to save lives. All we seem to hear from the student nurses is complaints about the level of their pay, and then about their stealing. Do they not care? I see them walking past sick patients who are in trouble. One man lying stark naked in bed who hadn't had a drink for eight hours or more, yet the nurses were oblivious at the other end of the ward, chatting and laughing!" It was not the first time for me to hear this kind of talk. There were some frustrated people at the hospital. Somehow, they battled on.

"You know Philo?" she asked.

"Yes, I know him," I acknowledged. "He is a good friend of mine," I added.

"You know, Dave, what he says is mostly true. But the rest of us don't know what to do about it. It's like he is trying to reveal our nakedness! What he says is often spot on. We keep on working here, like at the hospital, but it can be very hard at times to see a light at the end of the tunnel. Will we ever hand over the mission hospital to nationals? If we do, how long will it last? Maybe a week? It's been decades since the hospital was founded. You would have thought things might have changed. But they never do." I sat still listening attentively.

"Some people are tired of Philo's questioning," Mildred went on. "It's not that he is trying to upset people. He is just talking about things that he is trying to process in his head. He might be innocent, but extremely provocative. Sometimes when he talks about the secondary-school teachers he might as well be talking about our nurses."

"Good news," Mildred added after a pause, changing the subject. "We have a surgeon in prospect. We have been without a surgeon for six weeks. An American surgeon has agreed to come for twelve months. Hearing about the urgency of the need, he is ready to come in two weeks' time."

"How are the other new staff members doing?" I asked Mildred.

"Okay, as long as they don't realize what is happening, and before they talk to Philo," she quipped. "You know I have said things about Philo, but the missionary hierarchy really seem to like him. It's not every single young man who devotes three years of intense consistent service as he has done. Neither have we heard of him getting involved with any girls, despite being a teacher at a girls' school. Anyway, what about our Bible study?"

We planned our study. It was to be on the second chapter of 2 Corinthians. Afterwards, I asked Mildred for a lift back to the mission, to help me get to the local shops. (The shops were about three miles from the mission.) "I've talked about Philo," Mildred said, as she was driving back, "but maybe I need to add something else to fill you in."

"Okay" I said. "Please speak up as it is hard to hear you over the engine," I added. We stopped and picked up some hospital workers on their way to work, then she carried on.

"Francesca Pitcher was here last week." Francesca had at one time been a headmistress in a Zambian secondary school, and was with us in official capacity from the British office of the mission. "She has come from the UK to interview UK personnel. She overheard us talking about Philo over dinner one day. We jokingly asked her 'What do you think?' We thought she might laugh. Instead, well, Francesca is quite a serious creature, she told us quite a lot, particularly about Philo's achievements. She went on to tell us 'Philo is the only missionary I have known who in a three-year term, while teaching full-time at the secondary school which operates entirely in English, has acquired conversational fluency in Bantu—or for that matter in any other local language. In addition to teaching agriculture and other topics like maths, geography, chemistry and biology at the school, he has done serious ministry. I know that Sunday alone is an extremely busy day for school teachers, spending hours and hours at services and giving devotionals to pupils. Philo has faithfully attended Bible studies led by the Zambian teachers. He has taught classes of TEE (Theological Education by Extension) to local pastors. He has been involved in outreach to local churches over weekends, led by his teacher colleagues. He has attended seminars together with Zambian colleagues. He has travelled extensively, visiting mission stations and other projects, then he has written reports about such visits. He has lived with Zambians throughout his stay, and not made any girls pregnant! Even more amazingly, he attended a gathering called 'Saturday Fellowship.'"

"It was amazing to hear Francesca read out that list to us," Mildred went on. "What she said was correct to my knowledge. The case of 'Saturday Fellowship' is interesting. We missionaries here on the station have long met together every Sunday evening. It was 'missionaries only' so that we could discuss and work through our issues, and receive Bible teaching. Well, the senior Zambian staff at school and hospital wanted to join us. After all, they said, they were operating at professional level using English, so how could they fail to understand what we were talking about? The missions' leadership at the time refused. They felt that missionaries needed their own space. As a reaction to being blocked from 'Sunday Fellowship', the Zambians started 'Saturday Fellowship' on Saturday evenings! We felt they could become a group of rebellious troublemakers. In due course 'Sunday Fellowship' was opened to Zambians. 'Saturday Fellowship' continued. It was exclusively Zambian, and strictly so—until we heard that Philo had joined them! It appears he became an integral member of the group, who would walk from the school to the hospital and back with the Zambian teachers for the fellowship on Saturday evenings, on a regular basis. He never made an issue of it. When we heard about it, we were astounded."

CHAPTER 11: SURVEY NOT FROM HEART

Sometimes, at the mission station, passions could get whipped up. This was going to be one of those times. It all started rather innocently in a Bible class. One of the hospital doctors was teaching a Bible class to pastors. A citation from the book of Philippians was the spark that ignited the debate. Especially that "faith without works is dead." Discussion continued amongst Zambian pastors after the class. In the meantime, a minister from a church in the USA was visiting. This man had a church of three thousand people in Ohio state, USA. His church, I later discovered, had made a major contribution towards the cost of the new hospital wing. The presence of that new wing had been essential for the advancement of the nursing school. Bruce, as the pastor was known, was a thick-set man with a full crop of bushy hair. Sitting around the table with him that midday, from the volume of his contribution to table discussion, you might have thought he was preaching to three thousand people in an open field.

Doc who had taught the said Bible class sat opposite me, the visitor alongside me. "How much do the unskilled workers at the hospital get paid?" Bruce, the visiting pastor asked. Doc (Robert) told him.

"That's not very much is it!" Bruce declared. We were taken aback by his confidence.

"It is more than they would get paid working for the government," Doc responded. "In fact, the amount they get paid working with us here equals the salary of a primary teacher."

"You couldn't buy a decent Sunday lunch for two in the USA for the amount you pay a worker for a week here," Bruce said. My hairs stuck up on the back of my hand! The doctor's wife went red. Their maid who was serving us at that very moment, stepped on the cat. The cat let out a resounding scream. That series of events might have been quite funny, if I didn't have to see the expression on Doc's face.

"That may be," said Doc.

"It's not may be," Bruce declared, sticking the dagger in a little deeper and wiggling it around, "it is as true as your heart is black."

The moment he pronounced the term "black," a flower pot that had been destabilized by the running cat fell to the ground with a clatter. I burst out with a loud "ha ha …," but no one else was laughing.

"Be careful before you come by here accusing people," Doc responded, deadly serious.

"I am saying what I know. I have it from the horse's mouth. The foreman not only told me how little the workers are paid, but also showed me the receipts. He also told me that you are the one who determines wage levels. I have been sending thousands of dollars to support the work of this hospital, thinking I was sending money to Christian men, not to racist animals!" Bruce shouted loudly.

"Thank you for the good food," Doc said nodding to our hostess as he stood wiping his mouth. "That was an excellent lunch. I have a seriously-ill patient who needs urgent attention. Good day, Dave. Good day, Bruce." He walked briskly out of the door.

Bruce's tirade is largely unrepeatable. It was long and aggressive. Those of us who remained sat in stunned silence. Bruce's grasp of counter-racist measures in the USA were being transferred lock, stock, and barrel to Mubantu Mission Station. If he only knew half of what was going on! We had an extremely hot potato on our hands. How dare we missionaries (he was unaware that I was not actually a missionary) be so racist! The volume eventually dropped.

"Sorry to find you are so upset," I interrupted. The volume rose again. "Things don't work here like they do in America," I added. We managed to dissuade Bruce from going to search for the local police.

Tensions ran high on the mission station for a week. Some opportunist Zambians were not slow to try to take advantage of their new-found advocate. Workers downed tools. The police did come—someone called them. They did not stay long—fortunately. The following day the field director made the ten-hour road trip from Lusaka to Mubantu. (The plane was transporting medical personnel to Eastern Province in Zambia, so was not available.) The day after that Bruce left with the field director.

A week later I met Philo outside some of our local shops. "Hi Dave," he greeted me. I hadn't seen him, so he startled me. "*Mujibyepi?*" (how's things), he asked me.

"Hey Philo, it's you! I'm not used to having white people appear from shops when there is no vehicle around to show their presence," I exclaimed.

"I've got a new job, have you heard?" Philo asked me.

"New job, haven't got a clue," I replied. "Hope it will pay well," I added wryly.

"Well, not that kind of job unfortunately," he told me. (Philo and the other missionaries lived off charitable donations from the West.)

"Well, what sort of job?" I asked. "Look, I am in a bit of a hurry. Why don't you jump into the truck and I will give you a ride back to the mission," I added, before he could give me his answer.

From the town to the mission airstrip wasn't very far. But it was far enough for Philo to be able to inform me of further developments arising from Bruce's visit. Bruce wanted someone to talk to Zambians and to Europeans in the area about development. He left Zambia determined that he could find a better way for his church to use their money. The mission director had asked Philo if he could engage in a small research project on Bruce's behalf. It was Philo, after all, who was our resident agriculturalist, one who also had a better grasp of local goings-on than did many. Now Philo was excited by this prospect. He even agreed to make use of a motorbike to pursue it.

I never did get a report that I can remember from Philo directly about his research. I did get a report from Doc a few months later. "Remember the interesting lunch with Bruce?" Doc asked me, waiting a little pensively for my response. The issue that Bruce had raised was a difficult one. I was still troubled by the issues of right and wrong that he brought to our attention. How could Doc teach African pastors about God's love, while sucking his workers dry with miserly wages? At the same time I also realized, unlike Bruce, that American race-relations couldn't simply be transferred to Africa as if context made no difference.

I had to make do with Doc's report on Philo's research. "Philo drew two main conclusions from his research," Doc told me. First was that it was not practical for a mission station to pay its workers ten to forty times as much as other Zambian workers were getting paid. (The salary differential between Zambia and European countries tended to be of between a factor of ten and forty.) The jealousies and fighting for employment at the mission would be too intense. We needed to remember that government employees working at the hospital and school were themselves on the low side that Bruce condemned. Bruce needed to take on the Zambian government, not the Mubantu missionaries. Philo's second conclusion was even more perplexing. Philo asked over thirty people a list of questions about how to bring about rural development. He asked the same forty-eight questions in the same way to Zambians as to ex-pats. "Zambians gave the right answers," said Philo to Doc apparently, "but were unmotivated and unanimated by discussions about development." So much so that Philo reported that while his interviews with Europeans were often very lively, he would be in danger of falling asleep during his interviews with Zambians. Doc concluded that while Zambians got Philo's development questions with their heads, they did not always get them with their hearts.

Philo's three years were nearly over. As it happened, I left Zambia a few weeks later, also for the UK. I'd landed a two-year contract with a big company in Manchester, which meant I could spend some time with my sister, who was not only living there, but was engaged to Derek, a local guy.

As usual, the missionaries arranged a farewell meal. Everyone contributed a pot of something. Philo was excused—being a bachelor. (Fellow missionaries didn't trust his ability to cook anything decent. Probably quite rightly so.)

"Philo—we'll see you in England in a few months," I told him.

"What will you be doing there?" Philo asked. I knew that Philo was going back to study for a Master's course in rural development at university.

"Two-year contract with a UK company," I told him.

"How are things working out?" I asked Philo.

"You know, Dave, amazing," Philo told me.

"Oh?" I asked.

"A few days ago, I wanted to make a video of the school to show to supporters back home," Philo told me. "I managed to find someone who could loan me a video camera. As a formality, I asked Rickson for permission. He refused me permission!" Philo said. Why on earth he should refuse his permission I had no idea.

"Why did he refuse?" I asked.

"Because they suspected that I would use the video to make money for myself on the back of their poverty."

"You mean that you would use the video in the UK to impress on the people how you were working with the poor people, so as to get more money?" I asked.

"Exactly," Philo replied.

"Well. So, no video?"

"Later they allowed me to video the farm, but not the other school buildings or activities," Philo replied, "on the basis that it was on the farm side of things that I was most involved."

"I hope to see the video when we are in the UK," I said.

"You will," Philo proclaimed. "I love it when the girls sing as they cultivate by hand. Farming is much more fun here than in the UK—where we sit alone in cold, noisy, dirty tractors for hours and hours."

Another of Philo's comments also made me think. Philo had worked hard in developing the school farm. (Philo was not full time on the farm, he was also teaching. Yet much of the school farm had been transformed.) Philo thought he was enabling the Zambians to continue benefitting from the same project. As he was soon to leave, one of the teachers commented, "Now we will have to find another European man to run the farm." That was just one comment. But to Philo it was a very sobering comment. He could do what he did because he was a white man! He thought he was doing things for Africans to continue them, but at least according to this teacher, an African would not be able to take over from him.

CHAPTER 12: UNIVERSITY CHALLENGE

"I felt really good," Philo told me a few months later, as we sat drinking tea at his new university. Philo had started his Master's course in the University of East Anglia (UEA). "Walking down those wide corridors through the concrete jungle of the university made me feel as if I was someone important," Philo said. I guess he was comparing the aura of the university with what he had been experiencing there in rural Africa, out in the sticks, cut off from civilization.

Philo's reaction to going back to the UK was starkly different from mine. Being in Zambia had helped me to put thoughts of Cindy to the back of my mind. Moving to the UK, an English-speaking European country, revived them. I saw, for the first time in years, many girls who looked like Cindy. For a while, I longed to remarry. Philo took time with me as I shared this issue with him. Philo had a good listening ear, and a pastor's heart. I did not remarry. Philo's concern for me, added to my respect for him, and my willingness to listen to his issues.

"They gave us a pre-course course," Philo said. I asked him to tell me more about his course at the university.

"What's that?" I asked.

"It was for dimwits like me who had never done serious arts studies," Philo recounted. "It was a crash course in everything that we needed to know that we had missed out on. It was things like political theory, economics, sociology, a bit of anthropology."

"That sounds very *highfalutin*," I said, speaking as if I was a country bumpkin.

"By the time I had finished that month I knew I was on the wrong course," Philo told me.

"What!" I replied, "what for?" We discussed what Philo said in a lot more detail than I will recount here. UEA is considered to have Marxist leanings. That is what Philo was kicking against. His professors were telling him that underdevelopment was about the wrong soil, not enough rainfall, lack of access to capital and so on. Philo knew that it was hearts that needed transforming! The topic of changing hearts was not on the curriculum. Or at least it was very nominally so. There were, Philo told me, *occasional* mentions of witchcraft as a barrier to overcome in order to achieve development. Most of the time any thought that majority world poverty arose from people's own understandings of life and not from their environment, were not on the agenda at all.

I had to laugh when Philo told me that as a result of the above his grades became lower and lower as his studies progressed. That was because he got to believe less and less of what was being taught at the secular Marxist-oriented school. A breath of fresh air came to him when he was directed to sociology and anthropology. These people had, in Philo's view, more of a clue. They studied people *as* people, and not just as victims of economic forces as did all too many Marxist development experts.

In a few months, my sister was getting married. She had visited me in Zambia, so Philo had met her there. She was to have her wedding in the Scottish Highlands. It was not easy for me to convince Philo to come. I almost had to pay him to convince him to part with his books over a long weekend! He eventually agreed to take a train to Aberdeen.

The day after the wedding and before Philo was to head south for his studies, he and I had opportunity to experience some breath-taking scenery. The Scottish Highlands are phenomenal. It was almost as phenomenal to find that it was not raining. We drove into the mountains and parked the car. Then we walked up and down along wide and narrow paths enjoying the brisk Scottish air. It was Philo's first time ever in Scotland. After a lot of climbing, we found ourselves above a long slope of scree.

"See that tree with the fork in it right down there?" Philo said, pointing right down into the valley.

"Yes," I said, "to the right of those fir trees, as we are looking."

"Yes, that's the one," said Philo. I couldn't for the life of me see what was particularly interesting about that tree. "Isn't that next hill the one we have to climb over to get back to the car?" he asked.

"Hmmm," I looked carefully. "You're right."

"Do you think there's a path from that tree, up that hill?" he asked.

"Where there is no way, we can make a way," I responded. The thing he said next was the last thing I expected to hear from him at that point.

"Race you to that tree," he said.

"What!" I looked at him in astonishment.

"You chicken?" he asked. An overdose of youthfulness had evidently overcome Philo.

A minute later we shot off in unison on our crazy venture. Philo went off like a train, his legs pumping like pistons. I shot along behind him. I was soon puffing like a buffalo! We ran and ran—it was probably about two miles. It felt like a 30-degree descent. Our pace had slowed a little. The scree slipped noisily under our feet. My rucksack was crashing up and down on my back. Philo was maintaining about fifty yards of lead. It looked like Philo was going to win the race. "This is crazy!" I thought to myself. But then I had to laugh! (To myself that is.) It was Philo's first time in Scotland. He did not recognize the colour of green that lay in the final hundred yards between the end of the scree and the tree. It was dense furze! Philo was making a beeline straight for the tree. I curved off to the right to avoid the furze. He didn't. He glanced back just once or twice. He must have wondered where I'd gone, then wondered why I had taken a detour. Philo was ahead. He was faster than me. I saw the gap between myself and the tree narrowing but, because of the route I took, Philo was soon much closer to the tree than was I. Then I noticed his pace slow. His ankles, then his knees, disappeared from sight. I could almost hear him thinking, "How on earth am I going to get through this furze?" He disappeared altogether, then reappeared, evidently having stepped into a hole or tripped over some furze. By this time, I was laughing crazily as I jogged! "Bam," I hit the tree with the palm of my hand, long before Philo did. I was still puffing like crazy while laughing like crazy! When he drew closer I saw Philo's face was screwed up in intense concentration. It took two minutes before he arrived, collapsing on the ground beside me, his feet plastered in mud, and his trousers torn. I laughed and laughed and laughed. Fortunately, he didn't take offence.

"That was sly of you," Philo told me.

"Hmm?" I grunted.

"You saw that, what, furze is it?" he asked.

"Yes, it is furze," I said, "and yes, I saw it coming."

"I didn't," he added.

"I know!" I said, laughing louder again.

The base of that tree provided a good resting place. We sat on a log, and ate our rather shaken sandwiches (prepared for us by my aunt). "That was quite a lesson," Philo said.

"What do you mean?" I responded.

"The obvious route from our original vantage point was not the correct route," Philo observed.

"I see," I said.

"So then, it is possible to stand at a certain place," Philo added. "From where you stand, you see things in a certain way. We could have been a whole group. The whole group might well have advised me to run the way I did. Yet they would all have been wrong."

"Good point Philo," I said, while wondering where he was heading.

"That's it!" Philo turned to me. He added, "That is what is happening!"

"What do you mean?" I asked. I still wasn't exactly clear what he was getting at.

"It is happening in terms of Africa. The West stands on their hill. They are sure they know how to help Africa to reach a 'better' destination. They direct African people down a course which makes sense to them. They have money, so African people agree. Then they run off down the scree, yet there is a lot of furze at the bottom!"

Philo was sure he was onto something, so I paid careful attention. "Go on," I said.

"It's crazy," Philo told me, "in fact crazier than you can imagine!" At that point, we got an incredible view of a large bird above us, soaring down to us from where we had come. I like to believe that was my first sighting of a golden eagle. "People at the university. What are they teaching us? Whatever it is, the things they assume about Africa are not true," Philo added. "I was there for three years. In those years, I lived with nationals and I shared in their lives. I even acquired some fluency in their language. Our lecturers have not had that experience. They do not know what's going on. They are running almost entirely on the basis of what they could see from the hilltop. They are running blind!" Philo exclaimed.

"That's an incredible claim, Philo."

"But true!" he responded. "While living in Zambia I could hardly believe what we were meeting. One thing though—I became sure that I was not fooling myself. We saw what we saw, at least, I saw what I saw and I heard what I heard. I was not going to come back to the UK to study and forget all that. That would be silly. I wanted to apply what I had found in my studies. The university doesn't want to let me do that. Professors have all their own theories. The theories are not 'wrong.' They are right, according to the way they think about them. But they are wrong for Africa." Philo stopped there. He seemed to want me to argue with him. I did not have words with which to do so.

"I have been able to read some anthropology," Philo went on in due course. "I thought anthropology was for pansies. Now I see that what they are writing about is there," he added. "Even there around Mubantu. I've read a book about the Bantu people. What it describes is incredible. It describes them as being bound by witchcraft. It is true." Philo stood. He unstuck his trousers from where his sweating had made them stick to his buttocks. "I'm going back this summer," he said.

"What, back to Zambia?" I asked.

"Yes."

"Will they let you?" I asked.

"I've written to ask," he responded.

"Why?"

"To see if it's true." Philo said. "If it is true, that blows the mind."

"If what is true?"

"We are trying to develop Zambian people by telling them to do things the way we do them (with some contextual adjustments that make sense to us). But they are stuck in their fear of witchcraft!"

"Hmmm," I said.

"Absolutely stuck, hand and foot," said Philo. "Can't move, stuck—worse than was I in that furze!"

"Really?" I asked.

"Yes," said Philo. "Most ironic. What people who are 'stuck' in witchcraft need is the gospel of Jesus, but what we missionaries are all too busy giving them are medicine, agriculture, English, projects. You name it."

Philo planned his trip back to Zambia. He realized that if he wrote his thesis quickly enough, he had two months to spare before his next course. He planned to write quickly. He was set on making the visit. He booked his flight. Then, about three months after sending his original letter, he got a reply saying, "Don't come!"

"My flight was already booked, so I had to go," Philo told me later. "I'm sure they will understand," he added.

I was not so sure that they would.

A few months later it had become clear that they didn't understand! "Why have you come back to Zambia when we told you not to?" was the response Philo got from people in the mission when he arrived. Not only did the missionaries have that understanding, but also many nationals. Zambians and missionaries had been talking about what Philo might do when he got back to Zambia. The question regarding his summer visit had gone to the church council. The church council could see no reason for Philo to come then, when he still had another year of study in the UK ahead of him. They wrote a letter to Philo to tell him not to come. Then Philo appeared. He was labeled as a rebel. "Ouch!" That must have hurt! How to become unpopular in one easy stroke: ask for permission, assume you will get permission, be refused permission, do it anyway. Philo's halo had slipped, as far as Zambia was concerned, and seriously.

Philo told me all about it later, a few months on. When Philo got to Mubantu, Rickson helped him. The school teachers anyway tended to be a little rebellious. Having Philo come, contrary to the advice of the national church council, was no skin off their nose. Philo just wanted somewhere to stay, a position from which he could find out "Is it true?" Was what he had read in the anthropology books actually happening? If so, why weren't people responding to it? He and Rickson looked high and low, but could not find anyone in the nearby villages willing to take on a white man as a visitor for a month. That was very discouraging. What happened next was related to Philo's prior three-year stay.

Philo had, in his time teaching at the school, spent a year in Zambia living with his housemate, Tichi. After that year, another house became available. Tichi went to do some further study. Philo was given the available three-bedroomed house to himself. Observing these events, an entrepreneurial young man called Bremmy had come onto the scene. One way for a Zambian boy to make a way for himself was to latch onto a white man. Bremmy decided to try his luck with "lonely Philo," who was living by himself. One day Philo came home from school to find Bremmy preparing a vegetable patch in the garden around his house. "I don't want you, and I don't need you," were Philo's words to Bremmy. Bremmy kept coming back to continue his work every day regardless. Those words were insufficient to deter Bremmy. "Okay," Philo told him in the end, "I accept. Grow some vegetables for me." Bremmy did, and Philo paid him a little.

A month or so later it transpired that Bremmy wanted to go to school, but that his home was far from the school. Philo's house was much closer to the school he planned to attend. Philo, of course, had a big house. So the question arose—can Bremmy stay with Philo? "What!" was probably the reaction of most of the missionaries at the station. It was bad enough Philo staying with a Zambian teacher. For many missionaries, there was no way that he could take in a Zambian boy to stay with him. The boy was not even known—his family lived nearby, but were not especially connected with the mission. There was, however, an American missionary living on the station who did have two local girls staying with her. "Yes, it can be done," of course, she had to say. Just how much gossip it generated, I do not know, but Bremmy moved into Philo's house to stay with him.

"All his worldly possessions, apart from the clothes he wore, fitted in a little cloth bag," said Philo, when he eventually explained all this to me. Now however, Philo was faced with a dilemma. "The question now was— how are we going to eat?" Philo told me. "Unlike when I was staying with Tichi, now I was in charge of the household. I was gravitating towards the eating of European foods—as would be expected of me. But now—to buy European delicacies (as of course was the status of European food in that obscure mission station) would be expensive. It would also frankly not work." African colleagues could become very resentful if they were to discover that this village lad, who had just appeared at Philo's door, was eating bread, cakes, pies, tarts and ice cream! In that area, people's diet was often maize and beans for day after day. Giving Bremmy European food would easily raise his diet to a "higher" level than any other Africans for miles around! (In postcolonial Africa, what is European is taken by many as being implicitly better than what is traditionally African.)

Another alternative would have been for Philo to set up a dual-food-system. In such a system, Philo would eat European food, but Bremmy would access another cupboard, and eat Zambian food. "How on earth could I police that?" Philo asked himself. "I would have to keep my cupboard locked. Or—what was I going to do if Bremmy stole my food, yet I had put the temptation in his face?" The only practical solution that Philo saw, was that he must, with Bremmy, eat African food. He and Bremmy would share one food cupboard and Bremmy would be free to take what he wanted when he wanted it—as if he was at home. Hence Philo ate African food, cooked by him or Bremmy. He ended up thin as a rake.

Fast forward to the time of Philo's visit after completing his Master's thesis. By this time, Bremmy had moved back to his parental home. Meanwhile, no one else was ready to take a white man to stay with them in their home for the six weeks or so Philo had available, it seemed. But when Rickson approached Bremmy, he welcomed Philo with open arms! After all, Philo had previously had Bremmy stay with him.

"It was just amazing in so many ways," Philo told me after he had come back from his trip. "I was just a few miles from the mission. Over the hill was the mission station. There things were crazily busy. People were rushing to save lives at the hospital. Students were running to beat the bell to class at the school. Programs and projects and deadlines were the order of the day. Busy, critical, desperate, important, vital, foreign-funded work was being done. There in the village, things were very different."

"At one point, Bremmy's baby sister got sick," Philo told me. (Bremmy was the firstborn in his family.) "Mum took her baby to hospital. She had been given some high-protein soya flour to prepare regularly for the baby, to improve its diet. She made soya porridge once in the whole week before she was due to go back to the hospital," Philo observed. "That was in the morning before she took him back!"

"One day, I was sat in Bremmy's hut reading," Philo recalled. "His mother was outside cooking. A visitor came along, a man in his late thirties or so. He sat and talked with Bremmy's Mum for almost an hour. He did not have a clue that I, a white man, might be sitting in that hut in the village. So he chatted freely. What struck me was his analysis of conditions in the village. Everything that was happening seemed to be determined by witchcraft (*balozi*). Events, successes, failures, deaths, illnesses, causation, relationships—all were arising from witchcraft!" (Philo emphasized that his language knowledge was too limited to get all that was said. But he got enough to clearly grasp the above.)

"It could appear that people did not have a care in the world," Philo shared with me. "At night, we would sit and talk around the fire (or glowing embers). We might be fifteen people. I didn't really know who was who. I certainly did not know who was whose wife and who was whose husband. It was not that people did not have troubles," Philo observed. "But they did seem to handle their troubles in certain ways," he added. "If everything is caused by witchcraft, that rather changes the nature of personal responsibility," Philo pointed out. "The witch was always to blame. What people had to do was to try to avoid the impression of being envious (because envious people were accused of being witches), and to avoid as far as possible attracting the envy of others. Hence poverty was in many ways desirable," Philo explained.

"I also walked around and chatted to other community members. I already knew many people, but previously had not known what to ask or what to listen for when talking to them. Conversations with people this time were revealing. The terms mentioned in a book that I had read and the practices referred to were still alive," Philo told me. "On one occasion, I visited an old friend who had a farm in the neighbourhood. Now I was coming to him with new eyes! He showed me his crops and his land. Our conversation went to the time of year when food became short. When Zambians use English, they refer to that as the 'hungry season.' 'Why not plant more crops so that you have enough food for the hungry season?' I suggested to my friend. He clearly had a lot more land available than he was planting. 'But if I have spare food during the hungry season, I either have to give it away, in which case I don't benefit,' he told me, 'or if I eat well while other people are hungry I will get bewitched.' That was a no-win situation. I was amazed."

Philo, however, faced a dilemma. The one dilemma I have already mentioned—missionaries and even (presumably) some nationals, were talking against him. This was mostly because he appeared to have disregarded the clear instruction from the church council not to come. He also came face-to-face with a wider dilemma: "What I was discovering was challenging what my missionary colleagues were doing," Philo conceded. "This very same poverty that I was trying to solve, arose from their fear of witchcraft. This was the crux of the matter. What those people needed, it became clearer and clearer, was God's word. They needed a deep faith in God and in the Bible with which to displace their terror of what witches could do to them," Philo explained. "That however was not at all accepted wisdom," he went on. "Mission societies were busy running projects like hospitals. Even where there were Bible schools, they operated in English, thus concealing African issues from view. Missionaries were very concerned with helping people to improve their lives in many ways. They did not see that such would happen by itself as people became true believers in Christ."

Philo eventually showed me a copy of a letter that he wrote, but never sent. He addressed it to Francesca Pitcher, head of personnel for the mission back in the UK at the time:

August 1992

Dear Francesca,

Receive greetings in Jesus' name from Zambia.

You will be aware that as I write this letter I am in Zambia. I planned to make this trip back in March this year. I wrote a letter to the field to inform them of my intention to come and to ask for their approval. By the time May arrived, I had not yet received a response. I decided to go ahead and book my flight and make arrangements. A few weeks later I received a letter from the church council asking me not to come. Unfortunately, I felt it was too late to change my plans, so I trusted they would be understanding.

My main reason for coming back was so as to put my feet back onto the ground in Africa. As a result I have on this trip confirmed things that I had not at all understood during my previous three-year term. I discovered that people in the community around Mubantu are deeply engrossed in witchcraft. It has been a shock to discover just how much their lives are oriented towards avoiding being bewitched. In the light of this, it seems to me that our priority as missionaries should be to help people overcome their witchcraft through a knowledge of God. In this respect, many projects are a distraction because they draw people to foreign money more than to the gospel.

I look forward to discussing some of these things with you. I cannot see myself coming back to Zambia to do agriculture after my next year's missionary training course. I would much rather attempt to engage people's lives with God's Word.

Yours appreciatively,

Philo

"Dave, help me, what should I do?" Philo urged me. He was back from his trip. I could see that a combination of things were changing Philo's perspective. It started with teaching for three years in Zambia. At the time he knew nothing about anthropology. New insights and experiences had opened his eyes, and study had further revealed things to him. Philo was a hot potato. You couldn't hold him. What to do? Philo already felt condemned by the mission, because he appeared to have despised their authority. He also feared that if he told them the truth as he perceived it, they would not appreciate him. He was about to spend a year at a missionary training college. Would they appreciate what Philo had to offer?

Philo told me that he had sent a copy of the letter that he wrote to Francesca to his friend, Richard. "Look Dave," he said to me, "I have a really depressing letter here from a colleague. Richard and I were good friends at agricultural college. He wanted to give me a high-earning job in the company he formed. His company continues to prosper. Indeed, it looks very much as if had I been there, I might have been a wealthy person already worth a few hundred thousand pounds. Over the years, Richard had continued to be encouraging. But not now!"

Philo passed a letter written on a computer and with a colorful heading. I looked at it. Then Philo read it out, and as I looked into his eyes, I saw pain:

Philo. Trust you are well. Thought I ought to write to you straight away. I got the letter that you sent me. I was amazed. I feel I really should warn you. What are you doing? I know that what we talked about was ways in which you were going to help the poor in Africa, that is in Zambia. I warned you years ago; don't get too religious! For goodness sake, the poor don't need more religion. They have enough of it as it is. Are you now going to encourage them to pray more? They shouldn't be praying, they should be out in their fields working, and they should be setting up in business. Let me tell you also that disappointments are normal in life. Believe you me, I know. One does not stop in the light of disappointments. One keeps going. You are faltering, and in a way that makes little sense. When I read your letter telling of how your own thinking is changing, I was angry! For goodness sake Philo, keep going as you have been going. Don't change. There are enough crazy religious lunatics around without your joining their ranks. This is what you should do. Either resign all involvement in mission. Then come back to the UK. Come and see me. I can't guarantee you a job as you are now. For all I know you might have lost touch with reality altogether. But, I want to talk to you. Maybe, just maybe, you are still up to it. Don't ruin your life by spending more time with primitive African people who can't organize their own economies.

Philo broke off to explain how he had, over the years, kept Richard up to speed by letter with the crazy things that were happening in Zambia. Then Philo read on.

If you can't resign and come back—stop rebelling! Stop **rebelling**, Philo! Do what you are told as you are told. Probably the best thing you can do is to get a good wife. For goodness sake make sure she's English. Then, as you get to know her, ask her "Am I crazy?" If she says "yes" then make a decision never again to touch anything to do with mission. I am sorry to have to be so blunt. Someone needs to tell you. I care about you. I am not sure that those religious folks do.

Philo screwed up his face. His friend's words were hurting him. What really made this letter painful for Philo, was that Richard was in so many ways right. Philo's determination to do the right thing in the right way had lost him Christian missionary friends. "I can't see how Philo can survive this," I thought to myself. "He's getting battered from all sides. He's only a man."

"At the very least, Philo, you need, for the sake of your own mental health, to cut off your relationship with Richard." Philo looked at me. His look was hard. I could say his look was sad—not surprising given the battering he was getting.

"I like well-meaning, honest, intelligent people," Philo remarked. "I believe that is the category that Richard falls in to. *He means well.* I am waiting for God to enlighten him over what he is missing, and to change him."

***

On returning to the UK, Philo needed to see his own church pastor. The following morning, he had to leave to make other preparations for his coming studies. That evening was the only time available to see the pastor. "I'll be visiting the hospice tonight until 8 p.m.," said the pastor over the phone, "meet me then at the hospice canteen."

"There's something here," I said to Philo, "when your debriefing with the pastor is to be at the hospice!"

Philo grimaced, raising his hands. "We're taking the devil to the hospice and leaving him there!" he declared.

Neither of us recalled ever having visited a hospice. Both of us were struck by how clean, friendly, prosperous, and generally pleasant it was. I think Philo like me, was thinking of some of the dark, dirty, and smelly contexts in which people were dying in Zambia. In Zambia, it was not unusual to find a dying person alone, lying on the earth floor of a smelly, poorly-lit hut. I did often wonder who was clearing up the urine and faeces for them. I never asked. This now was a British shape of death. Sterile, yes, but death nevertheless. Another difference I discovered: slow death in the UK could be accompanied by joviality on the part of the dying. Why? Because of the use of morphine. Morphine is very difficult to get hold of in the developing world. That is through fear that it would be abused and create addiction. As a result, dying people in Africa were often racked in continuous acute pain.

"Sit down here, Philo," the pastor said. "Dave, is it?" he asked me.

"Yes," I replied, "a friend of Philo's."

"Welcome. I hope you don't mind my meeting you here?" said Clive, the pastor, waving his hand to point to our surroundings. "This place closes at 9 p.m. so we have an hour. What are you drinking?" Clive had pastored the same church for over twenty years. People especially valued him for his teaching. He was a man familiar with troubles, as his wife frequently suffered from severe depression.

Clive was ready to listen to us. "You start," Philo told me. I explained the situation, then Philo filled in some gaps.

"Philo, I fear that you have rightly identified a potential clash with authorities in mission. Also, you have identified ways in which mission institutions can become self-gratifying. I acknowledge that the message you have to share, while it is good and even more important, it is right, may upset some mission agency structures. It might not do so, but it might. You are right, I am sure Dave will agree with me here also, to show great respect to the leaders God has put in place to guide you. Those leaders, however, also know that the church is the bottom line. They are an agent of the church. They are not the church, but only a part of the church. They depend on the church. Your message, as I hear it, is not counter-to church either in the UK or in Africa. Be faithful, above all things be humble, be prayerful, seek God's face. We will stand with you."

At 9 p.m. exactly the lights flashed. We were the only ones left in the canteen. Walking towards the car park, a nurse approached Clive. She passed on a message. "She has gone," she told him. Clive nodded. Death is the bread and butter of hospice business. Some lady had finished her walk. "What was I going to do with mine before someone says that about me?" I asked myself. Perhaps Philo was thinking the same thing.

CHAPTER 13: MISSIONARY TRAINING COLLEGE

The year after his MA, Philo attended missionary training college, a place, one would think, that would not attract too many rebels. Someone training at a missionary training college shouldn't become victim to negative peer pressure. We'll see!

"You know, Philo was somewhat in trepidation at the prospect of going to missionary training college (MTC from here on)," I told Elaine.

"Oh?" she responded, "that figures." Elaine was one of the tutors at MTC. She was a slim lady with a pleasant demeanor, combined with strangely piercing eyes.

"So how's he getting on?" I asked.

"He's a big problem," she responded.

"Why?" I asked.

"Lots of reasons."

"For example?" I asked again.

"I might have said too much already, Dave. These things are held in confidence. But I am telling you straight—he is a nuisance and a headache. Why ever he wants to be a missionary, I don't understand, and how he will ever be one, I don't know either." That was the brief conversation I had with a MTC staff member one evening. She had come to give a presentation at my church. I was taking her back to the railway station. It was sobering. I called Philo the following day. He said he was okay. He didn't seem to be okay. I realized he was choking back tears!

"What's going on, Philo?"

"Come and find out," he said.

It was two weeks before I could get to meet Philo. I had to make a trip to Norway in the meantime. He said he needed his head sorting a little. I met him in Hampshire. We walked through the beautiful New Forest. We talked as we walked.

"It's hard to know where to start," Philo shared. "I was allocated a room at the college. My neighbor turned out to be a rebel. We were all new. We needed a mate to hang out with. He was not a good choice, but he was who there was. You know the kind of stuff that my heart and mind are full of. "Of course!" I started telling him. I am not sure that he understood. But he agreed all the same!"

I gasped a little. "That doesn't sound like a good start for engaging an unconventional set of theories in a missionary training college," I thought.

"There is a problem in language," Philo went on. "We used to have staff meetings at the school in Zambia. They were in English. In these meetings, much was decided. Often what was decided was not acted upon. Decisions were made, then ignored. Or so it seemed to me. That is mission in practice. I couldn't separate such practice from my comprehension of the reality of mission, when one begins to hand over to nationals. This, together with the presence of my rebellious neighbor, encouraged me to be slack in 'doing what I was told' by the college authorities, whenever such might have clashed with 'what happens in Africa.' After all, people should learn about mission in practice. When they were in class telling students 'don't expect what you find said about a people in English to be true, and don't expect people in other cultures to do what they say,' then the lecturer concerned should have been able to add 'as Philo has demonstrated for us.'"

"Philo, that's incredible!" I said. "You mean, that you willingly flouted the rules of the college in order to be a part of the message of what mission to Africa is really like?"

"That's it," Philo responded. "That might be incredible," he added, "but it is true. Are they serious about engaging the majority world or not? But, you see, I was being encouraged to do the same. Not only by my rebellious neighbor. Also by the college authorities. They kept telling us, even in the introductory sessions of the college, that they were there to teach us about mission as it happens, not theoretical stuff that we couldn't apply."

At that point, we came to a large clearing in the forest. On the far side of the clearing were some of the famous New Forest wild horses. I took some photographs. Then we moved on up a track with a gradual incline approaching a hill. "I don't know if what I did was right or wrong," Philo went on. "You know, seize the day, as they say. I have been of the conviction that the mission field is a place where one should learn. Those are some of the clear lessons that I learned. Now the people at the college were saying the same thing. Many of my colleagues had much less exposure to non-European cultures. How should they learn, if we weren't going to teach them? Not to learn would be to make endless mistakes.

They needed to learn. This college seemed to be the place for such learning."

"Come on, Philo," I said, "you knew that the message you had to share was unconventional."

"Yes, I did," he replied, "hence I was so nervous before going to college. Remember though—that you encouraged me to share openly! Well, that's what I have been doing." We walked silently for a while, then Philo interjected, "What else should I do? Had my experience in Africa been 'real'? I think yes. Was it incredible? Also yes. Should I now ignore all my experiences for the sake of getting a training that was preparing me for the very experience? Why? How? Tell lies? Say nice things just to please people?"

We continued in silence. The wind blew in the trees above our heads, but we were sheltered from it. The rustling of leaves underfoot at times became noisy. "So what did your tutors say?" I went on to ask Philo.

Philo was silent for a moment, then continued as follows: "Near the start of our time, we were asked to write an essay outlining our pre-existing understanding of mission. I wrote such an essay, and handed it to my tutor. In it, I explained some of the things we have talked about. How a foreign culture can really catch you unawares. The fact that African people need the gospel more than they need development. The fact that often missionaries and nationals might not be on the same page at all. I wrote all that, and handed it to my tutor. I was very nervous at the time. I said to him 'This is what I have written, but I am concerned that it will clash with what MTC is teaching.' His response was 'Don't worry about that. That's what we are here for. We are here to help people to articulate what is in their minds so as to have their thinking broadened and challenged.'"

I started laughing. This was all so crazy. The only thing to do seemed to be to laugh!

"Go on then," I said to Philo.

"Well, you see, I was emboldened."

"Yes, I see that," I responded.

"I trusted them," Philo said to me. "I had to trust them. You can't relate to people and make progress unless there is trust. It seemed to me that a lot was at stake. The lives and prosperity of millions of people in Africa, for example. We had to do things for them. There is hunger, and starvation, and suffering in Africa, that you could call 'unnecessary suffering.' It is unnecessary because it could be prevented, at least much of it, if people would only grasp what's going on, and then respond appropriately. I don't mean to say that it is 'simple' like that. But, yes, I think it is possible. It requires us, Westerners, to do things differently. That is what I was trying to communicate. I had to trust the staff at MTC or there was no point in being there. I had learned things. They had to agree with me. I was on to something. But I did not know that they would turn around and hit me because I was being open."

We got to a three-way junction. "Which way here?" Philo asked me.

"I don't know."

"I thought you knew where we were going?" Philo added.

"Hmmm," I said. The New Forest was a fascinating place to be. It wasn't always easy to know where one was. "Okay. Let's try that way," I suggested. Philo agreed, so off we went. "Look Philo, it seems you have totally misread and disoriented the MTC. What they offer was just not meant for someone like you."

"OK," Philo replied.

"Well, do you agree?" I pressed him.

"Yes, you may be right," Philo responded. "But is that my fault?"

"Who knows? The point now though is that you are in a pickle."

"You can say that again!"

"So let's recap on that one," I said. "You enter MTC with a great deal of trust in people there. At the same time, you are terrified at the prospect of having what you are going to say rejected."

"Yes," said Philo.

"Your fear was closer to the mark than was your hope and trust."

"Hmmm," Philo agreed.

"You saw yourself as a bit of an experienced missionary hero. The staff of the college took you as a rebel."

"Hmmm."

"Your tutor continued to encourage you to express yourself, when the warning bells should have instilled a spirit of caution."

"Hmmm."

"He was meanwhile getting increasing levels of negative feedback from others, but was too busy with other things to be able to appropriately respond to it, so he didn't tell you."

"Hmmm."

"Meanwhile, you express your desire to go back with the same mission to the same place you were at before."

"Hmmm."

"Because they trusted you, they called you for an interview early on, thinking that there would be no issues."

"Hmmm."

"Probably, they consulted the leadership in Zambia."

"Hmmm."

"They discovered that there had been some issues regarding your more recent visit there."

"Hmmm."

"Then the mission consulted MTC."

"Hmmm."

"They discovered that there were major issues there."

"Hmmm."

"You had not been told openly that there were such issues, partly because it was anyway considered too early for you to be given an interview, and partly because your tutor was too busy on other things."

"Hmmm."

"You were told after your reference had been sent to the mission?"

"That's right," Philo responded.

"You had a very difficult time at the interview that should have been a formality, extending your term as a missionary with the same people in the same place."

"Hmmm."

"It turned into a severe rejection. You expected a conversation on 'what exactly will your ministry be,' but were faced instead with people questioning you on all scores."

"Hmmm."

"Wa wa wa wa wa!" I laughed, and Philo laughed, but not with joy.

"In effect then," Philo said, "those trusted relationships that I had built up over the last five years are all gone."

"No wonder you were almost in tears when I called you that day! You are in a mess, and you could easily end up becoming a mess," I told Philo.

"You know the amazing thing though," Philo added.

"What?"

"I thought that would be the end of relationships with my supporting churches. But it was not. My supporting churches are all still ready to back me for what I am called to do, and where I am called to go. That is a miracle."

"Yes, truly a miracle," I responded. "So then, what is it to be?" I asked.

"I don't know yet," he responded. "The obvious thing is to go back to Zambia, but independently of the mission."

"That sounds rough."

"Yes it does. But I will do it, if God wills."

Meanwhile, I was aware that Philo had to contend with some very strained relationships at the MTC. There he was, having made a stand as to what was the right way to do mission. In the meantime, the staff of the college, in some ways very overtly and in some ways inadvertently, had condemned that stand. They had not only condemned his stand, they had condemned Philo! They had labeled him as "non-missionary material." Now, after our weekend, he was to go right back into the middle of all that. I asked him whether he shouldn't pack in the course? He didn't want to pack it in. His reason also was good. People often don't appreciate someone who gives up on things before having completed them. He was still on track to get a certificate. He had not yet been thrown out! The money was there for him to carry on. No-one had told him to pack it in. Meanwhile, as I had discovered from Elaine a few weeks before, he was the rancid smell in the noses of the college staff! Philo had to go back to the very place that had deprived him of five years of relationships and friendships. He had to do so smiling, as a Christian. The staff of the very place might "hate" him. Not in the literal way of "hate," one hopes at least, not as Christians. But they might "hate" him as he was opposing what they were saying, and saying that it was the ignorance of the staff of the college on matters concerning mission in practice that had put him into a pickle. If staff saw Philo talking with other students, wouldn't they be suspecting him of trying to provoke an insurrection? The alternative would be for Philo to stay, but to say nothing. He agreed that he should not be "vocal." But, knowing Philo, and given the importance with which he held the issues concerned, he would not be silent. He would tell the truth to those who asked it from him. Then he would also be expected to go to class. Many of the things taught, and the way they were taught, Philo had already said he struggled with. The lecturers would have to put up with the fact that they had a disgruntled rebel in their class, who frankly did already have a lot of missionary experience, but who had a stand that was at loggerheads with what the college was teaching! Not only was he at loggerheads with them, but he was effectively accusing them of having botched, through their incompetence, his mission work! (I mean incompetence, for example, in having told students that they were free to speak openly about their concerns, only later to have told a student that the way he talked had undermined his chances of going back with the mission and to the country and people that he loved.)

Philo was now in a mega personal dilemma also. He had committed himself to lifelong service in the developing world. His experience and what he interpreted as God's calling indicated that the way forward was not agricultural projects, but Bible teaching. Now the "experts" who should have been cheering for him, were condemning him! He was "blacklisted," and he had no-one to go to, and no-one to go with. What were the chances, after all, of any other mission agency taking Philo on, given that the prestigious missionary training college he was at, and the agency that already knew him the best, had kicked him into the ditch? On the other hand, amazingly, his supporting churches were still supporting him! Philo and I spent some time in prayer together.

One answer came at MTC, a month or so after my time with Philo. "You know, we have an African man here from Holima," Philo told me on the phone. "He is apparently the bishop of an indigenous church. Everyone is amazed at him. He just seems to be so African. Even the way he came to MTC in the UK is amazing. God spoke to an Anglican vicar who happened to meet him in Imbigen, that he should support him for studies in the UK." Philo went on, "The other morning, I was very discouraged, (as I was on most mornings). I was sitting at breakfast with some student colleagues. Usually I did not feel free to talk to students, as when I articulated the pain in my heart, I was simultaneously attacking the college. That morning though, by one means or another, I shared my pain. Those two students, just at the breakfast table, agreed to pray for me. They prayed especially that God would open a door for me to go back to Africa. After breakfast, I walked from the dining room, towards what we call the 'main building.' At the door of that 'main building', the above-mentioned African bishop approached me. 'Come and work with us in Holima,' he said."

"Wow! That's quite something! So, are you going to be able to take him up on his offer?"

"I took it as a call from God," Philo told me. "Let's be honest, that bishop was inviting a lot of people to go and work with him. For all I know, he saw me being prayed for. He is no fool—he has learned about the ways of European people! He knows that we have emotional crises. But, so what, that looks like a potential opening."

"You know one thing particularly amazing about what you have just told me," I related.

"What?" Philo questioned. "No."

"I have not told you yet, but I have accepted a new job in Holima to start at the end of this year. Wouldn't it be amazing if we ended up in the same area!"

"Impossible!" Philo exclaimed.

"Where is the bishop from in Holima?" I asked.

"Haven't got a clue," he said. "Okay. But I tell you what else."

"Go on," I said intently.

"My supporting churches are coming out in favor of my going back to Holima with this man, even though they do not know him. Even though I have never been there. Even though I know almost nothing about the situation!"

"Those people in the churches do believe in you!" I said enthusiastically.

CHAPTER 14: CUTTING WEEDS

True enough, I had a contract to work in Holima. Philo was also off to Holima. Indeed, it was amazing that we would be together again, this time in Holima. That should give our friendship a chance to develop further. Philo was to precede me by a few months. In the early days, I was told at the time I was to be based in Imbigen, whereas he was straight out into the villages of Western Holima.

His time at MTC had, by his own confession, been the worst year of Philo's life. The rejection he had received was acute. All the hopes that had been there for his future in Zambia on the part of fellow missionaries and others as well as himself, were dashed! For Philo, that was an excruciating blow. It's hard to know just what he might have done differently to avoid all that. The position of the MTC was such that perhaps a clash was inevitable. Philo shed more tears that year than he had ever done before, or since—to date. The heart-felt desire that God had put in his heart, to work with African people in their own way, was not proving easy to fulfil. Many might have thought that the thump he got from the school and mission would have been sufficient to deter him from ever going back; but not so.

"This garden has not been tended for a couple of years," a lady in his hometown in England told Philo one day. He had been advised not to rush back to Africa. Instead, his Pastor Clive told him to hang around until October. Philo became the voluntary gardener and handyman for anyone in the church wanting help. This proved to be a good way of getting to better know people in the church. So there he was, focusing on an overgrown garden. His remit, to solve the problem.

"We'll have a go," Philo told the lady. That was the start of "slash-and-burn" British style! (Some Zambian tribes are renowned for their slash-and-burn farming systems.)

"Thanks for a good job," the lady said later. Well—she had to say that, as Philo was a volunteer. She might not have been so impressed if he had been paid to do what he did. Philo did various jobs for folks including painting, weeding, clearing away rocks, laying slabs, and digging up potatoes. His heart was not really in it. His heart was far away, but he did what he could.

Before rejecting him outright, the mission had told Philo that being sent to Africa to do church work was different from going to do agriculture. To do church work, one first had to prove one's ability in the church in the UK. So, you had to learn what to do in the UK, so as to be able to teach Africans how to do it properly.

"Why not learn from Africans?" Philo asked me once. According to mission policy at the time, that would not do. Implicitly, the suggestion there was that Africans weren't doing it right, so it did not make sense to learn from them. "It was like missionaries had to be some sort of super-people," Philo told me, "super-prepared to always know better and tell Africans what to do."

Philo was not rejecting the basis on which he was being advised outright. He was, however, desiring to be vulnerable to Africa. He was pleading to be allowed to be vulnerable to African people! This was disallowed. Often someone who asked to remain in their home country ended up stuck there. "Stuck" that is, like, typically, married, or failing that, engaged. Then getting back out to the field becomes much more difficult. Philo was convinced that someone from Europe who wants to minister in Africa should go there when young. Young men are told the truth about what is going on. Older men with grey hair are bamboozled, fooled, and easily isolated from African communities. This is because they are given too much respect. Also because by the time they get to the field they are set-in-their-ways. They are used to living in a certain way. It becomes very hard for them to engage another way of life, never mind value it. Just imagine a man who has lived hand in glove with his wife for thirty or forty years before heading out for Africa. Quite likely his number one priority will be to look after her. He will continue to treat her as number one. Even if that meant driving a 4x4 to all the places to which African colleagues were walking.

"Please come and help us fix a wall collapsing outside our house," asked another lady from Philo's home church.

"I'm not a mason," Philo told her. "I can only do simple jobs."

"You can do it!" she told him. Philo was a little wary of this particular woman, and her tongue!

"Come along Saturday," she said. Philo agreed. What Philo did not realize was what the same lady was saying to single girls in the church. Her message to them was surprisingly similar to what she had told Philo. Except, that is, that their purpose for coming was not to mend a wall.

"What on earth is this wall going to be like?" Philo thought to himself, after parking his car. He was stood at the door, tools in hand, ready to go. "One wouldn't expect church leaders to dress like that," Philo thought when Sue came to the door. He was by then still oblivious of her plan for the day. They went in, and there was her husband shrouded in newspaper, putting down a cup of tea.

"Sue has a plan in mind for you today I gather, Philo," he said, grinning.

"Yes, that's right," Philo replied.

"Hope it goes well," he said. "I'll be leaving you to it. Do check that you have all the tools that you need. If you are missing anything, let me know in the next thirty minutes and I can give it to you before I leave. Sue doesn't have a clue where I keep my tools. It's probably better left that way too," he added. Philo nodded.

Seconds later the wall in question came into view through the patio window. It was about two feet high. It separated the lower and upper part of the garden. It was in disarray. Different shaped rocks were scattered hither and thither. Just as Sue opened the veranda door to the garden, the doorbell rang again. Philo heard a female voice greeting Sue. Philo recognized the voice. He wasn't sure straight away who it was. It was Mandy.

"Hi Mandy," Philo said. She smiled back. Her dress style also struck Philo as rather radical for a Christian girl. Now, how to go about repairing that wall? As Philo was bewildered and musing just how on earth he would repair that wall, he glanced up. Now there were three girls with Sue. He went to collect some more tools from the boot of his car. Two more girls were at the door.

"Come in," he said. He got back to the wall only to find himself called again for a cup of tea. Now there were nine girls sat around the table.

"Philo, I'm off. You got what you need, or shall I bring you out my tools before I leave?" Philo requested a crowbar. He brought him a straight metal bar about four feet long.

"Yes, that might help," said Philo, who was still trying to formulate a plan to tackle the wall. The front door closed. Sue's husband was gone. Philo was left in the house with the nine girls. They were dressed, well, yes, they were dressed, Philo told me, but not very much. It was time for a cup of tea.

"No wonder people told to do church work in the UK first before going to the mission field ended up getting married!" Philo thought to himself. He had only another six weeks to see through—what if it had been two years? "Was it the devil who had sent the girls or was it God?" he asked himself. He had been in the house alone with Direnes (Tichi's niece) in Zambia, but she was culturally very distant. These girls were "his own people." No snooty missionary would tell him off for courting one of these. In fact, when he thought more about it, some snooty missionaries may be very glad if he courted one of these instead of going back to Africa alone! Perhaps that was why the mission had insisted that he stay in the UK for at least two years. It was a trap!

Philo was very aware of the need for sexual purity if he was going to serve effectively in Africa. Messing with local girls was not going to stand him in good stead. In theory—and this is what some advised him, he might marry an educated African woman. If she was educated, so the thinking went, she would be much like Philo in understanding. One thing that was ignored was money. Girls do like money. To stay with African people in the way that Philo wanted to would require a kind of voluntary poverty. What African girl would accept voluntary poverty if she knew her husband could earn ten times as much back in his home country? Even more pertinently—what African girl could resist family pressure to benefit from access to wealthy Europe just because her husband, who could earn ten times as much at home, was stupid enough to live voluntarily as a poor man in Africa?

After drinking tea, Philo was allowed to go back to work. He was still trying to fathom which rock belonged where in the wall he was to reconstruct. Meanwhile, as he went to work, one of the girls came to help him out. She became his conversational partner and right-hand woman to assist him with his task. That carried on for about fifteen minutes. Then she left. Another one of the girls took over her role. It was as if there had been some signal for the girls to change. Philo did not know what that signal was!

Philo's mind was working on three tracks! First, he was trying to work out how to fix the wall. Another part of his mind was trying to work out what the girls were doing, while getting bamboozled by the beauty, who within full view of the other girls chatting not many yards away, had become his helpmate. The third part of his mind was processing the relevance of all this in terms of his anticipated return to Africa. The wall progressed in fits and starts!

Were Philo to marry a European girl, then he just might find one who had the same conviction as his own. That seemed pretty unlikely though, Philo thought to himself, while looking a little blankly at rocks. So, she may agree that one needs to give up a great deal to serve God. Some single female missionaries indeed were of that ilk. They did great work at enormous personal sacrifice to benefit the poor and the heathen. In return, they typically got some authority, respect, position, and pseudo-male status. (Single women on the African mission field often achieved levels of respect in the local community that they would very much struggle to achieve at home in the West.) What if they had to make all these sacrifices, and their reputation was instead as a wife of so-and-so? Would things still look the same? That is, assuming that no children were forthcoming. But what if the same lady gave birth? Would she, and the grandparents of the children, be happy for the children to be brought up in abject poverty because of some crazy missiological notion of their father? That sounded very unlikely.

Philo had by that time already known a few missionary couples who tried enrolling their children into the same school as local African children. They might have started with the best of intentions. But, practically, it could not succeed. Their children ended up bullying local children, who were in awe of the presence of Europeans. African teachers were afraid to discipline European children. (What European parent would want their child to be caned by an African teacher anyway? The kind of discipline that is normal in much of Africa is these days frowned upon in the West.) The quality of education in local African schools tends, by European standards, to be diabolical. The teachers who teach in English themselves, by European standards, typically have only a very basic grasp of the language. The list goes on and on! Perhaps the only practical option for marrying on the field was to marry a very obedient, humble, sterile, European lady! Could Philo explain such to this group of girls?

The system of switching every fifteen minutes or so continued. Part of the deal for Philo was plenty of tea and an excellent lunch. By the time Sue's "onslaught" came, at least Philo was a bit prepared for it. By this time all the girls had had their "shift."

"You should get married, Philo," Sue told him straight. Sue was not unattractive. She had a sharp voice, and a domineering style. She liked to be the centre of attention, and often achieved such, successfully dragging others into her emotional roller-coasting. She continued before he had a chance to respond. "Men like you lie in bed at night thinking about girls. That is not healthy, especially for someone who wants to serve God. Better you have a wife!" That was, literally, a bit below the belt, Philo thought. These were Christian girls, but no less girls for that. There was no guaranteed screen to stop worldly matters from infesting Christian gatherings, Philo realized! It was almost as if the pastor of the church had set this up. Philo would be working thousands of miles away, out of eyeshot and earshot of everyone else in the church. Could he be trusted? Would he make a mess? Would he prove an embarrassment to those who sent him? Could he stand up to being seduced by beautiful women?

A big part of the problem, of course, is that Philo would have loved to have had a wife. That was the stuff of his dreams. One day he explained — it was the stuff of his wildest dreams. The harsh reality also remained the case, however, that marrying would greatly increase the likelihood of Philo's having to leave the field. It would instantly double it; two people were twice as likely to have serious medical ailments as would one. Quite frankly, if a couple is working in mission in Africa, things may be much more difficult for the woman. A woman is more likely to deeply desire to return to her home country than a man. This is still assuming that there are no children. Children yet more radically change the scene. Even should a couple remain on the field, the demands made on them with children needing to be brought up in a way not later to disadvantage them in the West, can be enormous. It is not impossible for a missionary family to live in the field at great expense, but to have very little time for church work with nationals. Child-rearing on European standards, including the educational demands of children, is a vast and complex enterprise that takes much time and effort, and brings endless missionary families home from the field.

"Don't think you will be respected as a single man in Africa," Sue added. The other girls seemed rather nonplussed by her directness. This wasn't a concerted attack on Philo by a group. Sue was the one attacking. The other girls were shifting their eyes to the side, as Sue's were constantly seeking to lock into his gaze. Unfortunately, Sue was all too right. Single people remain children in the eyes of many in Africa. The amount of respect they are afforded will always be limited.

Philo did not reply to Sue. Sue was trying to help a girl, whichever one Philo might have chosen out of her nine visitors, to get a husband. A girl is made, even in the West, by having a husband, or at least many consider it to be so. That was a fair aim. She was also taking pity on Philo. The poor fellow, in her eyes, was desperately lonely. Philo had something else in mind. He had seen people suffering. He had realized the ignorance of the West in the ways they attempted to engage so as to help to relieve suffering in the majority world. He had hope in the gospel of Jesus. He believed God had called him to a difficult task. He believed God would want him to bring change to the system. Was he ready to put all that at risk for the sake of one woman? Is one woman more important than all of that calling? Not for Philo, no way!

The best ice cream Philo had ever tasted rounded off the day. The wall was—well, it could probably be said, that it was better than it had been. The stones were less scattered than they were originally. Philo drove his borrowed car home.

CHAPTER 15: TO WARMER CLIMES

The date of 13th October 1993 gradually drew closer. Philo's flight was to leave for Holima that day. The return was open. Philo had acquired a place on a MA course in theology in London that was to begin in September 1994. He had almost a year available to get his feet back on the ground in Africa. This time though, not back to a familiar place where he already knew the language, as he had hoped, but to a different country. A vast unknown! At that time, he knew one person in that whole country (I had to finish my UK contract first before flying out to Imbigen). That was an African bishop. The same bishop had a reputation in the MTC of being "very indigenous!"

Bishop Philip was waiting for Philo at the airport in Imbigen. He was slim, medium height, and liked to dress well. He had a magnetic personality — he was the kind of man one wanted to be with. He had a very empathetic spirit, and the gift of talking in a way that left his listener encouraged. While a leader of many, he was keenly aware of individuals in a group. All that of course — African style — that English words cannot really encapsulate. Once Philo reached Philip his freedom was gone. That is, he longed to have a white face welcome him! Then he could have gone to a European home. Perhaps meet a European family. Had some chocolate chip cookies with ice cream. Had some affirmation from his own people. But there was no white face waiting for him. Instead, these were black faces who were leaders of Pentecostal churches. They were the ones into whose hands he fell. These were the colleagues of that Holiman bishop who had acquired the reputation for being "so African" at MTC.

Philo had gone back into the famous other realm of *The Lion, the Witch and the Wardrobe*! Relocating to Africa means that "everything had changed." Aside from the foreignness of everything, Philo remained under a dark cloud of rejection. That rejection had numerous ominous undertones of guilt and of condemnation. The words of his tutor at MTC rang in his head "you are a problem … when I tell my wife I am going to meet with you that day, she takes pity on me … none of the staff of the college like you …." Now Philo was flaunting all of that! Months after completing his missionary training, he was already on his way back to Africa. Of all the students to have graduated, he might even have been the first to get to the field. Others had much lengthier and drawn out preparatory procedures before they could leave for foreign climes.

"From the airport, we went to the home of a brother to the Bishop," Philo told me on one occasion. "We stood in a circle and prayed noisily. I expected to drop dead there and then. How could I flaunt the advice of so many of the people I so respected, and get back to the field and survive? They would then tell of me, I imagined; 'Philo was just a rebel. He would not listen. Everyone told him not to carry on. He was not cut out to be a missionary. He went anyway. Well, now he has got his just dessert. Young people should listen to their elders.'" It was not easy to flaunt all that well-intended advice. Not easy at all. Philo couldn't believe himself that he was being forced to do it: ignore the advice of fellow missionaries who were charged to take the Christian gospel. The kind of people who wrote the hero stories of faith that Philo had found lined up in the guest-house bookshelf in Lusaka on his first day in Africa! They were the people whose faith we are all in awe of. Philo had had to go behind their back and against their will.

From the home of the brother of the bishop called Okach Owach, Philo and Philip went to a guest-house for the night. Okach Owach was a short, thick-set builder by trade, a businessman. His house was alongside a slum. The house itself was decent by African standards, but decrepit by UK standards. It was always an adjustment going to Africa, to find that everything was under-maintained, neglected, and dirty. This time was no exception. Driving through the streets of Imbigen in Philip's rather dilapidated old Peugeot, they arrived at a run-of-the-mill guest-house. That is where Philip paid for a room for the two of them. Philo was struck by his comment: "I like it here. It is quiet because it is run by Muslims. You don't get people drinking here." Philo slept well, he tells me, in his bed on one side of the room, until about 5 a.m. Then sleep ended. Philip, in the other bed in the room, in a fashion that Philo had gradually to get used to in the days, months, and years ahead, started praying noisily! Philo wasn't sure whether he was praying in an African language, or whether it was glossolalia. He went on, and on, and on, and on, until both of them got up, an hour or two later.

That day there was a long drive to Deja. Philo was surprised to be asked to drive. He accepted. Eventually, having left Imbigen at about 11 a.m., they arrived in Deja around 8 p.m. It was raining. It was miserable! They drove across a dirt field into a shanty town. In the middle of this smelly slum, known by some as a "residential area," was a large house in the centre of an open area of mud. (It was sandy, so the mud was not sticky.)

The air was thick and pungent. It was as if the still air of the night in this flat densely-populated place was filled to saturation by the pungent smell emerging from endless scattered pit toilets. Surely a lot of people did not even bother using the pit toilets? Many were full anyway. There were pigs running around to clear up the mess if anyone chose not to use a toilet. (Philo once shared how a friend of his had told of her experience. She had to defecate in an open field with nothing but foot high grass to conceal her activities. Out came the poop. Seconds later a pig stuck its nose out from the grass and swallowed it, still warm!) Philo followed Philip into the house.

"Welcome home," Philip declared.

"Home?" thought Philo. "This is it? This will be my home!" What could he say? He had set out to live with the African people. The experts had told him he was a fool, and that he should give up on being a missionary. Now he had arrived at his destination, and this dank, putrid, smelly, muddy, rainy, and hot place was it! In the house, the air was even heavier and stickier than it had been outside. Noisy, unsettling prayers ensued, then pitch-black faces came to greet him in the dim glow of a paraffin lamp, with coarse voices saying *"Ruoth opaki"* which he was later to discover could be translated into English as "praise the Lord." The air was putrid. There seemed to be no ventilation to this house. "How many days can I possibly even survive here?" thought Philo.

People were coming and going. A good number of them wanted to meet and greet their very pale-skinned new visitor. "I am pastor so and so," then, "I am pastor so and so." "What were all these pastors doing in that house that night?" Philo asked himself, flabbergasted.

"I still couldn't believe that this would be my home," Philo told me later. "But I had no choice but to accept it. I was destined to live in this miserable, dank, hot, smelly, dark place—perhaps for years, surrounded by all these strange people!"

Philo couldn't understand what was being said. Then at about 10 p.m. he was told "Okay, let's go."

"Go where?" he responded to Philip.

"To home," he told him.

"I thought this was home?"

"Well, sort of, but let's go home now," Philip repeated.

"Wow! There is hope for a better place after all," Philo thought. They filled the car. Philo was still driving, back into the dark slum on the rainy night. They drove for perhaps an hour, way up some hills to the North West. Then off the tarmac up a muddy track, then onto another muddy track, through some iron gates into a homestead. Here there was grass, there were trees all around, and the air was cool, pleasant, and clean.

"Welcome home. This is where you will be staying," Philip told Philo. Enormous relief! Philip's wife, Clarice, had clearly been busy in the kitchen. A slap-up meal was awaiting them, before bedtime—which was well after midnight. What a day!

Much could be said about Philo's early days in Holima. "After I had been there a week," Philo explained, "it felt like three months. Just so much was foreign. So many new experiences." Endless people, many of them pastors, continued to come to Philo. People came asking for money. They were very hospitable and welcoming. Although—just not the same as Zambian people had been. Many knew English and could speak to Philo in English. But as soon as conversation reverted to their own language, which it did quickly and often, usually as soon as they started speaking to each other, Philo was left in the dark. Their language was not the soft flowing of Zambian Bantu. It was coarser and more abrasive. People wanted Philo's money. They came with sad stories of death and illness from which Philo could rescue them. At least he had learned that much in Zambia. He did not give them money.

Taking mefloquine might not have helped in this respect. (This is a malaria prophylaxis that Philo was taking—that it later came to be known could give people nightmares.) Philo would wake up at 4 a.m. or 5 a.m. in the middle of vivid demoralizing dreams. Still racked by guilt and plagued by his memories of MTC, he could only pray that God would save him from a terrible fate. The staff of MTC and their damning words haunted him. He wanted to go home! Most of all—he wanted to talk to European people. Really just any European who could say some calm assuring words. There were three rather unreliable phones about two miles from where Philo was staying. Philo looked up the phone number of a mission organization in Imbigen. He had nothing to say, but he just wanted to talk to a European. A puzzled lady, an American, came on the phone. "What do you want?" she asked. Then the phone cut out.

Philo was not recommending that a new missionary to Africa should go alone to live in a strange country on the basis of having just one friend, as he did. He felt he had no choice. A mission agency would not have taken him. He had been rejected by the missionaries who knew him well, amongst whom he had served. He had no choice but to go and simply plant himself in a place. He had no choice but to accept whatever hospitality his hosts had to offer. The amazing and wonderful thing was that Philo's churches in the UK did continue to support him.

Philo's arrangement did have advantages. Philo went with great vulnerability. He found himself totally in the hands of his African hosts. If he was to succeed in his ministry from there on, it would be thanks to them.

Things could have gone wrong. Philo had to trust in God to look after him. Through his approach, Philo needed the people to help him. He could not succeed without them. In that sense, he was like the missionaries sent by Jesus. They were told not to carry provisions. The difference was that, whereas they travelled within a familiar Israel, Philo went to a totally foreign people, thousands of miles from his home.

Fifteen days after his arrival in Holima, Philo hit breaking point. He went up some stairs to the bishop's office. This was a few miles from his home.

"Come in," he was told. Philo walked in, then burst into tears.

"I can't cope," he said. He did not tell Philip about all that happened at MTC. But he did make it clear that he could not cope.

Fortunately, Philip was wise as to what to do. Within an hour, Philip was ready to travel. "Let's go to Deja," he said. He drove Philo to Deja, and took him to one of the tourist hotels. One with a view over a large lake. There was a spare room. The room overlooked the lake. There were a few European people staying there. Not that Philo could talk with them. They would wonder what he was at. They would probably try to convince him to go back to the UK straight away. The hotel, though, resembled white men's things. Philo did not have a stream of people lining up to talk to him and ask him for money, whose agenda is unfathomable. Instead, he could sit alone undisturbed. Instead of being told what to eat and when, he ate what he wanted when he ordered. He straightened his head. The next morning as he sat on the veranda and watched the sunrise, a deep relief flowed into his soul. Finally, he was at peace.

Philip had quite likely thought that was the last he would see of Philo. Contrary to such expectations, three days later Philo went back to continue his residence in Philip's rural home.

Richard wrote Philo a letter around this time. I include it here:

Dear Philo,

Receive greetings. I gather you are back in "darkest Africa!" I hope you are enjoying the mosquitoes, lions, and vicious natives.

Having read some of your latest news, I have been prompted to write to you again. I am almost at the point of telling you that whenever you come back to the UK, you should never visit me. Your life is an embarrassment, Philo. It seems you have made so many enemies, that you have now been forced to travel back to Africa entirely alone. You mean that none of your old "friends," as you used to describe them, are there for you anymore? You must be about the only white man in the world who has launched himself into a poverty-stricken village as you have done.

There are some things in life that are important. Had you learned them properly, then probably we'd be in business together. Consider my previous offer for you to join me in business partnership to be well and truly closed. I don't want you. We recently had a class reunion from the agricultural college. Your old mates are laughing at you. Then also, I met someone from your home sending church. They didn't realize that I knew you, but they told me a little about you. Some people there despise you. You know why they despise you? Because you are racist.

I can only recommend that you come home, sooner rather than later. Then, try and pick up your life. Get a job, man! Like a normal person! Someone might still take you on to drive a tractor for them. Or maybe to muck out their cows. Maybe you can wash eggs or something.

Say hello to the natives for me, who you think are stupid.

Richard

CHAPTER 16: PROPER MISSIONARY

I was not very familiar with Imbigen. Because I had a friend working in one of the banks in the city, I asked him to reserve a vehicle for me. I was due to travel to the north, to Mimbwa, as soon as I arrived. That was to be for the first meeting that I was to be involved in on the continent of Africa since leaving Zambia two years previously.

Having booked well in advance, I had few concerns. I went to the car-hire agency. I was met by a man in a kiosk (small shop) outside the compound. He was a short, squat fellow, with an air of "couldn't care less" about him. His dress seemed surprisingly informal given the role that he was fulfilling. He gave me the paperwork. He showed me the vehicle that I was to take. Everything seemed in order. I handed over the cash he wanted. He gave me the key to my vehicle. I piled my bags into the back. I went to have a light lunch, and expected to begin my journey an hour later. Fortunately, there was a small place offering snacks nearby, so I did not have to go far. (I wanted to avoid taking the vehicle and re-parking it where it might have got damaged or stolen.)

While eating, drinking tea, and checking some of the documentation in anticipation of my meeting, I heard some raised voices. Some of those voices were American. I ignored them. Twenty minutes later five Americans sat at a table beside mine. I couldn't help but hear what they said. It seemed to pertain also to me.

"How can they tell us that no vehicle is available, and we made a booking months ago?" said the older man, who I was later to discover was called Martin. He was forty-five or so, longish hair yet a balding head. He had probably been slim before he had reached his middle years. By the time I saw him, he was a little flabby.

A younger man, Andrew, responded. "Now we have searched the whole area. The only vehicle people are prepared to make available to us is three times the price. We can't just be taken for a ride like that," he said. Andrew was tall, wore glasses, slim, perhaps thirty years old, seeming very alert and on the ball.

"There is no vehicle available for another two days," the older man reminded him.

Andrew's voice came to the fore again. "They tell us that the vehicle we booked was also booked by an American who is heading for Mimbwa. Because he got here first, he was given the vehicle."

That mention of Mimbwa disturbed my reading. They carried on talking about an American who was to go to Mimbwa. They did not seem to notice my presence. It appears that my vehicle had been double-booked! Had I arrived thirty minutes later then quite likely I would have been in the pickle that they were now in. I coughed. Andrew looked in my direction.

"Hi. I'm Dave," I said.

"Good to make your acquaintance," said Andrew.

"I couldn't help but overhear some of your conversation," I added. Andrew kept his eyes on mine. His accent indicated he was from the West coast of the USA. "You wanted a vehicle, but someone else has already booked it on a trip to Mimbwa?" I asked.

"Yes, that is what we have been told," Andrew said.

"Weren't you on the BA flight that came in this morning from London?" I asked him, as I realized where I had seen him before.

"Yes, that's right. You were on the same flight?" he asked.

"Indeed, I was sat behind you, a few rows back. My name is Dave," I repeated. I stretched out my hand. He reached out from where he was sitting. That manoeuvre for him was an awkward one, but he managed to reach my hand and introduce himself as Andrew. "Look Andrew, I seem to be the American who has your vehicle. Where were you planning to go?"

Andrew turned around and asked the older man "Where are we going?"

"Deja," I heard the reply.

"Can I join you?" I said.

"Sure," he responded. I stood up and moved into their circle.

Before long we had made our acquaintance. I told the men that I was the American going to Mimbwa, who had the vehicle that they had also booked. I offered for us to drive together to our destinations. Although a bit of a detour, I could travel through Deja to get to Mimbwa. They agreed. I loaned them my key. They put their bags into the back of the vehicle. It was a minibus—the sort one can take into the game park. Within an hour we were on our way. I drove half the way and Andrew the other half.

Except at one point, where a fallen crane blocked the road, we made good headway. The dual carriageway out of Imbigen became a single carriageway. We climbed higher. We had some of the most fantastic views over the Rift Valley available in East Africa.

"Is Deja your final destination?" I asked.

"For today, yes," Andrew acknowledged.

"So tomorrow?" I asked.

"On to Swaro," he said.

"Swaro!" I exclaimed.

"Yes, that is a few miles out of Deja," Andrew responded.

"That is amazing," I said.

"Why?" Andrew asked, a little puzzled.

"A friend of mine is staying in Swaro."

"That sounds unlikely. You know Swaro is a pretty small place," Andrew said.

"So who will you be meeting in Swaro?" I asked again.

"A fellow called Philip, who is a bishop to an indigenous church." I couldn't believe it. The man said that with a straight face. I was shaking my head in disbelief.

"I know Philip," I said in due course, "or at least, I know of him."

"Well that's a bit incredible and rather unlikely," Andrew responded. "We are going to hold a crusade and a week of teaching at his home."

"A friend of mine is staying there with him," I told him. "His name is Philo. I was together with him in Zambia, and now we are together in Holima. He's been here a couple of months."

"That sounds unlikely," Andrew responded. "Is there a fellow …" he started asking Martin in the back.

"Is he American?" Andrew asked me.

"No, British," I responded.

"A British fellow staying with Philip?" he continued.

"Never heard of him," I heard Martin say.

"Where is he staying?" Andrew asked.

"With Philip in his house near Swaro," I replied.

"That is very unlikely," Andrew told me. "You won't find a white man staying there. That's out in the village."

"Well, it may be out in a village, but that is where he is staying," I repeated myself, adding "He met Philip at a Missionary Training College in the UK."

"Well, Philip has been at a college in the UK," Andrew conceded. "He came back a few months ago. Martin is not very pleased."

"Why?" I asked.

"Bible colleges don't teach right," Andrew told me.

We were late arriving in Deja. I took my new-found friends to their hotel. From there I took a taxi to the home of the boss of my company who was living in Deja. "We were expecting you in Mimbwa tomorrow, not in Deja today!" he told me. I explained everything. "There's a bed here for you," he said. His wife managed to conjure up a very good meal. As I ate (they had already eaten) I learned about this area. "The people here are deeply steeped in their traditions," I was told. That sounded familiar from Zambia. "As a result, this is one of the least developed parts of the country," my boss added.

"Do people's traditions determine their economic status?" I asked him. I was very interested in that idea, after what Philo had told me.

"You'll see!" he said.

A strange thing happened to me that night. I had come from the UK to a land with very foreign customs. There was very much entirely new in what I was meeting. Then I arrived in this very "domestic" situation; my boss's home. My boss's wife, to me at least, resembled Cindy! I said nothing, but it took me a long time to get to sleep that night. I was longing for the kind of domesticity that my boss enjoyed! Allowing myself to cry was what eventually gave me peace. Having been married, even if only for eleven months, left me with a memory of what "might have been!" I was not jealous of my boss, or I think lusting after his wife. I was just suddenly very sad not to have Cindy's company.

A little mysteriously the following morning my boss said, "Come back here for lunch."

"But I am heading for Mimbwa," I told him.

"Don't," he said. I looked at him, then shrugged my shoulders, and off I went to the hotel to collect my colleagues.

In the morning, we drove up the very hill Philo first ascended that wet night in October. I couldn't believe what was happening as I drove up the hill. I had heard very little from Philo. "He will be amazed to see me turn around the corner!" I thought to myself. Martin had obviously made the trip before. He had no trouble directing me. Unlike in Zambia, this part can have rain almost all year around. There were many large trees. We passed through a town that I called "Banana town," due to the hordes of women who came running up to us so as to sell us bananas that were perched on their heads. Some miles on, we turned to the right, then left into Philip's village. Mud was still pretty slippery following the previous day's downpour, but we made it. I didn't see Philo.

"Is there a fellow called Philo who stays here?" I asked a woman after we had arrived.

"You mean a white man?" someone responded.

"He's gone across the river," I was told.

I left just Martin and Andrew that day. The other three men came with me to Swaro. Suddenly we saw Philo walking on the side of the road with a Holiman colleague. I flashed my lights. He ignored me. I parked after passing him, and shouted "Philo!"

He turned around and recognized me, then came to greet me in incredulous disbelief. "Dave. How on earth did you get here? I wasn't expecting to see you for months!"

It really does blow the mind to think how we were together in Zambia, and now were together again in Holima. Philo filled me in on his last two months. He told me of the discouragements, and that he was learning Swahili. I told him that I was heading back to Deja that very day, for lunch.

"There's something fishy going on," (Deja is on the shores of a large lake) I told him. "But what I do know is that I should be heading for Mimbwa."

"Mimbwa is a long way off," Philo told me. "If you were in Deja, that would be amazingly close." Just twenty-five miles in fact. When I got back to Deja, it was as we were hoping. Some exchanges were happening by telegram with Mimbwa. Our manager in Deja managed to convince and cajole the Mimbwa office into accepting that that I should be based in Deja. None of this was my doing. I was a pawn in a greater act! I was to live in Deja.

I did chat with the three men I was with going back to Deja. "We have teaching seminars and a crusade starting tomorrow. That's what we have come for," they told me.

"I felt very junior," Philo told me later. "The whole experience was quite overwhelming. Martin would sit with us at mealtimes and between meals, and he would not stop talking. He would talk, and talk, and talk, and talk. His talking was not quiet. He talked with a loud voice. The bigger the group, the louder the volume. But even when there were just four or five of us around the table, you could easily hear him outside the house."

"So, what was he saying all the time?" I asked.

"Good things. That is—biblical things. He would expound on the Bible. He would encourage us to be diligent in following Jesus. He would expound on theology. He would tell us how important it is to read and follow the scriptures. Especially, he told us how to be a good leader. He explained the task of elders."

"So why did you feel junior?"

"While he was doing that I was asking myself—is that what you do?" Philo responded. "I felt guilty. I would talk about the Bible in the evening, if asked to share, at select times. He would talk all the time. I felt like a very inadequate second-class missionary. In fact, to be more precise, I did not feel like a missionary at all. I felt like an imposter!"

"Wow," I responded.

"I asked myself 'how did Jesus do it?' I mean—the Gospels depict Jesus as talking and teaching a lot. His voice always seemed to be heard. Maybe that's how he did it—raise his voice and keep talking. I run out of words!" Philo said.

"So what did Martin make of you?" I asked Philo.

"I guess somehow I was an embarrassment. Once he realized that I had attended the same 'wrong' college as did Philip, obviously whatever I taught would be wrong. So he has been largely ignoring me."

Martin was big, Philo explained. He had big words. He had big plans, and he had big stories to tell. He oozed with confidence. He knew what he was doing! This was not his first visit. He had been around before. On previous occasions, presumably, he behaved similarly. This time his coming was part of a pre-planned program. On his second day, by 11 a.m. or so, we had a gathered crowd of seventy-odd people. After some songs, Martin and his colleagues taught the people gathered under the tarpaulin. Martin made sure that a few pictures were taken of him surrounded by black children.

"You are planning to live out here?" Martin asked Philo.

"Yes, God willing."

"What do your family think?" Martin added.

"That's a good question," Philo replied. "Actually, they have put up no resistance," he added. "I keep in weekly touch with my parents by letter," Philo revealed to Martin. "Although I am sure they miss the grandchildren they might have had, they seem very much to appreciate what I am doing."

"What about your siblings?" Martin added.

"Same" said Philo, "as far as I know. They don't try to make me feel guilty."

Philo was sent to tell a pastor about Martin's coming, and to encourage him to attend the meeting. The pastor's wife was stooped double over some dishes when Philo got to her home, he later told me. This was standard for washing dishes in the parts of Africa Philo knew about. Women worked stooped double doing their work almost at ground level, while standing. That might look excruciatingly uncomfortable, but to them it was simply their normal working posture.

"Wait, he's coming shortly," she told Philo. For once he did wait. On many occasions someone telling you, "wait, he is just coming" could mean almost anything. The person encouraging you to wait may have no idea where the person concerned is or when they might be coming. It is considered bad practice, though, to discourage a visitor from waiting. It is considered bad practice, generally, to discourage anyone, in fact. It is almost always better to tell someone what they want to hear. That makes for the most amicable relationships. So, if you are looking for someone, you will be told, "they have just left and are coming back right now," even if the person is not expected back till evening. Think how bad it would look if a visitor is told, "no, they are not here, so there is no point in waiting," only to have the person turn up two minutes later. That kind of situation must be avoided at all costs.

Considering "being encouraging" to be more important than "telling truth" is something a new missionary has to learn about. Philo had told me many stories of how this used to frustrate him. Using public transport brings this to the fore. You are waiting for a bus. You don't know when it will come. It seems to be delayed. You ask someone, thinking that perhaps they know when the bus is due. Invariably they say, "it is just coming." On hearing that, you feel good. You may even pick up your bag in anticipation of boarding the vehicle. Ten or more minutes later, and the bus has still not come. Then you have to ask yourself—how did this person actually know that the bus is coming? Of course, they did not have a clue. They saw you were discouraged or frustrated. They wanted to encourage you.

Philo sat waiting for the pastor. There was little reason for him not to wait, as the task he had been given was to talk to the pastor, and invite him to the gathering concerned. The pastor's wife went into the house and got a chair. Philo sat, as the lady of the house carried on working on her dishes. "I did not know that you were Rick's wife," Philo said to Nyaseme. She did not respond. Philo had seen her often at family and church events. She was more thick-set than most of the women, so easy to remember. He had also frequently spoken to her husband. But he had never actually seen the two of them together. He only knew that Nyaseme must be Rick's wife, because he found her washing dishes at Rick's home!

"Can I ask you something?" Philo said to Nyaseme.

"Go ahead," she said.

"Why don't women walk with their husbands?"

"What do you mean?" she responded.

"Like when you go to church, do you go together with Rick?" Philo said probing.

"No."

"So, why not?"

"Men don't have to look after the children and do the housework," she said. "They can go whenever they like. I have that work to do first." As she spoke, she was moving a set of three or four plates from one bucket to another. There was no hot water in this dish-washing process. But there was a bucket for washing, a bucket of clean water for rinsing, and then a rack where utensils were laid to dry in the wind and the sun. The plates rattled in her hands. Philo was struck by the fact that he, the man, was sitting. She, the woman, was working.

"So the only reason you don't walk to places with your husband is because you have housework to do?" Philo pressed Nyaseme. (We called her Nyaseme. Literally this meant something like, "the daughter of," or "the fertility from," such and such a place, in her case from Seme.)

"Why should I walk with him?" she asked Philo in turn. Philo didn't respond. He was waiting for her to explain her statement. They were silent for a minute. "So, in England," she asked, "do men walk with their wives?" Now how was Philo going to answer that question? Couples in England are encouraged to go to places together, and holding hands no less. Philo had not yet seen a man holding a woman's hand in Holima. Couples walking together is a good thing in England. Philo thought that surely such a rule was universal, and it must be a good thing everywhere.

Eventually Philo said "Yes, but why don't you do it here?" Nyaseme glanced up to see if he was serious, giving him an embarrassed look. Her eyes said, "why should I need to walk with my husband?" Philo realized that she was wondering why he was insisting that she check on her husband! Hmmm. That had not been his intention. Not that she couldn't trust him to walk alone, but that the two would desire to walk together!

As Philo was thinking on this, a cyclist turned the corner, dismounted, and proceeded to push his bicycle up the hill towards where the two of them were talking. Philo realized that this was Rick. He was about thirty, a big man, with a smile that always seemed to have a twist to it. Philo explained what he was there for, causing Rick to disappear into the house to prepare himself for the gathering.

Ten minutes later a female voice called Philo into the house. He discovered that Nyaseme's sister was staying with them. When Philo entered the house, tea and bread were already on the table. Rick and Philo sat as the sister served them. Going to stay with one's married sister is a favorite ploy for getting oneself noticed by boys to whom one is not related. Nyaseme's sister did appear, from what Philo could tell, to be behaving well with that purpose in mind. She was about seventeen, and very friendly and helpful. After a prayer, Philo asked Rick the question he had been asking his wife.

"Do you ever walk together?" Philo asked him.

"She wouldn't want that!" he responded. Philo gave him a quizzical look. Rick had apparently come across this question before. He had been to a Bible college at which he had learned things from his European tutors. They had told him that for them it was important to walk with their wives, and to sit next to them in church. Rick's wife came in at this point. She appeared to have finished washing the dishes. She picked up a big basin of dirty clothes and walked off down the hill with it on her head. "If you see a woman walking alongside a man, she's probably a prostitute," Rick told Philo. "As for sitting next to your wife in church—why? No way would my wife sit next to me in church," he said. Philo looked at him quizzically. "Don't you know what happens to a man, especially if she is his attractive young wife, if he sits too close to her?" Rick asked, seeming to think that perhaps Philo was a little naive. Philo didn't respond to that question. He realized that a very normal and respected practice in the West was taboo in his new homeland!

Sometime later, Philo was sat with Rick in Philip's home. People were sat around in a circle. "Is your wife coming?" Philo asked Rick.

"She isn't," Rick responded. He looked at Philo and read the question in his eyes. "Pray for her Philo. She hasn't been to church for three weeks." He didn't tell Philo why she hadn't been to church for that time. Philo supposed there was some issue. Perhaps there had been a falling out between her and another woman in the church? Rick did then take Philo back to his prior question. "There is a way of telling who is married to who in a context like this," Rick told Philo.

"Hmm?" Philo responded. A group of women had just walked in the door. Each in turn was going around and shaking the hand of every person in the circle.

"In a circle like this a woman will greet everyone but her husband," Rick said to Philo. "You can tell who the husband is—he is the one who she doesn't greet!" Sure enough, now that he knew what to look for, Philo observed a woman skipping a male member of the group. That must have been the husband!

Some things that Martin taught were especially interesting. "The Bible says that in church a man needs to sit next to his wife," Martin told the gathered crowd. In that African village, no one wanted to do that. Where exactly in the Bible he got that from Philo did not know. After lunch it was crisis time. "Every woman sit next to her husband," Martin insisted. "If you do not do that then you are not a Christian!" he added. He started commanding individual women. They were so embarrassed, they ran away! It took Philip's intervention to diffuse that crisis.

Martin asked us, "Why was Moses put in a basket and left to float down the River Nile?" We did not know exactly why. "The basket could not float down the river, because it was put amongst the reeds," he said. He never did explain to me why that was important.

"You ask me what they made of me?" Philo added talking to me. "They could hardly believe that I had only been there for two months," he explained. I was a bit puzzled—why exactly should they not be able to believe that? "When they heard me speak to people in my two-month broken Swahili they were amazed!" Philo said. "They would stand and look at me, mouths open. Then they would ask 'How did you learn to speak like that?' 'I am learning Swahili,' I told them."

"We need to send people to live here so that they can learn Swahili," Martin said in due course.

"I was rather awestruck by it all," Philo told me. "Unfortunately, it did not end well."

"Oh?" I queried.

"Martin wanted people to follow a certain leadership structure. According to him, we should not have pastors. The Bible does not say every church has a pastor. It talks about deacons and bishops. I agree with him. That wasn't wrong. Convincing the African folks though was more difficult. One afternoon, he told Philip that he was going to build him a Bible school. He was promising to bring sacks of rice to give out to the poor. (He had already brought a couple of sacks.) Then he was going to buy Philip a new car of his own to use in ministry. That night he laid down his conditions: Philip must take his people out of his current denomination. He must join Martin's denomination. From there on, no one would be called a pastor.

"That night," Philo told me, "Philip refused. Try as he might, Martin couldn't convince him. The next evening when I got back at 7 p.m., I saw them leaving. Martin and his people got up and left at dusk, leaving behind the evening meal that had been prepared for them. The relationship between Philip and Martin was over. I was stunned. All those words. All that wonderful long-term friendship. All that teaching—hinged on Philip taking his people into Martin's church! Then it was all over. Philip refused. Not everyone refused, however. Philip lost quite a lot of people to Martin. In a way, I really liked Martin's approach. He was strong for the Lord. But he tried to bulldoze his way through. When he found poor pastors looking for his money, then it worked. Philip was not ready to be bullied. Yes, that is what it was in a sense; bullying people. It was as if he was building the kingdom of God on the back of money. People paid attention to Martin because of his money. Anyone who didn't want his money, needn't take any notice of him anymore."

"God and his kingdom should not be built on the back of money," I said, after hearing Philo explain all that.

CHAPTER 17: START A SCHOOL

"I have found out the reason I was offered this job in Deja," I said, when we met a few weeks later. At that time, Philo was retreating to Deja every two weeks or so. Once in Deja, he would book a room in a guest-house. He would spend the night in Deja. Then the following day he would travel back to Swaro to continue life in the village. It would have been good had I been able to offer him something better. I was only in very temporary accommodation myself. Why would Philo do this every two weeks? "To keep my head straight," he used to tell me. Life in his African village was in a way very relaxed. I don't think he would ever say that the pace is fast. But it is wearing on a European! Having to fit into people's incomprehensible (to a European) ways of doing things was strenuous. So, as I understand, Philo would make a trip to Deja just so as to be able, for an evening and the following morning, to be away from the constant pressure to fit in to the pace of local people.

On one occasion, I was around when Philo came to Deja. We sat in the dim light of the few remaining light bulbs in a hotel. Most light bulbs seem to have blown. Philo told me that two weeks before at that hotel at about 10 p.m., a scantily-clad girl had asked him whether he was lonely or looking for company.

"You know, Philo," I said, "many people do not stick a job here for very long."

"What's the reason for that do you think?" Philo asked.

"It is a stressful place to work in. I was offered a job here. I felt privileged to have been offered it. I still do feel privileged. I have also discovered that the average duration for people in my job is six months."

"That's not very long for a permanent position," Philo quipped.

"I find the pressure I come under to give people money to be wearing," I added.

"You have discovered that," he replied.

"But it is constant, Philo," I reiterated. "Constant, constant, constant!" I said driving the point home.

"It is a pretty gross situation," Philo admitted.

"It's hard to explain that to someone who does not live here," I said. "Every engagement of nationals with Europeans seems to be a way of getting money out of them."

"That reminds me of Zambia," Philo said, "except perhaps here the pressure is even more intense."

"We have started a school," Philo told me.

"That sounds impressive," I responded. "Tell me about it."

"It's a bit of a long story," Philo added.

"That's okay. I'm in no hurry."

"Like you said," Philo shared, "everyone wants to know what you are wanting to do. It's like they are wanting money, as you have suggested, but again not entirely so. You know that I have come here from Zambia, convinced that it is having a knowledge of God's word that will help people. So, my proposal is that we teach God's word."

"Oh, sounds great," I agreed.

"This of course had to happen without foreign money or I wouldn't be able to know whether people are interested in God's word, or interested in the money that would come with the project," Philo added.

"Sounds like that could be the catch."

"Well, yes," Philo responded.

"Do you want another drink?" a girl asked us. They had tea for Philo and coffee for me. One heard rather unpleasant things about these guest-houses. Sometimes I would take a room, and find condoms stashed on a shelf. One wonders how often the bed one is sleeping in has been used for adultery or fornication. The presence of bargain guest-houses has made all that rather easier.

"Local pastors arranged a meeting," Philo went on. "There were about twenty of us gathered. The agenda—to establish a Bible school. I stated categorically that I neither had money or access to money for such a project. They could not believe me. They knew that having a European man land in the village, they had hit a jackpot. The European man didn't seem to want to leave. Many European men came and went. This one came and stayed. But he did not appear to want to do anything, apart that is, from learning Swahili, and teaching the Bible. He did not start any projects. Hence local folks thought they should start one for him. His role (i.e., my role), would, of course, be to provide money. I did not want to stop them setting up a Bible school if that is what they wanted to do. I told them plainly I would be very happy to be a part of the school, but I had no money to give them."

"Having been in Zambia and then here for a while, I know that they only wanted to start the Bible school because they were looking for a means of getting money out of you, Philo."

"I know, Dave. But what could I do? I think teaching the Bible is an excellent idea. That's what they said they wanted to do. I was willing to help them (in fact I had already started), and I told them plainly that I had no money. The extended meeting of pastors happened," Philo went on. "Together they decided that a Bible school should be set up. Then they appointed a committee to run it. I was to be a member of that committee. My role was to be that of co-ordinator. That's the title that they gave me. I accepted it—what else could I do? At least the title I was given wasn't fundraiser, even though that is what they expected of me! Had it been 'fundraiser' I might have refused. Co-ordinator sounded okay though. It was ambiguous enough. All I know was that I had no intention of funding whatever project I was going to be working with."

I laughed a little, albeit under my breath. I could clearly see the sense in what Philo was saying. But it was far from normal. It was far more normal for a European to work in a project that they were also funding.

"At the end of our meeting the chairman, who was to be the chairman of our Bible school, stood up to give a closing speech. In his speech, he described a dream that he had. In his dream, he told us, he saw money coming to him out of heaven. Local church leaders continued to behave as if they had confidence that I would provide money," Philo went on, "except in our meetings. When they pressed me to raise funds in Europe, my refusal was unnerving for them. Perhaps I was serious and our project would never take off? Then they would be the fools who failed to milk the European man. I did not want them to look like fools. Hence I told them often and categorically 'I do not have any money, and I do not intend to raise any money.'

"Another church from Europe was paying the rent for some buildings for use by the church. The bishop made a room available for us to use as the Bible school office. That worked for a while. Eventually though, he was told, 'You mean there is a missionary from the UK using an office that we are paying rent for? Why doesn't he get his own office and pay for it?' Then we had to vacate that office. Until we moved out, our project had indirect help from the other European donor who did not know that they were helping us. We even had a typewriter of theirs that we could use. But when they found out, they pulled the rug."

Philo was probably far too enthusiastic at the beginning. He got some books for teaching theology from Imbigen at a knockdown price. He told his new students that he would only charge them the knockdown price. He would, in other words, waive any transport cost. The students were very grateful, and Philo felt good about it. Unfortunately, on the day the class was due to start, all of the students said they had no money on them. "Okay," thought Philo. "To facilitate the progress of the class, I'll give them the books now, and collect money later." After all, they were all ready to start the class. (They were to meet in the hall, the rent for which was paid by the European church.) Philo made a mistake. "I was wrong to have done that," he admitted. Philo handed out the books, expecting to be paid later. He never got any money for any of them! Unfortunately, such naive thinking, that people would do what they said they would do, encouraged the committee to think that eventually they would be able to get money out of Philo. This inspired them to keep calling meetings, during which they would spend hours pressurizing Philo to give them money!

"We were having one of those meetings," Philo explained, "when the suggestion was made that board members should contribute to help to run the teaching program. That seemed more of a reasonable system, so after considerable pressure over an extended time, I contributed the amount that was required, about US$3. Philip was also with us (he was the patron of the school), and he was receiving a lot of money from various donors, so he did likewise. The others never paid. Then on another occasion it was agreed that all board members should contribute a weekly amount to the kitty. None of them did—and neither did I by that point, as I knew it was a ruse," Philo added.

"You know, I tried to explain things to them," Philo told me.

"But they couldn't hear," I responded.

"That's right!" Philo said. "I explained that for theological teaching to be contextually relevant, it would have to be locally funded. Money comes with strings. Outsiders wanting to help us with funds would also want to dictate what we taught, how we taught it, in what language we taught it, and so on. Therefore, I stuck to my guns, in the interest of the relevance of our proposed teaching. I think they understood this. But I think it was also so wildly beyond their own expectations that it could not register. Their whole interest was basically in money, so no case would do for not bringing it!" I listened intently in amazement. Thankfully, my own time in Africa enabled me to appreciate what Philo was saying. By providing money, a white man digs a grave for his own projects.

Philo continued with his battles. I, as others, could only follow him from a distance. Sometimes he seemed more encouraged. Sometimes he seemed less encouraged. That went on for years, as the extension Bible school went on for years. Here's a synopsis of what happened over those years, and some of the things that Philo learned—things of much relevance for mission and development to date.

"It was encouragement and discouragement," Philo told me. "Round and round," he added.

"But why?" I asked him in a conversation we had some years later.

"I didn't know then, but I do know now," Philo answered. I told him that response alone was not very helpful. Could he explain?

"Philip was my host in Holima," Philo said. "I actually stayed in his house the first eighteen months. I wanted to learn how to behave as a Holiman, or as a local tribesman, in order to become as much as possible a regular member of the community. That is, so as not to do things that might cause offense, and push people away. I've already explained how this helped me to understand that you never leave a visitor standing at the door. You invite them in. Not being able to understand how to behave towards visitors could be very troubling."

"Philip was the bishop. He was the bishop of my home church. He was by nature an encourager. I believed that he spoke truth. Could I come out to call him a liar? Well—no. So, I thought, Philip says the school will work. Okay. I was seeing more and more that it couldn't and wouldn't. But, I thought, no, I will believe him! I will believe the words of the senior African. Surely that's the thing to do."

"I had in mind," Philo went on, "many parallel situations in which the word of African leaders was taken as pivotal or decisive in decisions made by outsiders. The outsider can only do so much after all. Then they have to believe the native person, or not. I was aware that many projects floundered. I refused to accept that was because African people were evil. Not to say that they are angels either. They are people—so there is good and bad. I was going to believe that African leader, the bishop, to the bitter end, so as to get to the bottom of this situation, and by implication others like it."

"One always came away from a meeting with Philip encouraged," Philo said. "He had an incredible strength of character. Philip exuded confidence. That's how he ran the church. I came from time with Philip somehow convinced that the project (i.e., the school) must work and will work!"

"The same often applied to engagements and conversations with other African people," Philo went on, "if to a lesser degree. Now there were those who said we wouldn't go anywhere without foreign money. I have already mentioned that. It was clear to me though, that such was not the case. That is to say—the kind of people we were intending to educate had time available. Typically, they had a bicycle or such means of transport. Just looking at what they did with their time, it was, as a rule, clear that people are capable of making time for a class like ours. That is—they made time available for other things. Why shouldn't they make time for us? It was their choice!"

"Whenever, almost invariably, I engaged in conversation with African people, they expressed that they were very keen on this project. They believed it would work, and almost always they were themselves willing to become students. In the vacations, often we visited people in their homes. They were heady times!" Philo said. "By the end of the vacation we knew that our classes were going to be bursting at the seams!" He added, "The same applied even to volunteers who came to help us. At times, we had a significant team. At the time, I did not fully realize that they were all hoping for my money. Not only did I not realize that. I refused to realize it! To have realized it would, after all, have been to say that if our classes didn't end up filling, Africans were liars and conmen. At all costs, that is the conclusion I did not want to reach! Hence, I believed, and believed, and believed, that our project, which logistically could work, actually would work, starting tomorrow. Yes, it was always tomorrow, next week, next month, next year that things would be different. Okay, I thought, let's wait it out and see!"

"I guess it is clear, that if I had backed off, then the word would have been; 'if only you had been patient till tomorrow, next week, or next year, things would have been different.' I had to keep, keep, keep, believing, and carrying on."

"Ironically," Philo added, "going back to Europe had the same effect. That is to say, whenever I went to visit the UK, typically for a few months every two or three years, things changed in my head. To put it bluntly, the way Africa and Africans are perceived in the West would not allow what I was experiencing in Holima to be true. I mean, that was the case in many ways. Just for example, there is the publicity put out by mission agencies. Similarly, the literature put out by development people. In both cases, the image they portray, and this is frankly the one British people get, is of African people who receive, react, do, and behave, *as if they are British*. The publicity is pretty much always, let me say, about successes. These, those, and the other people were having successful theological education programs. Those, and those, and those, were guiding successful development projects. All those terms and words were giving an image of Africa that was contrary to my experience. While in the UK my head, i.e., my comprehension, would adjust. The problems and insurmountable obstacles that I constantly met on the ground in Africa disappeared! They became unbelievable, almost. The more I stayed in the UK, the more field reality shifted in my head."

"That would come to an end when I got back on the ground in Holima," Philo went on. "My first week back was typically full of sobering reality checks. Remember that I could touch down right at grass roots. Due to my language knowledge, I could hear things said first-hand. Because I was not a project administrator, or significant donor, I related directly with local people. I would be rudely reminded of the reality, and that all that optimism in the West was largely, well, empty."

When Philo told me all that, I just had to interrupt him. "You know Philo, what you said is just fascinating, and is, well, revolutionary. I can hardly believe how simply you are able to explain things that fox people who are involved in mission and development."

"Well thanks, Dave," Philo said.

"Do go on," I encouraged him.

"Oh yes, something else I want to add," Philo said. "That is—I was determined not to give excuses to people who might want a scapegoat for our school should it fail."

"What do you mean, Philo?"

"For example," Philo said, "if students go to class and find the teacher is not there, or is late, that could quite quickly knock their motivation for continuing."

"Okay," I said.

"So I made very sure that I never missed, and I was never late. To help to ensure that, I would get to the location of a class one hour early. Then, even if I had a puncture, if it rained, or if people wanted to talk to me on route, I would still be well on time. Never once should a student say, 'I got to the class on time but there was no teacher so I left again.' I was always there. When we had other teachers, I would do my utmost to ensure that they did likewise."

"Wow," I said.

"So then, day after day, for eighteen years, people would promise that they would come to class. They would praise our school. They would say they love God's word, which is what we were teaching, they would say all the right things, but they would not follow through. They did not come."

"Now I need to qualify that a little. We did have students. At times, we had about twenty plus people come to a class every week. The bottom line always seemed clear; people came because there was a white man involved. A white man who potentially had money. They would keep coming as long as a prospect for some financially lucrative career or material gain seemed to be in prospect. When such was no longer the case, they would stop. There were a few temporary exceptions to that rule. But the rule held very strongly."

"Perhaps I need to add," Philo said, "that this could be because I'm somehow substandard. Maybe I'm not very clever. Well, you will have to judge that. I think though, frankly, in UK terms, I am as good as the next man. Not exceptional. Not incompetent. The other thing to consider here is that we did have many teachers. Over eighteen years perhaps we had fifteen or so African people at one point or another, seriously committed to helping us teach. Sometimes they would report having been deceived by the constant optimism we were fed by the bishop, in vacation time by prospective students, and so on. Frankly though, in sheer attendance at their classes, they did no better than I did. They also experienced the kind of deceptive-enthusiasm I've already mentioned, followed by late-coming, followed by people who had expressed great interest just dropping out, followed by many classes ending up with zero students. The problem was not my inadequacies; other teachers failed as badly as I did."

"Despite the great optimism, class after class failed abysmally. If we went to a new place, there would be some interest. This, I had to realize, was people hoping to benefit from the pocket and influence of the white man. When that was not forthcoming, promises came to nought. In case you might be wondering about the teachers I talked of, Dave—we had some teachers, because when they taught for us half-time, we also gave them opportunities to advance themselves at a known Bible college by studying there the other half-time. In fact, we offered them half a scholarship each."

"So what you are saying, Philo," I said, "is that many, many, good encouraging words were empty. You are also saying that you were determined by all means not to draw that conclusion. Yet it looks like that's the conclusion that you have drawn. If all those Holiman people were full of optimism that ended up groundless, does that not mean that they are indeed liars and deceivers—what you tried to disprove from the start? In addition, you seem to have said that African people are only interested in money! Can you explain all that?"

Philo thought for a while. Then he said the following: "If a European were to come to my home area in Africa now, and want to do what I did then, my response to him or her would be much the same as that of my African colleagues to me then." Then he qualified his response in this way: "That is not entirely true. I continue to be a supported missionary from the West. I would not need that European's money. Then of course, not all African people were after my money at the time either. Many were polite, encouraging, and left me alone. I guess that is how I would be to such a new missionary."

"So then," I said to Philo, "You would also be a liar and a conman?"

He responded "Europeans do not learn. To reach a people, if you do not intend to enslave them or confuse them or exploit them, you must use their language. Then you must be able to continue hearing what they say. That means, in effect, that you should not bring outside resources into what you were doing. If you bring in such resources, then people will compete for those resources. Just bring the gospel!"

So I asked "But didn't you yourself learn quickly not to use outside resources?"

He answered "I did use some outside resources at the start. It was, like, to get things going. Remember the opposition I talked about having had in the UK to my approach? Instead of having people supporting me in taking a vulnerable approach, European people were attacking me. I also started by using English, for the first few months, before I was confident enough in local languages. I knew I had done those things. I kept things small and at a minimum. I had to be seen to be doing something that European people recognized, like extension Bible teaching, so that supporters could understand me. You see, I was working with African people according to donor pressure, not according to the African context. From a European point of view, perhaps, I was testing the African and finding him wanting. Actually, I was testing the West and its approach, and finding it wanting."

Philo paused. I was about to ask another question. Then instead, he added: "Remember also, Dave, that I had a reputation to live down. The church leaders I related to in Holima were not fools. They already had experience with Europeans. They knew the game was money. They know us well! If you squeeze a European, money comes out. I still have not lived that reputation down. I cannot. There were too many Europeans doing the money thing."

"But," I responded, "surely if a missionary like that came, you would help him or her by explaining things. Surely, if it is as you say it is, then you should warn them?"

"That is up to them, if they're ready to listen, then I might. You realize though that to do so is at risk to myself? The current system has a lot of benefactors. The fact that it does not work doesn't mean that there are not people profiting from it. There are. Many. For me to try to explain things to a new missionary is like cutting my own throat. It would be making enemies. Enemies on both sides that is, of Europeans, because they enjoy the prestige and activity of being generous patrons, and of Africans, who have become dependent on the patronage."

"I get it," I said.

"That is why," Philo added, "a new missionary or development worker coming to the field should not expect either local people or expatriates, including missionary colleagues, to tell them the truth. They should expect, in other words, to be told untruth; you could say, lies. They should expect to be conned. I do not see another way as things are. They must be as wise as serpents and as innocent as doves. For an Englishman or American to come to Africa with money in their pocket, expecting to engage with African people using the English that Africans have learned in school, is sheer folly. Until someone gets away from that model, well, they are absolutely between a rock and a hard place.

"People come from the West. They have an idea. They have never thought about how it might work in this context. They cannot so think about it, because they do not know the context. You learn people's contexts, in that sense, as you learn the language. Learning the language as you engage with their ways of life (not in the classroom or from books) is a way, no, *the* way, of discovering the meaning-categories that people live by. Foreigners want to implement their ideas without ever going through that process. You might say someone doing that deserves to be ignored. They should take their time first. Yes, you are right, but they also bring money. Sometimes big money. It is hard to ignore them, because of that money. Some people will ignore them, but others will take the chance and engage with them in the hope of getting some of that money. Often they do get some money. But to take someone like that seriously, is a very dicey process. Money is divisive, and causes arguments, disputes, and suspicions. It is very hard in that process to avoid lying and deceiving. Who should you blame though? It is the foreigners who bring that temptation and put it into people's faces. It is lots of foreigners, and they keep on doing it. If they want to be respected, they should stop."

"What you're saying is true," I said. "What you have proved in your eighteen years of dedicated extension Bible teaching is, yes, that African people responded to you as liars and conmen because they had no choice! What you have revealed is the folly underlying the approach by the West to mission and development using outside languages and outside resources."

Part II

The Roho Church

CHAPTER 18: A TRUE BUS ADVENTURE

One day, Philo confided in me. "A certain pattern is developing. I don't know what to do about it."

"What's that?" I asked.

"You remember Saturday Fellowship in Zambia?"

"Yes. That's the fellowship that was set up *in opposition* to the missionaries' meeting on Sundays."

"You know that I joined them?"

"Yes, I remember."

"Later, when I went back to visit, after my MA, leaders of the church run by the missionaries cast aspersions on what I was doing and why."

"Yes, yes, of course, I remember all that."

"Well, it put me in a funny position. A position, that is, in which my own people were condemning me, but my African colleagues were accepting me. Well, it has kind of become a trend. I am not sure that becoming over-accustomed to working only with African churches is necessarily a good thing."

"Why on earth not?"

"They're not my people, and it is important to be accepted by your own people."

"Okay. So then, you seem to fear that identifying with an African church can be a kind of escapism. Is that it?"

"Yes, I am afraid that I have been attaching myself to people who do not really understand me in depth, our cultures being so different, but, I have been accepted by them. So, what exactly does their acceptance mean if they do not understand me? I feel a bit like someone who has lots of good friends, but doesn't relate at all to their family."

"That would make you into someone who sounds like the prodigal son," I answered. We both laughed at that. To reach others with the gospel can make one appear like the very prodigal son whose example we should be avoiding!

Philo said in a low voice, "But then—you know who that resembles in the New Testament? I think it resembles the attitude of Paul."

"Maybe. Yes. Got it! Jewish people were unhappy at the time with Paul. To them, he had abandoned the true ancient faith. He was compromising it to fit the Gentiles. So, some Jews hated him."

Philo reflected further, "So then I am a new Paul, jammed between angry Jews and just as concerned Roman authorities; Roman authorities who were also against the gospel, thinking that it would undermine the authority of their gods. Missionaries are in trouble! Once they identify strongly with other people, their own people condemn them!"

"You should have explained that to Richard," I commented, as Julie walked onto the scene. Julie was my sister, whose wedding Philo and I had attended in Scotland. She was an intelligent blond, slim, attractive, of medium height, with a pleasant smile.

Philo jumped up, "What are you doing here?" he exclaimed, with an enormous smile on his face. He ran up to Julie and gave her a massive hug. He had not known that she would be visiting Holima. Her husband had some work to do in Imbigen, so she was with me for a few days' visit. It had been around 20 years since Philo and Julie last met, at Julie's wedding!

After an exchange of greetings, Julie asked, "You were talking about Richard as I came in, Philo—is it the Richard that Dave talked to me about? He said the man has been troubling you?"

Philo looked at me. His relationship with Richard was not a secret, but he looked surprised that I'd told Julie about it.

"I told Julie about Richard." I looked at Philo, hoping he wouldn't mind.

"Seems he made things very tough for you," Julie said.

"Well," Philo asked, "does Julie know the latest?"

"No," I said.

Julie gave me a sidelong, quizzical look.

"Tell you later," I said. "Look, this story needs a proper telling. Let's keep Julie in suspense till we find a good opportunity."

"For goodness sake tell me at once!" Julie demanded.

"Look, Julie," Philo said. "Here we are sitting at the bus station in Deja. Not a good place to tell a story. Why don't you come home tomorrow, then we can sit in the shade of the tree in front of my house and tell you the full story in the way it ought to be told." Julie was reluctant to have this bit of suspense prolonged. Philo and I insisted. It would be good, anyway, to visit Philo at his home.

"A serious note," Philo said. I knew what was coming.

"My home is a very African home. I don't have too many visitors. You are welcome, but let me be up front about the conditions."

"What do you mean?" Julie asked.

"There are two rules I ask my visitors to keep. One is not to give gifts of any kind to people they meet at or around my home. The second is not to instigate ongoing relationships. That is, be friendly with everyone when you are at my home; but once you leave, don't follow up with relationships thus formed."

I could see that poor Julie was very confused by those instructions. Philo could probably not see that. Julie frowned and looked at me with a look I am very familiar with: the look she has when she wants her own way. I signalled by shaking my head that she should say nothing more. Moments later Philo was off. He knew his way around the bus station possibly better than me, and there was a particular bus he was after.

Once Philo had left, Julie asked me: "What was all that about rules at his home? What kind of host is that who gives his visitors rules?" We were by then walking. It took a few minutes to get away from the throbbing crowds.

"Philo knows what he is doing. Unfortunately, Europeans often behave in ways that cause a lot of disruption to people's homes and families. Philo is simply trying to protect his children from the kind of messes that Europeans make. Over here, if you give gifts to an African community that consists of extended families, you can create enormous tensions arising from people's jealousy. Having a *white friend* can be like handing out a nugget of gold. Philo doesn't want to ruin relationships in or around his home. He does not want to be a walking bank or to be perceived as such."

Julie had not reflected about the fact that white people who think they bring wonderful blessings wherever they go, can also create severe problems for indigenous communities.

"And what is all this about Richard?" Julie asked me in her most persuasive tone of voice, which had worked with me many times before. I would not tell her anything. She would have to wait till we got to Philo's place the following day.

* * *

The following morning Julie and I agreed that we would take a bus, which would leave us within a half hour's walk of Philo's home. Walking back to the bus station, we got many of the usual hassles. I tried to avoid making eye-contact with people selling anything and everything along the road. As soon as one made the briefest eye contact, their eyes and then their whole disposition would pull you towards them. I jokingly said at times — if you were not careful you would end up on a bus or in a *tuk-tuk* (a motorized rickshaw) going to some place to which you had no intention of going at all! You would end up going there just to please that person.

Julie was more liable than I to that. I observed her struggling to avoid making eye contact with people, while being interested in what was going on around her. Matatu touts, as they called them, that is, young men trying to fill buses, would at times physically drag a woman into a bus against her will. That is not to take her where she did not want to go, but to force her choice as to which bus to use. Sometimes before forcing her, these men will have already grabbed the bag of the woman concerned and put it into the bus of their preference.

The route on the main road that went nearby Philo's place had many buses traveling on it. Hence, we had choices to make. In the end, I took Julie's hand, to make sure she didn't get waylaid so that we wouldn't be disconnected from one another.

"When is this bus going?" I asked the one conductor.

"Right now!" he told me.

We sat inside it and waited thirty minutes for *right now* to happen. As we sat, an endless flow of salesmen offering everything from handkerchiefs, screwdrivers, pictures and beans, tried to draw our attention and make eye contact, amongst a constant chaos of voices, as more passengers were noisily being recruited and sometimes almost pushed into our bus. Some of the young men that we assumed were fellow passengers got out minutes after we had sat down. Clearly, their role was to make the bus appear to be nearly full; they had no intention of going anywhere.

Eventually, we were off. Our journey was uneventful. It might have been more interesting if Philo had been there with us, because he was fluent in both dominant languages of the region, Swahili and Striden. That meant he could understand what was said in a crammed bus. Sometimes such understanding could be very entertaining, he tells me. We were more ignorant—with mostly ineffective ears to comments quite likely being made about two white people in this crowded situation.

We reached our destination, alighted, and started walking the last two miles or so. The route was still a little muddy and slippery from the rain of the previous afternoon. Curious locals might have wondered what the two of us were doing on their village path.

"Where are we going, Dave? Are you sure this leads to Philo's place? These paths don't seem to lead anywhere except into the middle of an African village," Julie said.

I laughed, a bit more to myself than out loud. This did rather strike people about Philo's home. If you didn't see Philo himself, or at least didn't get to his bedroom, which doubled as his office with a shelf full of Bibles and dictionaries, you wouldn't know that there was a stranger living there. Everything else was thoroughly African, including the toilet, some would say, and they would be right. Philo's toilets left much to be desired as far as Europeans were concerned. Julie's reaction was not wrong, nor surprising. Truth-be-told though—although some of the local African folks might have wondered what we were doing on their village paths, others probably assumed that we were heading to visit Philo.

Sure enough, we caught up with an old man walking in the same direction as us. He was walking with a stick, very slowly and with a limp. The positioning of his hat on his head was particularly noticeable. Instead of sitting squarely, the tilt of his hat gave the old man an odd appearance. His expression was such that one could not have known whether he was smiling on the inside, or miserable.

"You must be going to visit Philo?" he said, when he found us beginning to pass him on the path.

"Yes," I replied.

Julie looked at him. Hearing someone mention Philo's name helped to reassure her that we at least weren't just totally lost. The old man started singing Philo's praises. Folks around, or at least some of them, seemed to appreciate Philo. He said some things that reminded me of things Philo had told me in the past. I know that Philo was fluent in speaking Swahili, the regional language, and Striden, the tribal language.

"He knows Striden, Swahili and Lile," the old man said. He stated that as categorical fact. There seemed to be no doubt in his mind, according to what he said, that Philo was a fluent Lile-language speaker. But Philo did not know much Lile at all. This was a discourse style that Philo had warned me about. In European English, one might have called it telling lies. If you thought in this community that people were, therefore, liars, you would be misunderstanding them. To praise people, especially patrons, is normal. (Philo was staying with orphan children, so in at least that respect was a patron.) Truth, when it comes to the giving of such praise, is almost irrelevant. A similar misunderstanding occurs with contracts: Europeans say that they agree, then the discussion is done: it is a contract. In most of Africa, it just means "I am listening," and it is the start of the discussion, not the end.

I had, after some time, finally understood that. "How many Europeans didn't?" I often asked myself. Europeans believe in notions of objective truth that are very hard for people here to grasp. Hence, they believe what they are told as if relational truth were objective truth. Philo is right, I thought to myself, that such error underlies endless difficult issues in relationships between Europeans and locals in Africa.

We eventually moved ahead of the old man and his slow pace. "He told us Philo knows three local languages, whereas Philo has only told us of two," Julie commented.

"Hmm," I said. I didn't feel up to trying to explain that to her at the time. Explaining African notions of truth to European people can be fraught with confusion. It results in some Europeans having a low opinion of Africans.

"You must ask him about …" as I was talking, Julie slipped in the mud! She was there beside me, then suddenly she was gone.

"Sorry, sorry," I said.

Standing up again, her dress was embellished with a big brown splodge of mud! It transpired that she was carrying a spare skirt for just such an eventuality, which she was able to put on when we got to Philo's place. Let me also confess—it was not only Julie who was slipping and sliding in the mud that day. I had come very close to falling over two or three times.

"Why did you say *sorry, sorry*? It wasn't your fault that I slipped," Julie said. By that time the ground had got a little firmer.

"Oh," I exclaimed. I had to think about that one. "I've picked that habit up from the locals."

"'Sorry' isn't an African word, it's an English word, so how can you say that *sorry, sorry* is African?"

"Yes, I know it's an English word, but it's also a translation of some African words. In Swahili, it would be *'pole, pole'*, and in Striden, it would be *'mos, mos.'* Striden is the name the Striden people themselves use to refer to their language," I added.

"So, you mean *sorry* doesn't mean sorry?" Julie replied, without perhaps thinking about what she was saying. Reflecting on her words though she was right: *sorry* doesn't mean sorry! That is, *sorry* as used by local people won't mean the same as does *sorry* by a typical English person!

"You are right," I said, "sorry doesn't mean sorry. This could get confusing!" I thought: how can a word not mean what it means?!

"When African people use English words, then they no longer mean what English people originally intended them to mean or think that they mean," I said to Julie, reflecting on what she said. I needed Philo's help on this.

We still hadn't reached Philo's place though, so I had no choice but to have a go at explaining this myself. "Sorry is for people around here a translation of *mos*. 'Mos' is said (i.e., 'sorry' is said) to empathize with a person who has stumbled. It implies a kind of collective embarrassment at someone else's misfortune. As if you're stumbling is somehow partly my fault, hence I apologize. Sorry, but sorry certainly isn't sorry anymore."

"That's confusing," Julie frowned.

"Yes," I conceded. I wanted to drop the topic, as I was beginning to wonder if any words still meant what they once meant.

"That's Philo's home," I eventually said, as we turned a corner, having walked up a steep bit of hill.

"What. Those two houses?"

I glanced at Julie. She didn't seem very impressed. Her pace slowed. I could only imagine what was going through her mind as she looked for the first time at Philo's rough-looking accommodation. Philo was happy to acknowledge that if this had been England, his houses would long ago have been condemned and demolished. Julie had not yet seen half of what was there. The inside of the house, as I perceived it, was worse than the outside. And Julie had only seen the latter, then at a distance.

"Come on, Julie, we are nearly there."

CHAPTER 19: RAISING CHILDREN

As we scrambled up the steep muddy slope taking us to Philo's home proper, a small child shot out of Philo's door and ran towards us. A second later, another, then in no time, five small children were running across the grass towards us.

I glanced across at Julie. I tried to look into her eyes. This was not a new experience for me. I knew how welcoming Philo's kids are. I am not quite sure whether I saw a tinge of fear, "What do these African children want from us?" or whether it was a mother's eyes.

"What beautiful children, and so endearing!" Her fear would not have been entirely ungrounded. That is to say—it is not unknown for groups of African children to run up to white people to laugh at them or to ask them for money. This time, though, they were indeed Philo's children who had come to welcome their visitors. After giving us joyous handshakes, they took our bags, and led us towards the door of the upper of the two houses.

Moments later Philo emerged in the doorway. He was also smiling. He made his way towards us. "Dr. Livingstone, I presume," Julie said to him! She had entered the spirit of the moment. It was great to see him on his home territory.

I did have to reflect. Here was Philo, more than twenty years after he had first come to Holima. This was where his endeavors at solving the development puzzle had taken him. Not all were led in this direction. I know that he was not the only European wanting to help Africa to develop. Most of them, though, occupied paid posts in the aid industry, did research at universities, attended high-level meetings in hotels, participated in intergovernmental discussions and fundraising, and liked fat budgets. For Philo, it meant living like an African villager, and adopting all these children! This was Philo's way of trying to get to a position of understanding what was going on around him. And it was proving very effective.

When Julie entered the house, she must have been struck by how dirty it was, according to European standards. That is not to say that preparations for visitors had not been made. On the contrary, the seats were covered with white cloths embroidered with flowers, the floor had been washed, and the house had been swept. The ceiling board had gaping holes in it. The walls were murky with dirt. I could sense, however, that she barely paid attention. Instead, her mind was doing overtime with the joy of finding all these children in Philo's home.

I prayed as we stood. Then ten or so children filed by to shake our hands. I judged them as being aged between seven and twenty, about half boys and half girls. Then the housemother and other ladies who were there to help her with the cooking did the same. Julie was just about bursting as we engaged in formalized greetings. It wasn't long before she came out with it. "Philo, what about all these children? Whose are they? Where have they come from? Do they live with you?" Somewhere along the line Julie had missed this piece of information. I know how much she loved children. I know that she and her husband had been trying to have children for years. She was bursting with wonder at seeing all these children in Philo's home.

"They live with me," Philo said. "They are orphans. Well, I don't consider them orphans. They are my children," Philo added.

"How many are there?" Julie asked.

"Twelve," said Philo.

"Twelve children! You mean that you live here in your home with twelve children?" Julie exclaimed. Philo seemed to be used to having visitors being so amazed.

"Yes, of course," he simply said.

I had often been amazed myself. I still was, but it was not my first time to visit Philo. Julie fired her questions at Philo: "How do you get the children? How old are they?" and so on. Philo explained. His was no orphanage. That is—there was no registered project there at all. All arrangements were made only under the church, not through government. That is not to say that anything was illegal, but it was informal. The children were "informally adopted," Philo would say.

"So how do you get a child?" Julie asked incredulously and excitedly.

"We approach a pastor from the vicinity, who talks to a relative, for example, the grandmother of any orphan child nearby he is aware of. He tells the relative about what we do, and how, and why. If the relative is interested, then she comes with the pastor to talk to us. There is a housemother who resides permanently with the children. Being a widow, she has devoted her life to looking after the children." Philo said, "So we describe how we live to the grandmother. We get to know her a little and to know about the child. Everyone has ample opportunity to ask questions. The pastor is there to assess what is going on and works as a potential arbitrator. We invite the grandmother back at a later date, if she wants to come back again, probably with other relatives as well as with the pastor, to talk some more. If she comes back, then we continue our discussion. If everything seems amicable, then we invite the grandmother to bring the child to stay with us for a few days, as a visitor. That means no strings, but a chance for the child to get to know us. When those few days are over, the child knows us. Then the child goes back to the grandmother or another relative. They can tell them what they want. The grandmother and other family members have a choice at that point—either to bring the child back or not. If they do not, then that is not a problem. If they do bring the child back, then we consider the child to be adopted."

Philo pointed out that although he took full responsibility for the children, (barring any major medical emergency, or perhaps another big issue that would have him go back to the family for help,) he had no actual legal responsibility for any of them. The family members could come at any time to take their children back if they wanted to. But they did not.

Julie could hardly believe it. It was as if she was about to stand up and give Philo a big hug! I had warned her about that though. In the community in which Philo was living, while it was acceptable that women hug women and men hug men, hugging between sexes was frowned upon. Deep mothering urges and instincts seemed to ooze out of Julie as she listened. Questions were also piling up in her head. What about this, and that, and the other.

"We bring the children up as African children," Philo explained. "It is up to me to adjust, not up to them. The standard, apart from that of the Word of God, is the local one. We eat local food. The children go to the local school. Their school uniforms get to be as tatty as anyone else's. We use the local language."

This time I was the one who interrupted Philo. "Permit me to ask again, Philo, why do you use the local language with the children? After all, the official language of government, education and business in Holima is English. You're an Englishman. If you were to speak to the children in English …."

As I was talking, an older looking woman ran past our window shouting; "Wa! Wa! Wa!" at the top of her voice. On hearing that, two children ran past us towards the outside door. Once outside, they also started shouting and running in the same direction as the woman had gone. Instinctively I rushed out to join them. I passed a very worried-looking Julie. Philo followed me out. By the time we got outside, one disappointed-looking old woman and two children were coming back towards us.

"It got it!" Philo said to me.

"What got what?" I asked him.

"The otenga," he said, adding "a black kite to be precise, got the chick."

Julie had by this time joined us. "It got a chick?" she said.

"Yes, afraid so," Philo said.

"Whose?"

"Not mine, I don't keep chickens. It was grandma's." Grandma, it transpired, lived just a hundred yards up the hill. The kite had daringly swooped, even though there were people around, and grabbed a chick, and disappeared with it. All the shouting, intended to scare the kite, had been to no avail. All that had got our adrenalin pumping!

"Does this happen often?"

"I am afraid so," he said. "We lose a lot of chicks that way."

"Poor chick," said Julie. "And why do you call her grandma? Whose grandma is she? Not yours, is she?"

"You remind me of a friend of mine," Philo answered. By this time, we had sat back down again. "This friend was corresponding over the internet with a woman in the UK. On realizing that she was an older lady, he wrote to her (in English, of course) "You are my grandma." He told me the lady was quite upset, and told him so.

"Right!" Julie said.

"Well, it is different here," I said, supporting Philo. Julie looked at me. "It is respectful to call an older lady grandma, or more accurately, my grandma or our grandma."

"How do you stop the kites?" Julie asked Philo.

"Difficult! You'll laugh though at what people do. They paint the chicks purple, to confuse the kite!"

"Hmmm," Julie responded.

"Shall I carry on?" I asked. No one answered, so I carried on anyway. "I was saying, by using English here at your home, Philo, wouldn't you give your children an excellent head start in the Kenyan educational system?"

"Yes, you're right, I would." Then Philo added a little cynically, while carefully checking our eyes to make sure we will get what he says, "That is the problem." Philo carries on staring at me. I encouraged him to speak more. This was too cryptic. Philo had more explaining to do!

"Look, if I talked to the children in English," Philo explained, "you are right, that they could end up doing very well indeed in the educational system in Holima. They would easily graduate to the top of their class. But that would quickly and almost inevitably, no, inevitably, bring enormous jealousies in its wake. Imagine the wealthier families around here discovering that the orphan children I adopted were all doing better than theirs in school. Next time we had a vacancy to take in a child, the whole community could end up fighting for that opportunity. Massive bribes would soon be changing hands. People would be mightily jealous of the child who succeeded. It could not work! It would generate conflict. It would drive me out of the village. That would not be living as the people do! That would be a kind of neo imperialism!"

Julie was gobsmacked. She had always imagined that teaching people in the majority world to know English was one of those progressive things that everyone should be doing. She had thought that passing on knowledge of English is a sure contribution to development. Now here was Philo, with a prime opportunity to do that for these dear African children, and he was refusing! And he was giving us good reason for his refusal. If he did not refuse, jealousy and corruption would drive him out of the village!

At that point the old woman, who had tried to scare away the kite, walked into Philo's home and sat down with us. She was of medium height for a woman, perhaps judging by her slight stoop, having lost an inch or two in later years. A bit startled initially by finding so many visitors in the house, she soon seemed relaxed enough with Philo. We stopped our conversation. Philo was talking to her. I could only get a few words of what he said to her in Striden. Julie didn't understand anything. In due course, the lady went into the kitchen.

"Who was that?" Julie asked.

"She comes from across the valley," Philo said. "We call her *Awuor Nyasaye*. When in church she likes to say '*awuor Nyasaye*', out loud, while the preacher is preaching. *Awuor Nyasaye* could be translated into English as 'I am amazed by God.'"

"So, what was she doing? Why did she just walk in?" Julie asked.

Philo looked a bit puzzled. Then a light went on in his head. "Did you expect her to stand in the doorway," Philo asked, "while we are all sitting in here?"

It took some time for Philo to explain this to Julie. "We don't do things here like they do in England," he told her. "When someone comes to the door, the first thing we do is to welcome them to come in and sit down. To leave someone standing in the doorway is considered very rude," he added.

"Oh," said Julie, suffering from overload of all the new things she was learning.

"English is a big problem in Africa," Philo carried on, bringing us back to our topic. That was one of his bold statements that he made while carefully surveying our eyes in case we misunderstood. Julie said nothing, and neither did I. We wanted him to carry on. "All other languages here in Holima come for free, basically, but English has to be bought. Updates regularly have to come from faraway England or the USA. So, this is dependency writ large. The impact of English on Africa, well at least Holima, is horrific, and Europeans themselves generally do not even realize it. There are many reasons why they do not realize it. English is very much a language of money. If you know English, you can get money. That's a product of globalization. Hence Holiman people easily justify spending money on English to draw on the benefits of globalization."

"But what is the catch then?" I asked.

"There are many catches," Philo replied, "including catch 22!" Julie and I laughed.

"English stops people from thinking their own way." That was another of his bold statements that begged justification. "It condones all the wrong categories. Look," Philo added, "we might not have time for a class on linguistics this morning. I cannot pretend to tell you everything in one short session! Let me just say one more thing for now. Local children, including my children, become very, very adept at their own language before they even step into school. Children learn very easily, very quickly and they learn a vast amount. That is the foundation on which schools in England build. When children enter the educational system, they already know a vast amount about the language in which they are to be educated. When children go to school around here, it is very soon made clear to them that their home language, the one their mother uses to speak to them and the one they use while playing with other children, is trash. At school, they must start again. As if that is not bad enough, the language they have to learn does not make sense in African contexts. It is a language with a long history in Christianity, in science, and in secularism, both in Europe and America. Bringing it to Africa is condemning African people to, yes, often new forms of servitude or you could even say, slavery."

"You have a way of putting things that puts other people in their place," I told Philo, after we had sat in silence for some seconds. Julie was frowning. I could not tell if she did not understand or if she disagreed. On the other hand, she was appreciating being a part of our conversation. I knew her well enough to understand that.

"I am sorry Dave. I don't mean the Holima *sorry* that means *mos* or *pole*," Philo added with a smile. "I see things that other people don't seem to see, or that they shut up about. You know, that is why I came here, to try to unravel the puzzles that are besetting European efforts at bringing about effective mission and development in Africa. Learning and using the local language enables me to listen. As a result, I hear things that almost no other white people ever do—as they are so intent on spreading English!"

As Philo said that, one of the children walked up to him and said something in Striden. Philo nodded to the child, indicating that he had understood. "Now the question is," Julie added, "will anybody in the West be ready to listen to you or not?"

After a pregnant pause, Philo said, "There's tea on the table, let's go"—revealing what the child had just told him.

* * *

Philo's home being African, meant ignoring a lot of the habits and *good sense* that Europeans tend to use. I had noted that at Philo's home when it came to hygiene. In gender terms, also, Philo worked on an African basis. Women and girls were in the kitchen. Girls were the prime ones to be trained to serve visitors. Some Europeans might find the children to be behaving in a servile way. Sometimes they think that it is their Christian duty to impose European values, like that "girls should not be subordinate to boys." That's all very well and good. But, and this is what Philo explained to me one time; such teachings should not come piecemeal. If one is going to influence a community, just encouraging certain specific behaviors without knowing the context in which that behavior occurs, is too limited. One ought to deal with the whole. Dealing with the whole requires accepting what is, before trying to change it! That can be a hard lesson to learn for some, who immediately want to make suggestions as to what African people should do and how. I know that Philo is wary about this issue. To some, especially Westerners, Philo's accepting of people as they are, is denying African people any progress!

The same girl who had whispered to Philo, was now standing there with washing water in a jug, and a bowl. Each of us, in turn, could wash our hands before sitting down at the table. The grass mat that was the ceiling in that part of the house was a little raggedy. Looking too closely, one might have wondered about the dirt that was hovering above the table we were going to eat at. Such things are best not thought too much about. The same girl who performed the washing duty, also very normal in this part of Africa, was responsible for praying for the food. That prayer for the food should not be confused with the *giving thanks* that goes on in British Christian homes. It can be a serious matter. It is very hard in Africa to separate *giving thanks* from *declaring the food clean*. Implicit suspicions as to whether someone has put magic into the food are thereby cancelled. This came to be another topic of conversation on that day, as follows!

* * *

"It's very sweet that the young girls work so hard and even say grace," Julie shared, after we had sat and started drinking our tea and consuming the bread. "It is very nice to find how grateful African folks are to God all the time. Tell me more about this language thing though. I still don't get it."

Philo looked at me. I had to laugh. The series of events and Julie's words leading up to her question were just so fortuitous. Someone who didn't know Philo well wouldn't have realized what he thought, but I knew him well enough. Julie, I think, didn't have a clue. Julie's few observations gave Philo the opportunity to lead her by the nose. He didn't miss it!

"So, what did the girl just do?" Philo asked, a little rhetorically.

"Well, she invited us to the table."

"Then what?"

"She provided water for us to wash our hands."

"Then what?"

"She gave thanks for the food."

"Did you understand what she said?"

"No!"

"Then how do you know that she was giving thanks for the food?"

"Well, I assume that is what she was doing."

"It is not a bad assumption, but why do you think you made that assumption? I mean, does that assumption come from your experience of living in the UK, or your experience of living in Africa?"

Philo added more queries. Julie seemed a bit upset. "Don't get upset, Julie. Philo is trying to teach us something," I reassured her.

"Okay," Julie said, and put on a brave smile. "From my experience of the UK," she conceded.

"Do you see what I mean about language then?" Philo asked in turn.

Julie looked puzzled. "No!"

"Well, you assumed, based on your experience in the UK, that what the girl was doing was giving thanks for the food. Presumably, she was directing that thanks to God, yes? So, then there are at least two things here: what the girl said, and what she intended by her saying."

Julie nodded; but she was still not getting Philo's point.

"I'm listening too, Philo," I said, to encourage Julie to continue to pay attention.

"What if in the tradition of people here, saying thanks is quite unusual, a new thing?"

"What, you mean there are people who do not say thank you?" Julie responded quizzically.

"Let's say so," Philo added, knowing that *thank you* is a new kind of expression for many African people, brought to them by Europeans.

"Okay, I guess that is possible."

"Then, those people are told, that as a Christian one ought to give thanks for one's food before eating. How will they receive such an instruction?" That question from Philo seemed to confuse Julie. She looked at me.

"Think about it, Julie," I said to her; "You have never been taught to say thank you. Now someone says, 'Give thanks for the food,' how will you understand them? They may well tell you how to do it, maybe they also demonstrate by doing it as you are watching, the next time you eat together."

"Well, if I respect the person and what they are telling me, then I will imitate the behavior, and as far as possible follow the instruction," Julie replied, looking at me.

"Right, you have got it, Julie!" I replied. "Now let Philo carry on."

Philo added, "Such a person, who respects the people telling them what to do, will comply with instructions. Remember as we say, that when white people came to Africa, they came with a lot of power (arms and political power, amazing technology, money and so on) so often came to be enormously respected. So then, African people told to give thanks before a meal, would certainly do it."

"Well, that's simple enough," Julie said, nervously.

"Saying 'thank you' doesn't exist in your culture, let's imagine," Philo added. "So, if you are told to give thanks, what will you understand yourself as doing?" Suddenly Julie looked puzzled. If I could read her thoughts, she was facing a double fix: how can someone say thank you when they don't know what *thank you* is, but how can they not say thank you, as their important visitor has told them to do just that?

"Perhaps," Philo said, "there is something that causes concern to people as they sit down to eat at someone else's table. Let's suppose there is such a thing, and let's suppose that the thing is putting poison into the food."

"Poison!" Julie started a little. Her eyes widened.

"Let me explain poison in a moment. If someone is concerned that perhaps poison has been put into the food, then in his mind before he eats, he would like to be assured that poison has not been added. If it has not been added then, just possibly, anything said at the last moment before guests tuck in, is likely to be understood as being to neutralise that poison."

"What's all this about poison?" Julie asked.

"I have noticed, and you will too if you hang around for a while, that whenever someone, i.e., a lady, makes food for a visitor or visitors, she will make sure that a member of her home is within the circle eating the food, or drinking the drink, with the visitors. Why?"

"I don't know," said Julie. I stayed quiet.

"Because, food prepared for a visitor might contain poison, but the hostess wouldn't put in poison for the visitor if she knew that her husband, say, was going to eat out of the same pot."

"Got it," said Julie, "but what's that got to do with …?"

"So then, when a visitor comes, they may well be wary that they are being given poison. Do note however that when I say 'poison' I do not mean a 'chemical' poison. I mean what one could in English call magical or witchcraft poison."

"You mean people here still believe in witchcraft?" Julie exclaimed.

"Hear him out," I said.

"You are trying to stop me explaining," Philo said. "People are concerned that, should they visit someone and they are the only one receiving food or drink out of a container, that they may be being given poison. Hence the typical host's behavior. People here, however, do not know about 'chemistry,' they know about *juok*. That's a Striden term. In English, we could say magic or witchcraft. That's what they are concerned about."

Philo paused, then went on. "I hope you are following me."

Julie and I both nodded.

"So then, someone comes to visit you, and expects to eat or drink what you have set before them, while wondering if poison has been put into it. Then before eating, the Christian host mumbles some words. With what are the guests likely to associate those words?" Philo asked.

"With … magic … witchcraft … poison …," she responded slowly, hesitantly, and in a hushed tone, one word at a time.

"Let me take over here for a while," I asked Philo. "Say the outsider has not only given an example of how to say grace before a meal, but has also taught the words to say, like 'Thank you God for this food.' Then *thank you* has become a way of declaring that this food is cleansed of bad magic. This applies whether the person is saying grace in English or their own language."

"Then" Philo interrupted, "if I, as an Englishman, hear *thank you*, then I tend to think it means what? *Thank you*! But it is quite likely that is not what it means."

"This is getting complicated again!" Julie said.

"Yes," Philo replied. "If I am using my mother tongue with African people, I am likely to be confused and to confuse them!"

I nodded. I felt like concluding, "These issues don't centre on one word, like *thank you*, they are all over and all through the languages we are using. Notice," I said, "you thought you might not have understood what the girl said, because she said grace in a language that wasn't English. Striden, yes Philo?" Philo nodded in agreement. "But, even had she used English, and said, 'thank you for the food,' that wouldn't mean that she was saying 'thank you for the food' the way we do. As Philo said just now, this isn't an isolated incident. This is what goes on all the time in translation between European languages like English and African languages like Striden!"

Poor Julie's head was by this point a little frizzled. Mine had been so when Philo first started explaining this kind of thing to me. Philo's head was full of these issues, and he could have kept telling about them all day as things were happening and being said around us, by us and by others!

By this time, it was hot. Around Philo's home is a lot of green. It was a singular opportunity to enjoy a good walk. Julie and I did not want to miss that opportunity.

"Before we go on to discuss business of the day …" Philo started.

"What business?" asked Julie.

Philo had some amazing news to share. "Richard, his friend from agricultural college, came out to Holima to meet him!" I replied.

Julie looked incredulous.

"Let's go for a stroll," I suggested to Philo. He was quick to agree. We wanted to keep Julie waiting a bit longer yet. Minutes later we were outside walking, and Philo was filling us in a little on his living circumstances.

CHAPTER 20: ARE MISSIONARIES A NEW KIND OF FOOL?

"The lower house is where the girls sleep," Philo said. He seemed to have been anticipating a question from Julie—if Philo has adopted orphan children that live with him, boys and girls, how does he keep them apart at night? "That second house where the girls sleep was originally a house built for a second wife of the owner. The owner had no need of either house anymore. So I rent them."

"What is that nice smell?" Julie asked suddenly.

"What smell?" Philo turned up his nose a little. "You should come here at night!" he said. He pointed to a night rose still ten yards away. Sure enough, the closer we got to it, the stronger the smell. "At night, that smell is even more powerful," he commented. "I'll take it with me back to England," Julie said jokingly about the night rose.

"Sorry, carry on, Philo," Julie added.

Philo went back to the issue of the owner needing the house. "Indeed," Philo told us, "per local tradition, the owner was not permitted to enter any of the houses. The Striden people have a tradition called *goyo dala*. Once a man has reached a certain stage in rearing his family, he leaves his father's compound and builds his own. Philo was living in the houses originally built in the father's compound. Once a man has *goyo dala*, he is not expected ever again to enter the houses he left behind. Should he do so, he will have become in some way unclean. Amazingly," Philo told us, "monkeys had taken up residence in his house before I and the children moved in! The house was too out of the way to be much in demand. While empty, local vervet monkeys took a liking for it."

"Why are there so many trees around here, whereas in some places one finds hardly any trees?" Julie asked.

"My best guess is to say that it is because, by some means, local residents got employment in Imbigen from early on. That is to say—family members had found paid employment; they did not need to fell all the trees and cultivate every little piece of land."

Julie was impressed by the walk. It took us over a stream and back through a small piece of woodland, as well as past several typical village homes. Everyone who greeted us knew Philo by name. That includes motorcyclists who passed us a mile or more away from Philo's home itself.

Outside the homes, we often saw women washing clothes or their dishes. Some men were in the fields cultivating. Others were keeping a wary eye on cattle. The cattle roamed free, but were redirected if they wandered too far or in a wrong direction. That could be either by a flying missile launched by the herdsman concerned, or by his running in the direction the errant animal was heading to deflect it back to where it should have been.

* * *

Julie noticed that children seemed to be everywhere. This was very unlike the UK where, nowadays, children concentrate on spending time on their computers and electronic games. Whereas in the UK there might be pheasants or other wild birds foraging, they didn't stand a chance in Philo's home area! Chickens had the monopoly! Everyone seemed to keep chickens. Those who could, kept cattle. Grazing was, however, in short supply due to rising population density and a preference for the use of land for arable production. By far the most common crop was maize, which typically also had beans planted in its midst.

Returning home, all three of us could sit in the shade of a large tree outside Philo's house. This finally seemed to be the right time for us to tell Julie something of the story of Richard's recent visit.

"You fire away," I told Philo.

"What?"

"About Richard," I told him. "What Richard learned has massive implications for development and mission in Africa in the future."

"Julie, do you want to know? It is quite an amazing story, but a long one," said Philo.

"I want to know; I have waited long enough!" Julie said.

"Richard is an old friend," Philo began explaining. "He and I met at agricultural college. We started there together for our undergraduate degree. We graduated together. I recall clearly the day of the closing celebration at the end of our studies. Richard invited me to join him in a lucrative business venture, which he had already launched. For me, it was either that or Africa. I went for Africa."

"He was disappointed?" Julie asked.

"Guess so," Philo said.

"Or was he angry?" I quipped.

"Not really, but at least disappointed. Richard always speaks his mind. And he also writes his mind in letters."

"That was painful for Philo," I added.

"Very painful. But I am sure he meant well," Philo said. "He evidently thought I had flipped my lid!"

"I am not surprised," Julie broke in, smiling.

Philo smiled, but otherwise ignored her comment, and carried on. "I don't know if he was depressed at the time he wrote, but he had a knack of making me depressed."

"I've seen some letters," I said, "very hard, bitter, attacking Philo. He could be aggressive and damning."

"Why?"

"Either because he wanted to put Philo right and was convinced he had gone seriously wrong, or because he is a psychopath who likes to make people suffer."

"I can see his point though," Philo admitted. "I think he is right that to be a missionary you have to be, at least, a bit of a fool!"

"You are not a fool, Philo!" Julie added.

"No. I mean it. Certainly, with respect to today's culture in the UK. Who respects someone who wants to spend their life sharing the gospel in Africa?"

It was a rhetorical question. Neither of us responded to it. In my opinion, Philo was right. In the UK at the time, plenty of people would have thought Philo's chosen profession incredible, if not laughable. Maybe this is less so in America, but in Britain? Richard was not so unusual in that respect.

"I think you do have to be a fool, though some people might wait to be told to go into the mission field. That in a sense is what is killing mission. In the USA particularly, mission leaders have to be very careful before they tell anyone to go and live in Africa."

"Why?" Julie asked.

"Insurance! If you are in a position of authority and you tell me to go to Africa, and then something goes wrong, my family could sue you for all you've got! That's why. A young person should not expect anyone to tell them to do anything radical in mission. They just have to go and do it off their own bat."

"That's it," I added. "Philo has explained this to me before. It means that young people preparing for mission should not be too intent to listen to their elders. If they do, they will only end up doing *controlling*, mediocre mission."

"How to get that message to young Christians in the UK is difficult," Philo added, "especially because people in missionary training colleges and mission agencies try to kill it!"

I was amazed, yet again, at the things that Philo came up with! So was Julie. She shrugged. "You mean," she asked, "that to be a good missionary you have to be able to reject advice you are given, and foolishly do your own thing?" We left her question hanging.

* * *

While we talked, there was some activity nearby. Some children were harvesting guavas off a tree. At that point, Julie went to powder her nose.

"She won't like it," I told Philo after she had gone.

Julie came back immediately. "Is that the only toilet?"

"I'm afraid so."

"It's not very clean," she grimaced.

"Sorry! It's good enough for me, and twelve children."

Julie made a grunting noise.

"Philo's place is not intended to be European-standard," I explained. "If you come to visit him, expect some things that you are not used to."

Philo laughed. "Sometimes expect things more African than Africa," he added.

"Sorry! Dave is right. You can go back into the trees there if you want to." Julie disappeared again.

When Julie was back, I started Richard's story again. Philo looked a bit embarrassed. "Richard was writing letters attacking and undermining Philo. Every time, he was making Philo depressed. Then he suddenly wrote to say that he was coming for a visit!"

"When I got that letter," Philo said, "I told Dave about it. I thought maybe Richard was coming to kill me off completely! Could I put up being with Richard for a whole week, with him just telling me how stupid I was, that I should go back to England, and that I was wasting my time? I didn't want to tell him not to come. But I did tell Dave that I needed his support for this!"

"Frankly, I couldn't give Philo much time," I said, "because of my work commitments. I might be living near to Philo, but mostly, as far as he was concerned, I might not have been on the continent at all. When I heard what was going to happen, though, I took four days off. For the first four days of Richard's stay, we could be a threesome. That means that if or when Richard laid into Philo, I could be there to take some flak."

"And I was very grateful. You know it's a funny thing. People who threaten your mission work are primarily not Africans, but fellow Westerners."

"What? How can you say that?" Julie exclaimed. "Remember that we, Westerners, are the ones giving the money that keeps you afloat."

"Certainly, I very much appreciate that they do as much—but that doesn't alter the reality I am referring to. You see, African people are generally in need in a way that Europeans are not these days. That's part of the patron-client system—everyone is always ready to be a client and to get something. Many people who have become big-time patrons in Africa are European missionaries. They usually only have a limited appreciation of the fact that they are patrons! It is not how they see themselves. African missionaries are less in a hurry to become patrons, because it costs. They also do it, but cautiously. The reputation of European missionaries around here is that they do it willingly and enthusiastically, even if they end up having no or almost no relationship with the client or clients. It means that the expectations of the locals are raised. When they see a missionary coming, that brings them a strong expectation that money could soon be flowing in their direction. That is what is dangerous."

"You mean risky, Philo?" I corrected.

"Okay, risky" Philo said, looking at Julie. "Once someone like you says to one of the children that you really like him, and that you intend to send money for his support, then the child might believe you, and I have been landed with a problem, a spoilt child always suspicious that I may be eating the money you intended for him."

"Sorry for having been shocked," Julie said. "I get this."

* * *

"Let us go back to Richard," Julie proposed. "Philo, carry on."

"So, Dave agreed to stay close during Richard's visit, and was I grateful! Richard came alone. He arrived at the airport in the morning. He came out of arrivals and ...," Philo paused, his eyes glinting. He got his reading glasses out of his pocket and polished them, for effect. "Well, he launched into me from the word go."

"No!" said Julie, leaning forward.

"Yes," I said. "He'd hardly said hi, when his tirade began."

Julie laughed. "He was like a man possessed," Philo said, laughing too.

"He was sure though, it seemed, that at the end of the week I was going back with him to England. Richard, by then, was not a Christian. He saw no role for a missionary in today's world at all, and he expected everyone to agree with him."

"In hindsight," I said, "the series of experiences we went through with Richard are quite incredible. One after another, as if they had been plotted. Somehow, providentially, Richard ran into one circumstance after another, that proved to bring a foundational challenge to his worldview. Julie—you may think we are somehow making this up. We are not!"

"From the airport, we went to treat Richard to lunch in Deja," I relayed. "That's not Philo's normal ilk, but it seemed right. We went to a good hotel in Deja and ordered a meal. There we were sat around a table. The table had four seats around it, so we occupied three of them. We took no notice of a light jacket hanging on the fourth chair. We didn't even notice it. We were engaged in conversation, when suddenly this burly American appeared. 'You're sitting at my place,' he said. We looked at each other. 'Here's my jacket,' he added, pointing to the fourth chair. Then we saw the jacket. Richard asked him if he was alone, and proposed that he join us."

"That was pretty bold of Richard. He is bold like that. The American sat down," Philo said.

This is what followed.

"I appreciate that, actually," the American said. We looked at him quizzically. "It's a lonely world around here," he added.

"Somewhere in his late twenties I guess he was," Philo said. "A decent-looking fellow. We did all the customary introductions. The American was called Rudd. Not sure what that was a shortening of."

He was the last to introduce himself.

"What do you do?" Richard asked him.

"I work in development, on the rice farms," he said, "volunteering, projects and all that."

Richard knew at that point that he'd found his ally. He turned to Philo and said, "There you go Philo. You should be doing something useful like that!" He obviously didn't anticipate what was going to happen next.

"Useful!" Rudd exclaimed. Rudd's nose twitched when he spoke. He sat nonchalantly in his chair. He was from the deep south of the US, he had already told us. Although those parts were known for their racist history, Rudd had been a rebel as a youth. He was determined to stick up for marginalized people. That's why, it appears, he had come to Africa—to make a difference for African people. His exclamation: *useful!* had us all turn to look at him. It's almost as if he had not realized what he said. "Sorry, kneejerk reaction," Rudd added.

"What do you mean?" Richard asked. "We've been talking with Philo here. I'm trying to encourage him either to use his time for something useful here in Africa, or to get out of here."

"Oh, I see," said Rudd.

"So, what's useful?" Richard was a businessman and used to negotiating sales with all kinds of people. On this occasion though he was beginning to feel he was going to be on his back foot.

Rudd added. "I have been here for two years, very nearly. I came thinking that I was coming to do something useful. Now I am just two days out of hospital." We all made empathetic noses. "Hypothermia," Rudd said.

"How did you get to be hypothermic over here?" Philo asked, concerned.

"Fell into a ditch," said Rudd.

"Does falling into a ditch cause hypothermia?" Philo asked.

"It does if you stay lying in the same water in the same ditch for twenty-odd hours," Rudd answered. "I fell in a ditch and laid there was because I was drunk. I tell you what, Richard. Before I came I thought that I was set out to do something useful. Holima has knocked that belief out of me. I did not anticipate what I was going to meet up with …." At that point Rudd's voice dwindled away. Tears welled up in his eyes. "I did not know before I came, and no one could tell me," he said. "Look—I already feel like I've gate-crashed your party. I can go and get lost if you want me to?"

"Go on," said Richard. Philo and I were nodding.

"What they tell you over there in the US is not what you find here on the ground," Rudd said to Richard. "It looks like your friends have been around for longer and would know better, the first week or two is all smiles, then the reality sets in. Life is cruel. People are hard to understand. Everyone wants your money. No one wants to work. Behind the smiles, it's all daggers. You try to help people in different ways, but all they want is your money. I tell you, I'm not the only volunteer to turn to the bottle. Most of us do." I saw Philo glancing at Richard. "Many of us volunteers get depressed. You must be some kind of giant not to be. That is what makes us turn to the drink. Trouble is that once drink has taken over, the mind no longer works well. So, I got involved with local women. I mean—there might be nothing wrong with getting involved with a local woman, but you need to know what you're about. White men are a prize catch."

"Uhha," Philo exclaimed.

"You have a choice of women. It's like they line up for you. I mean—not the decent ones. They're not around. But the others," Rudd added, then sighed. "So, I took a woman. A nice-looking girl. We went out. Of course, I paid for everything. That night I had already had one drink too many. Then this African guy turns up, and says the woman I have got is his wife. Ati, her name was, denied it. I told him to get lost. He did."

"Half an hour later," Rudd went on, "we were walking back towards my place. Next thing I know, I am lying on the floor with the oaf sitting on top of me. I tell you, I am not much of a pro when it comes to fighting, but I managed to get him right in the groin. The fellow bellowed in pain. The moment he jumped up in pain and then fell back, a motorbike was coming up the hill. The motorbike knocked into him, and sent him flying! The motorcyclist and motorbike skidded along the road on its side screeching noisily. Dave—you know the kind of thing they tell you? If you cause an accident, don't try to help the people, because you are likely to get lynched. I ran for my life. I am not sure whether they tried to follow me. I am not even sure if either the husband, if he was the husband, or the motorcyclist, are alive."

I coughed. "Did that happen in Ankara Street?" I asked Rudd.

"Yes."

"Two days ago?" I said. "The motorcyclist is dead," I announced. Rudd's face fell and turned white. "It was in the newspaper. Probably you didn't see it. The newspaper said that the cause of the accident was unknown. Nothing was said about anyone else being involved in the accident, just the motorcyclist."

Rudd was alarmed. He had killed someone, even if indirectly. He started shaking. "That's when I decided to get so drunk, and I fell into the ditch, I just laid there for hours," Rudd said. "I could easily have been dead by now." We were stunned into temporary silence. "This is a roundabout way of telling you," Rudd said, eventually looking at Richard, "that there's more to doing development than meets the eye. Development is today's big lie," he added. "Perhaps people used to tell lies about fairies. Nowadays they tell lies about development. I tell you what it is—it's dependency writ large. That is what is going on. Plus, it is control. Yes, if you can control what is going on in Holima from the outside, things move. If you don't control from the outside, they don't. Us volunteers don't control anything. The big men in America do that. We volunteers can see some of the things that are happening on the ground. They can't. They control through statistics. That's all they get to see … and sweet-talking of the big men in Africa. It's a big con."

"So, what's needed then?" Richard asked, mustering up the courage to come back into the conversation, having had his position obliterated!

There was a pause, then "A change of heart," Rudd whispered.

***

Julie was frowning. "So, did he ever confess?"

"You mean like go to the police and tell them what happened that night?" Philo said.

"Yes," Julie responded.

"Not that we are aware of—eh, Dave?"

"I don't think he did," I said. "It wouldn't have been wise. It would have put his neck into a noose for nothing. He probably did the best thing, leaving Holima, and drawing a line under it all. He was not directly responsible."

"So was he right about development?" Julie asked.

"About it being a myth, like myths used to be about fairies?" Philo asked. "It's not the first time I've heard it. You know about my experience when I was at university in the UK. I was amazed when he said what he did—because I thought, he was right—but many people in the UK do not see what he saw. His comment about fairies was interesting. It's true—people need myths to live by. The myth used to be about fairies. Now it's about development. What is happening to give Africa its economic boost is enabled by foreign control." Philo added.

"Hmm," said Julie, amazed. "Then, I guess Richard was on a learning curve!"

"After that meal, Richard was keen to see a bit of the town." I went on telling about Richard's visit. "Philo suggested that we visit one of his children. He has had children stay with him in the past, some of whom had since left and got jobs and their own families. That seemed a fair plan to Richard. It seems at the time he didn't know what to expect though. Richard insisted on using local transport. In no time, he sat squeezed into a shaky minibus with minimum suspension and a noisy, boisterous conductor. Richard kept quiet. A constant flow of his criticism of Philo had finally abated! He didn't exactly look worried sitting alongside us squeezed into that bus, but perhaps concerned as to just what he was letting himself in for, so quickly after arriving from the UK.

We stepped out of the bus into a housing estate. All we had to do then was to find the actual house of Philo's child called Laura. There was litter everywhere, stagnant water, open sewers, overfilled toilets, overpopulation, grubby looking mud houses and amongst all of that, children running around playing barefoot, wearing rags, apparently impervious to their decrepit surroundings. We leapt over endless stinking, stagnant puddles as we walked. Richard did not say much. Somehow, he had not anticipated the pain of the reality of this kind of poverty. No matter how often one might have seen it on TV, it is always hard from the West to come to terms with the reality of deep poverty. Now, because of his prior vocal opposition to and criticism of Philo, Richard was too embarrassed to speak up. Had he been actively criticizing Philo, that would have meant that his heart had not been touched. His silence indicated that he was at least busy processing things in his head.

"*Hodi*!" Philo said as we approached the door. "That's Eastern African parlance for 'look we're here standing at the door, can we come in?'"

"*Donji*," (something like "enter," in Striden) said a high-pitched female voice from inside the one-roomed house. The lintel to the door was very low. This house was in the corner of a small, muddy courtyard. Inside was a tiny sitting room. We all filed in. As is customary, we prayed, well, Philo prayed on our behalf before we sat down. A young woman in her twenties came to greet us, clutching a baby. Philo enthusiastically reached out and took the baby out of her arms. He and that baby were like old friends rediscovering one another. We sat down in a row facing the young mother. Four people, two each way facing each other, plus baby, was as many as the sitting area could accommodate.

Philo proceeded to talk to Laura. She was short and slim. She liked to laugh after completing every other sentence. I think she would have done that with everyone, and not only with us. I understood a few words. Philo introduced me, still speaking only the Striden language. He made a few comments to us in English from time to time. Laura spoke back to her adopted-father, also using Striden.

*   *   *

"Can I just interrupt the story there," Philo interjected. Julie was quite caught up in the narrative and was looking forward to hearing how on earth this adventure with Richard in a slum-house was going to work out. But, we gave Philo opportunity to talk.

"I just wanted to explain why I use so little English," Philo said. "I have already explained, that I don't see how we could survive if I was to use English there at my home, English being Holima's official language and for that and many other reasons, a language of money. As I said before, if I was to use it, I would be majorly advantaging my children. But then, there is also the question of consistency when it comes to language. I don't know when I should use English and when not. So, I just don't use it unless I have to."

"Couldn't you use English with people who understood it well, and other languages with those who don't?" Julie asked Philo.

"But don't you see? That's the problem … or at least one of the problems. I mean—that would be judging—I will talk with one person in English because I think they are educated, but I won't use it with another because she is obviously a country bumpkin. Should I have to make such a judgment call every time before I start talking?" Philo asked rhetorically. He let us think about his question in silence for a while.

"And …?" Julie added. Julie was obviously interested in this language issue!

"Talking with Holiman people in English makes me feel like a stupid foreigner," Philo stated. "It is like I am inviting them to deceive me, laugh at me, and despise me. It makes me feel like (at this point Philo put on a snooty voice), 'I don't care about you enough to learn your language even though I live here, but I do expect you to learn my language, even though it comes from thousands of miles away.' Doesn't that just show that I think I am more important than them?"

"So, we'll forgive Philo for having spoken a language we couldn't understand," I carried on.

"Wait a minute, Dave," Julie said, "what about other languages? Don't you have to make a judgment call on whether someone knows Striden? For example—might not someone be a Lile and not a Striden? Then you need to make an assessment of which language to use before you talk. Isn't that the same as trying to decide whether to use English?"

Philo responded, "Someone not knowing Striden in Holima today, even if they are in Stridenland, is not considered as something inferior. It simply identifies that they come from a different tribe. Not to know English in

Holima today, however, means you are—what—akin to an uneducated country bumpkin!"

"Everyone now satisfied with the language issue?" I reiterated.

"For now, yes," said Julie, but she was still frowning. I went back to the story.

* * *

Before long, tea and bread were brought for the visitors. Philo carried on chatting in Striden, occasionally bringing us up to speed with a few words in English. At other times the conversation did go to English, and included all of us.

When Richard had finished his tea and bread, he excused himself and went out.

I wondered what he was at, but thought, "Well, he shouldn't come to any harm." I assumed he would stay close by and not get lost.

About half an hour later, Richard re-appeared at the door puffing and panting! His eyes were wide with fright. He sat down, breathed a deep sigh of relief, then, looking from Philo to me, exclaimed "That was interesting!"

"What happened?" I asked him.

"Oh, nothing."

"Well, what was so interesting, then?"

"I am impressed by the way people here live, even though they have nothing," Richard said. His body language meanwhile told us, "Look, I'll tell you later."

In due course, we said our goodbyes. Laura, the lady of the house, accompanied us on our way—a young girl carrying a big baby. Then on we went.

"Hey, what happened when you left us?" Philo asked Richard, as soon as we were out of earshot.

"Tell you later," was his response again. Time was short. We had to catch a bus. "If possible, get us a bus with a bit more leg and wiggle room than what we had coming for this visit," Richard pleaded.

"We'll try." We took a *tuk-tuk* (motorized rickshaw) to the edge of town, and stood on the side of the road. Ten minutes later a bus turned up. We jumped aboard, and were headed up to Philo's home. Well, actually, not quite.

"Philo does have a base, apart from his home," I reminded Julie.

"Oh yes, at the mission station," Julie said.

"That's where we landed with Richard that evening. Philo has a room to use as he sees fit at this church's mission compound. That's nearer to Deja than his home anyway. That gives him security, twenty-four-hour electricity, running water, and companionship with fellow missionaries."

"Of course," said Julie.

"We've spent some time there. A wonderful place with very warm and loving people, who seem to appreciate Philo a great deal."

"So, this mission, of a liturgical church, have given you a room for you to stay in within their mission compound?" Richard asked.

"Yes, that's right," Philo responded.

"But they are not 'your mission', like, they are not responsible for you, they have not sent you, and they do not even relate directly to your churches back in the UK?" he added.

"That's correct," Philo said.

"So, although you live at the home we have yet to visit, you also have personal access to the facilities of the mission here?" Richard asked.

"Yes, that's right," Philo said.

"That's excellent!" added Richard.

"How do you get on with their liturgical approach to mission?" Julie asked Philo.

Philo's Christian background was very much with non-liturgical churches. His hosts were very liturgical. "I think liturgy is a very good way of consistently carrying truth in a non-corruptible way, even to people who are of limited literacy," Philo replied.

So, that's where we went together to spend the night. We had given them advance notice, so there was even a meal waiting for us. When we'd brushed and scrubbed up, we sat down to eat.

"Come on now, tell us what happened today," Philo said to Richard, who was busy consuming an Egyptian dish called *Koshari*. It is made of rice, macaroni and lentils mixed together, topped with a spiced tomato sauce, and garlic vinegar; garnished with chickpeas and crispy fried onions.

"You mean at the girl's place?"

"The house felt small and stuffy," he explained. "I wanted to go outside. Philo was busy chatting with the girl so, as you know, I just excused myself and went out. When I got outside, I was overawed by what I was seeing all around me. That is—I was filled with amazement as to just where I was and what I was doing. I mean—it's not every day that someone makes a visit to Africa. It's not every day that you get invited for a cup of tea in a slum. There, suddenly I was, with poverty all around me staring me in the face. Now I have often thought about the kinds of things I would like to do if I was to meet 'real poverty' like that. As you know there were many children around. One of those slum boys pointed at me and calling me *Mzungu* – that must mean white man, yes?" Philo nodded. "'What do you need?' I asked the boy. 'Pencil and rubber.' he said. I was by this time feeling good about what I would be able to do for him 'Where can you get a pencil and rubber?' I asked. He understood my English. He pointed. I indicated that he should lead the way. I was very careful that I was paying attention, so that I could find my own way back as well! We went some distance, then we got to a shop. I bought him a pencil and a rubber. He was beaming. I felt good to have helped a poor child in that way.

"As we were walking away from the shop," Richard carried on, "a friend of the boy saw the pencil that he was carrying. He evidently said, 'What about me?' So the original boy pointed at his friend. Can't do any harm, I thought, so I went back to the shop and bought another pencil and rubber. Then, the same thing happened again. Then, again and again! So, I realized, need was great, as one hears is the case in Africa. I bought fifty pencils and fifty rubbers. I mean—that's still nothing compared to the money one spends in England on Oxfam. Here I was where Oxfam rarely trod, I thought to myself! I started handing out pencils and rubbers, one of each to each of the children who came along. That's when the scene changed and got ugly.

"It became difficult to know who had already received a pencil and rubber, and who had not. Two boys started arguing. I presume that one was accusing the other of coming for a pencil and rubber twice. One boy hit the other. Then other boys went to stand with the boy who got hit. The boy who had hit him grabbed the pencil of the one he had hit and started running. Then another boy picked up a rock and threw it at him! It just missed the running boy's head! I couldn't believe what was happening. I tried to shout at them that they should stop fighting. They took no notice; they were by that time too engaged in their own disputes. At the original location of the argument, six to ten boys were now engaged in a rowdy brawl, scrapping and hitting each other. Out of nowhere it seemed, an older lad of maybe twenty or more appeared. His eyes were bloodshot, he appeared to be drunk or high on something. He reeled as he walked towards me. I didn't know Holimans would have such a dirty mouth. He started throwing expletives at me. You know; 'you …' and all that. He blamed me for causing the fighting. 'All you foreigners do is make us fight all the time!' he shouted at me. He looked like he wanted to fight with me. I started backing off. Then I turned around and marched smartly away. Before long I was running, with some of the boys taunting me. Fortunately, they let me go. I don't know how all that terrible fighting ended, although it seemed that I had caused it. That's why I came in puffing and panting, my mind in turmoil!"

***

"So what exactly went wrong?" Julie asked. "What did Richard do that he shouldn't have done?"

Philo answered her in this way: "I remember a new missionary couple telling me a story of something they had done while they were still new in Holima. One day they had bought some cakes. They had them in the car with them as they drove through Deja. Then, without thinking about it, out of compassion, when a street boy came to their window, they gave him one. A second boy came; they gave him one too. Five minutes later all twenty cakes were gone. The couple felt very good about having helped those poor boys. The following week they bought fifty cakes, especially with the intention of handing them out to street boys through their window. They did so. The following week they went back with the same car to the same place to do the same thing. They met up with a riot! They were forced to close their windows, blow their horn continuously and just keep moving until, eventually, they had left an angry mob of boys behind them. Their car was badly scratched. They were advised by the police to keep out of town for at least a month. The police told them, 'If you ever want to come back again, make sure it is with a different car. Never give handouts like that to street boys.'"

"In short—Richard had a lucky escape," I said. "Things could have turned a lot nastier—on him or on us, never mind on the boys he 'helped'," I added.

"So, did Richard realize what had happened and how foolish he had been?" Julie asked.

"I guess. He told me, 'I didn't realize that it was so easy to be so stupid.'"

* * *

The following morning, we were all there together at the mission compound. We gave Richard a tour of the compound. All around us were images and evidence of an ancient Middle Eastern Christianity that has survived to this day, despite often massive levels of persecution of the church. That applies both to prior and after the successful Muslim invasions in the seventh century.

On a beautiful sunny morning, such as this, the three of us quickly reached agreement that climbing the hill alongside the mission compound would be a good idea. Richard was fit, I discovered. People coming from the low altitude UK to our much higher altitude and warmer climate often had problems, but not Richard. We climbed the hill, it seemed, in leaps and bounds. From that hill, the more we climbed, the more of a grandiose view we enjoyed. Large tracts of land, including distant scattered low hills, emerged. We sat on a large boulder enjoying the early morning sun, surveying the scene for miles around. Deja Lake was clearly in view. Beyond the lake, we could see as far as its other shore. Much of all this land was occupied by Striden people, who are great fishermen. One of the hills we saw was of great local renown as being the location from which rain was made by local Lile people, on behalf of neighboring tribes.

One hundred years before, rainmaking had been a very fraught act, often resulting in unsuccessful rainmakers becoming highly unpopular, in early colonial days sometimes ending up in prison. The temptation to make rain was however too great. It carried a bonus—rainmakers were given extensive gifts in return for ensuring that rain fell regularly, and in the right quantities for people's agricultural needs. That very bounteous generosity of local people to the rainmaker was what made them think that if rain wasn't made to their demands, that they had the right to punish the rainmaker.

We sat relaxed on some boulders, staring out across the landscape. I was the first to notice a crowd of people gathered alongside the main road heading towards Deja. At first, I thought nothing of it. I had brought some binoculars. I focused onto that crowd. They appeared to be just standing on the side of the road. I asked myself what they were doing there. I asked Philo, "Why would there be a group of people standing on the side of the road?"

"That's interesting," he answered. "You are probably seeing that passing vehicles are stopping, maybe for a minute, maybe more, bus passengers are alighting and having a look at something, then climbing back onto their buses?"

"Let's see," I said.

Richard looked in the same direction to see what was going on. Without binoculars, it would have been difficult. I took five minutes to check on Philo's prediction. "You are right Philo!" I said. I still did not understand. I think Richard was even more puzzled.

"Can you see which way people are looking?" Philo asked.

"Yes," I said

"Try and see what they are looking at," he added. I did that. I didn't see anything. Philo took the binoculars. He identified the crowd of people I had been looking at. They seemed to be just standing and staring. I guess Philo knew what he was looking for. "It's two motorbikes," he said. Then I realized what had happened, but Richard still hadn't got it.

"What do you mean, it's two motorbikes?" Richard asked, puzzled. "Are they putting on a display?"

"No," Philo responded. He looked at Richard to check that he was serious. "An accident."

"Oh no!" said Richard. "So then, why are the people standing around?"

"They always do for an accident. For that matter, for any calamity."

"An African way of resolving a calamity is to surround it with people," I said.

"Hmmm, that sounds strange. What do you mean by that?" Richard asked. I think Richard was a bit tired of being "the ignorant one," but he had little choice. So much that was going on around him was way beyond his comprehension!

"Very good question," Philo responded. "I don't really know, but they do it."

"So, what do you reckon?" I chipped in. As I did so a large bus pulled up, twenty or so people were getting out to look at the scene. Then I noticed something else. "I see a cow alongside the road, presumably dead," I said. "And there's another car lying on its roof. People are standing on the upturned car!" I commented.

We were looking to Philo to give us an explanation. He had a go. "People like to swamp death and calamity with life," he said. That took a little thinking about. I could see that Richard was wanting to ask another question, but he didn't. "Funerals of course are a prime example of that, although I appreciate that Richard has yet to attend a funeral. Why? Well, let's say, to swamp the 'absence' of the person being buried."

"That's an interesting way of putting it, Philo," I said.

"But the same applies also to any sudden calamity," Philo added. "Someone's house burns down. People gather. A building collapses. People gather. A road accident, people gather. People will often *kesha* there, that is, stay sat all night at the site of the calamity (or the site, say, of the body of the dead person)."

"Why?" Richard asked.

"Here's some thoughts," Philo replied. "Partly, it's just a very natural human reaction, to want to be where the action is, so to speak. Inquisitiveness. It is also, a meeting with death. How many popular movies in the West are about death and calamity?" Philo asked.

"Well, lots," Richard responded, never really having thought about movies in that way before, though, I suspect.

"So, people are drawn by calamity. They want to share in it, to be a part of it, to be impacted by it. I think that's, partly at least, because of what the Germans call *schadenfreude*. People feel good when they realize how bad things are for others. There's also more to it than that, though."

"I expected as much," said Richard, feeling a little overwhelmed by the very different world he had somehow inadvertently entered.

"Road accidents are never 'accidents'," Philo said.

"I've heard that often also," I added. "Whenever there's something that we might in English call an accident, people around here look for a cause. In the West, the cause might be a brake failure, or a driver who had too much to drink. Here, that does not satisfy, and is not of primary importance. Of more foundational importance is 'why did the brake fail,' and 'why today, and just there,' or 'why was the driver drinking?' and if he has been drinking frequently, 'why has the drinking caused a problem on this occasion, but previously the driver got away with it?'" I said. I looked Philo in the eye, and he seemed to be agreeing. "This is why people care relatively little about how vehicles are maintained. Even when committees are appointed to investigate the cause of accidents, they may well not do it in a way we would expect them to in the West. They are not looking for a cause in anything mechanical, but in things spiritual."

"That's right," Philo added, "in people's hearts!"

"That's ridiculous," Richard interrupted. "How can someone's heart cause a road accident?"

"You note that Dave said 'spiritual', and I said, 'in people's hearts?'" Philo added.

"Yes, I did notice that, and wondered why you said that," Richard said.

"The term *spirit* can be quite confusing in the West," Philo went on, "that probably underlies a lot of the secularism we have today. People were believing in spirits, then spirits became redefined, the way they were redefined no longer made sense to people, so people stopped believing in spirits, so they considered themselves secular. That's why I prefer to talk about the impact of people's hearts."

"Fair enough, but still …," Richard left his sentence hanging.

"So, then you ask, how can hearts cause accidents?" It was clearly a rhetorical question by Philo, so Richard stayed quiet. "You love your wife and she loves you Richard?" Philo asked.

"Yes," he said, without hesitation, wondering where that question was leading. Richard's marriage seemed on all accounts to be strong.

"If you received a letter from her that told you that she no longer loved you and was leaving you, how would that impact you?" Philo asked.

"I would be devastated!"

Memories flooded back to me of the time I lost Cindy. That loss had made me turn to drink.

"Right," Philo said, "you might even be so devastated that, were you to be a motorcyclist, you would not pay proper attention to the road, so that an accident could arise."

"Well, I'd never thought of it like that before," Richard said.

"Start thinking!" Philo exclaimed.

Philo was making a good case. People's hearts could cause accidents! Separation, conflict, and disagreement were the kinds of things that troubled people's hearts. Hence the sign of solidarity of a group of people gathering around the site of a calamity, trying to right such a wrong, I could see, could be helpful. I think Richard was seeing the same.

"Particularly suspect also," Philo went on, "is the evil person. Few people will accept the idea that they are evil. On the contrary, here more so than in the UK, it seems to me, everyone makes out they are a good citizen and helping everyone. Yet, despite this, nasty things happen like that accident, the results of which we've just been looking at. This means that someone somewhere must be pretending. Someone must be pretending to be good, but have a rotten heart! That person can be suspect for having plotted things, like that accident. That person can, in English, be known as a witch. In other words, accidents are often considered to be caused by witchcraft." Philo was quiet for a while. "This is a big, big topic Richard! I don't think we will finish it this morning!"

Richard agreed that the topic in hand was a big one. Philo and I had said enough to give him a working understanding. But, a related question was bugging him. "You've said all this Philo," he said, "and it all seems to make sense. But why do I get it from you? Why is this not more widely known? Why are we in the UK so ignorant of these things?"

"Look, Richard," Philo said, "you Brits, and others want to hear about Africa from Africans. They in the meantime don't want to be laughed at. For many Brits, witchcraft is laughable. They think it doesn't exist. Africans get tired of being mocked. So, they hide the witchcraft, and when you talk about it to them, they will deny that it is there at all. You get a very silly situation, if Brits only want to be informed by native Africans, then the powerful people (Europeans are very powerful in Africa) are also very ignorant. To get accurate information, you need your own people to listen to the language of native people, then to translate it back to the West."

"Hey, and that's what you are doing Philo?" Richard half asked, half said.

"Yes," Philo affirmed, "as best I can."

* * *

At that point, I broke in to talk to Julie. "Here's the translation issue again Julie. I hope you are seeing it."

"I wasn't," she said, "but thanks, I am now."

"Now let me go back to Richard's story," I said to Julie.

CHAPTER 21: ARE YOU POOR?

"What about development then?" Richard asked. "If people are seeing hearts as causing all their problems, and if all their solutions are about 'correcting-hearts,' then how can they achieve the kinds of socio-economic development that the global community these days envisions for Africa?"

"Shall I take it?" Philo asked me.

"Go for it," I said.

"The solution, if there is one, to Africa's under-development dilemma, if it has one, is in the hearts of its people," Philo said. "That's why I work with the gospel. People need a new heart and a new mind. That's what the gospel of Jesus has to offer."

"And all this time I have been thinking that you are an idiot for doing gospel work," Richard conceded, "thinking that you should be doing *real development*, which is projects."

"Real development," Philo suggested, "is teaching people about God—the great Heart, the great Mind, the great Power."

After getting back to the mission, we met up with several Holiman people. They all obviously knew Philo very well. Philo talked to them in Striden or Swahili, as is his ilk. As he was doing so, Richard also engaged in conversation with one of the Holiman people there. I listened to Richard, because I couldn't understand a word of what Philo was saying. As he had recently come from the UK, Richard was not used to the Holiman scene. I guess he was still struck by how low the standard of living was around him, and how dirty things were, how under-developed the area was. Perhaps also surprised to see that, despite all that, people could seem to be happy. As they talked with us, they were laughing and smiling. They certainly weren't all long-faced and miserable, just because they were poor. So, Richard asked his conversation-partner, who was there preparing for a funeral, bluntly to his face: "Are you poor?"

I was myself rather taken aback by the question. Then, I was intrigued—what on earth will the fellow say in response to that question, asked by someone who evidently had arrived in the country only very recently? Perhaps the poor fellow had some difficulty answering the question. His answer when it came through was plainly stated. "We are poor," he said.

"You need help?" Richard asked.

"Yes."

"So, what kind of help do you need?"

This was one of those intriguing circumstances where East meets West. These were difficult questions to handle at any time. Now the poor Holiman fellow, who I believe was called Fred, had to think fast on his feet to know how to respond well to Richard. Added to his difficulty was that I was obviously over-hearing the conversation. Because Richard spoke quite loudly, so were a few other people. How was he going to respond to Richard, given that he had us as additional over-hearers? I knew that new visitors to Holima, as I guess much of Africa, were often coveted prizes. A new visitor from the West might be looking for a network of people to support. A local who wins over a new visitor could stand to gain an enormous amount from money sent, and further relationships that could be lucrative for years, or even for generations!

Fred thought quickly on his feet. He wasn't going to let this potential opportunity go by without at least trying. Most likely he was asking himself—why had Richard approached him rather than anyone else? One possibility, perhaps the best-case scenario, was that Philo had for some reason and in some way told Richard that Fred was especially deserving of his attention. If that was the case, he only had to respond to Richard in a way that would confirm whatever Philo had told Richard about him. That seemed a relatively unlikely scenario though—why should Philo particularly favor him? More likely—Richard was looking for a local to talk to, and he chanced on Fred.

Fred was, of course, fully aware of the imminent funeral at his home. Perhaps Richard would be interested in attending the funeral, and perhaps Philo and Dave could also be convinced to accompany him?

Fred gave Richard three options. "I have a Bible school and we need books," he said. "My oldest child should be in form II in secondary school, but instead, he stays at home for lack of school fees. My mother's house is in a very poor state of repair and I would very much like to build her a new one." He added, "Why don't you come with Philo and Dave to the funeral?"

"I will ask them. I would very much like to experience an African funeral. I guess they are very big and elaborate affairs." Fred assured Richard that he would be around for a bit longer, giving him time to consult with Philo and me.

"You heard that," Richard said to me. "What do you think?"

"Let's discuss with Philo." We sat on a step and waited for Philo to finish his conversations. We were trying to make eye contact without appearing to disturb his flow.

"Is Fred poor?" Richard asked me in a hushed voice, not to be overhead. "I'd only really like to help someone in genuine need."

"I don't know, but Philo might!" I wanted to wait for Philo to join the conversation to see how he would respond to Richard. For all I knew, Philo might be angry at Richard for being so quick to want to use his money in an attempt to buy friends, and maybe feel good about himself.

Rather than sitting with us, Philo waved for us to follow him. He had some plan in mind. He took us to his room. That was about as private a place as one can get. The rule for Philo and his room on the mission compound was that no woman was to enter. They treated him a bit like he was a monk.

We sat in a small circle in Philo's cell. Richard didn't hesitate for very long before he told his story. "I've just been talking to, er, Fred. I think you must know him?" Richard said looking at Philo.

"Yes, I know him."

"Is he the kind of person who needs support?" Richard asked Philo slightly hesitantly.

"What exactly do you think he might need support for?" Philo asked Richard, presuming that Fred had already told Richard.

"He mentioned three things." Richard told Philo what they were.

"They all seem to be worthy causes." Philo replied.

I could tell that Philo was, at this point, facing a multitude of dilemmas to which Richard was probably totally oblivious. I mean—everybody deserves support. Philo would say the same—we all need support. But now—why Fred? Why not someone else? Why not everyone else? Amongst the barrage of questions in Philo's mind no doubt, at that point, was also the idea that Richard might have taken a liking for Fred. He was obviously looking for someone to support. That could even help his business—if Richard finds a genuinely needy local person to support on his visit to Africa, then he commits his business to underwriting him, that could be excellent PR. But it raised the question—who would administer the support? There would be a need for accountability. Was Richard going to expect Philo to take up the accountability role? Was Philo going to have to police the situation, take pictures of what was happening, and generally be answerable for money that Richard might want to spend on Fred? And these were trivial questions compared to the main one: how much disruption would it cause in this small community?

Philo decided to make an appeal. "Please, please Richard, can you just leave off supporting Fred or other people around here." That was oil on the fire. I had thought that perhaps, because of his recent experiences, Richard's fire might have died. It was not so! Before Philo could begin to explain the reasons why he was asking Richard to leave it off, the latter was back in full force. Richard went for the jugular.

"That's it," he said, "out of the horse's mouth. Proof and evidence if I ever needed it. Dave is here to witness. You have a cold hard heart, Philo. All you care about is having people believe in your Jesus. You don't even care that Fred has a Bible school he is running. Probably you think you are the only one who can teach the Bible properly, eh?" Richard raised his voice. "You don't care that children are not going to school for lack of school fees. You don't care that an old woman is living in a terrible house with a leaky roof. You don't care and you don't care. Well, I tell you that I do. I have not come here just like a tourist to look at poverty, and then go away and tell my friends about it. I have come to help to solve it! You are trying to stand in my way. You don't even have to help me. I have the money! I have worked hard! You are now so selfish that you don't want Fred to have it?" Richard was angry, still stoking his anger. He added, "You just want to be the big white man. What do they call it—the *Bwana*!"

I expected Philo to come back at Richard with the same force, and to shout at him also. I guessed he was in turmoil inside. That was a serious attack on him from one he had considered a friend. To be honest—Richard had been attacking him for years. Was Philo a glutton for punishment or what—because he didn't seem to return in kind? That is—he did not attack Richard back. He just tried to take it all onto his shoulders. He had explained to me once why that was. He claimed to understand why people from the West behaved as they did. In short, we could say—according to

Philo—they were fed a constant diet of misinformation. How then can you blame them for reacting as they do? Why should Philo get upset with or over his visitors when they were talking from ignorance? "Forgive them, Lord, for they know not what they do," the words of Jesus, came to my mind.

And indeed, Philo was not upset. I am sure he was deeply hurt, but that is not the same thing. You could see that his lips were trembling. He remained with the question of how to deal with this looming issue. If he let Richard talk to Fred again, he could be inviting a headache that would take him years to overcome, if he ever overcame it! (That is, becoming the means of accountability for Fred's funds. Being blamed by Fred if funds came short. Being accused by Richard if funds were abused. Being tempted to conceal the truth from Richard for the sake of a quiet life. Being branded by his colleagues as having a favorite—pandering to Fred's needs, but ignoring theirs. All this would happen if Richard started supporting Fred financially.) I guess all those things and more were going through Philo's mind. Philo might have been tempestuous inside. But, he had been used to handling those kinds of situations before. He had to keep his cool.

"No way," said Philo calmly. "No way do you start offering or giving help to Fred. I brought you here. That is—I am the bridge that enabled you to get here. You come as my friend. If you have too much money, wait for another day when we are speeding along on a bus. Then, when no one can see that I am with you, you can throw the money out of the window at whoever is lucky or unfortunate enough to pick it up. Yes, we can go to the funeral at Fred's place. No way will I administer or provide accountability for you if you want to give funds to people here. If you want to tell Fred that I told you not to help him, then thanks for helping to dig my grave, Richard. Otherwise, don't go and engage in any conversations with Fred. If you do talk to him and he asks you about the money, tell him you thought he was someone else." Philo paused. "Let's talk more about it, but later. Right now, time is short if we want to go to the funeral and then get home afterwards."

"What do you mean? How long is this funeral going to take?" Richard asked. "Fred told me it was at ten. Surely it'll be all done by eleven?"

Philo said nothing. We began preparations to go to the funeral, then to Philo's home.

We had a good breakfast, compliments of Philo's colleagues at the mission! By the time we were ready to leave it was 11 a.m.

"No point in going to the funeral now," Richard said.

"Why?" I asked.

"Well, it'll be over. It was to start at ten!"

"It's not ten yet!" I said, wanting to play Richard up a bit.

He looked at his phone. "Look, it is 10.58 a.m."

"It may be 10.58 a.m. according to your phone, but it is not yet 10 a.m. African time."

"Do we even know where the funeral is? I assumed it would be here at the church?"

"Funerals don't happen at churches, over here. It is amazing how disoriented people can be when they think that all should happen here like it does in the UK." I thought to myself that the fact that we were using the same language with local people as we use in the UK added to the likelihood of this.

"How are we going to even find the place if we don't know where it is, and Fred has already gone?" Richard went on.

"But Fred is still here," I said. "See there!" There was Fred, an hour after the funeral was supposed to have started, by which time according to Richard's reckoning, the funeral should already have been over. Fred was standing and chatting where we had left him.

The funeral was not far away, so we all walked to it, with Fred as our guide. All the way there, Richard engaged in animated conversation with Fred. When we got there, the conversation continued. Philo and I were left just out of earshot. Occasionally, Richard would glance in our direction, as if to say, "Get lost." Richard obviously did not appreciate being told who to talk to and who not to talk to. He was getting sweet revenge.

According to his own explanation later, however, Richard's conversation with Fred gradually shifted gear and direction as it progressed. Initially, he had been probing Fred to find ways in which he might be able to use money that Richard was anticipating sending. Richard, at that point, obviously considered himself to have achieved something critical in making a personal friend of an African person who could, he anticipated, by receiving funds from his business in the UK, significantly improve his charitable reputation. To that end, he was already having a few pictures taken of himself with Fred. Philo was clearly not impressed. But he could not do much about it! His friend looked to be an embarrassment to him.

Then, Richard later confessed, the nature of his conversation changed, as Richard asked questions about what was happening around them. The house of the deceased, a father to Fred called Obonyo, had been renovated since he died. Yet Obonyo's wife had left him and he had no children, so no one was going to live in the house.

"Why have you renovated the house if no one is going to live in it?" Richard asked Fred.

"To save embarrassment to the family, because otherwise people coming to the funeral would see how decrepit his house was," Fred responded. Fred was presumably seeing himself as giving evidence for their family's need for money. Avoiding embarrassment at a funeral was usually a major need in his culture. Funerals, including those of quite poor people, generally needed a lot of money. Obonyo had no job and no money when he was alive. Now he was being given a stately exit.

"Where do all these tents come from?" Richard apparently asked Fred. Fred, thinking he was wanting to cover the cost of the tents, gave him an inflated figure, to make sure that should Richard pay for the hire of the tents (giving shade to the funeral goers) something would remain in his pocket. The real cost was high, but the inflated cost was extravagant! Richard was amazed. He began to wonder. He was taking Fred as a *poor African* deserving of his charity, yet Fred's family were renting expensive marquees at the funeral of a poor relative. Richard continued to be amazed as the tents filled. He later estimated that a thousand people attended that funeral. Most of those thousand people ate a meal. That meal included a generous portion of meat. Such a meal could easily have cost £1.50. Add to that, fizzy drinks being handed out, and cups of tea and drop-scones being prepared for people, food alone could easily have cost £1,700. The coffin alone, according to what he was told by Fred, cost £100. High quality, high capacity microphones and loudspeakers were rented. About a thousand chairs had to be hired for the day. There was an additional tent including dining area for catering, with professional caterers. The funeral event was not just for the day, Richard was told, it lasted a week. Obonyo had not died locally. He passed away while visiting his sister in Mombasa. Transport of the body had put the family back another £300.

Richard's head by this time was spinning a little. The cost of the funeral for this old African man, Obonyo, was spiralling to such a degree that, from what he knew of UK funerals, it was as expensive to bury a poor man in Holima as it was to have a funeral for a rich man in the UK!

"So, do the people who help at the funeral, like the priest who does the burial, need payment?" Richard asked Fred.

"Yes, and they charge a lot."

As events proceeded, Richard found more opportunity to find out about funerals. "Who are the people talking over there?" he asked Fred in due course.

"Those are our in-laws, that is—they have married girls who have come from this home."

"I thought you said Obonyo didn't have any children?"

"He didn't have any of his own, but his brothers' children are also his children."

Richard tried to take that in. "Why are the in-laws standing over there? Why don't they come to the front to talk like the other people are doing?"

"They can't come near their mother-in-law," Fred explained. Fred was, by this time, getting a bit tired of the level of ignorance of his visitor! "Look, are you free to go to your mother-in-law?" Fred said to Richard, with some frustration in his voice! (Richard remained quite confused by that exchange. He later asked us about it. We explained that mother-in-law taboos were very strong in these parts—such that many men tried at all costs to avoid getting close to their mothers-in-law. Of course, they had many mothers-in-law, just as Obonyo had *many children*, while having none.)

"What happens if you get close to your mother-in-law?" Richard asked. Fred looked at him like he was stupid. He couldn't even think how to answer his question. What did Richard want to do with his mother-in-law, he asked himself? Richard had to make do with silence as an answer.

The funeral event continued. The crowd gradually got larger and larger. Different tents were for different kinds of relatives. One row after another of relatives lined up to announce their names and presumably, Richard thought, to talk about the deceased. Richard asked Fred, "Why do you have such a big funeral?" We explained to him later that such a question quite likely made no sense to Fred. Firstly, because to Fred it was not a "big" funeral, as much as a normal funeral. Secondly, because he quite likely interpreted the question as a compliment—the size of the funeral reflects the prosperity of the bereaved family.

Fred responded, "We had to borrow most of the money." He surely thought that saying this would be a further incentive for his white friend to make an immediate contribution to the cost. Richard, meanwhile, was almost numb with shock.

We had agreed that at 2 p.m. sharp we needed to leave the funeral to go home. At the time we discussed the arrangement, Richard hadn't understood, but he agreed anyway. When 2 p.m. arrived, things were far from over. I signalled to Richard with my eyes and by turning my head in the direction we needed to go. The three of us, as far as it is possible for the only three white people in attendance to do so, crept away quietly.

As we walked, Richard was obviously brooding over the things he had learned that day. He told me later he was doing some sums in his head. If a thousand people attended the funeral, many evidently from a vast distance away, Richard was adding more costs. If on average they spend just 50p on transport, which is quite possible, that's another £500 for the funeral. Let's say those people were working for a wage of just £10 per day, then that's another £10,000 in lost productivity, arising from the funeral. Richard had begun to realize—that if he was going to help Fred financially, he would be subsidizing lavish funerals. He was no longer as convinced that helping Fred would necessarily be such a good use of his money.

Richard did not confess or apologize to Philo at that point. For all Philo knew, he had already entered agreement with Fred. Richard was confused, but too ashamed at that point to confess having intentionally aggravated Philo.

"That funeral has raised a lot of questions," Richard simply told us. "The whole event was vastly expensive! Where did all that money come from?"

"I don't know," Philo said. "Often people get into enormous debt. That much is clear. But the economy works that way anyway. People do tend to borrow where they can and spend as much as they can borrow. Over here, big ceremonies especially take a lot of borrowing. I don't know in detail. But there are a lot of people around heavily tied by debts."

"People going into debt a lot—that sounds like the UK or the US. Borrowing is the new way towards poverty!" I said.

"Certainly, there's parallels there—arising from human nature," Richard said. "There is a big European sector in Holima. Is that also what helps pay the bills?"

"Very much so," I said. "People with salaried employment and other means to access funds, some that we would consider corrupt, certainly contribute a lot of the money that keeps the funeral system buoyant."

We were walking on the road to get a bus. Our bags were starting to feel heavy in our hands. We walked in silence for a while. "That's self-imposed poverty," Richard said. "If we, in the UK, were to start living like that, constant large lavish funerals, just imagine! If the biggest event was the funeral, then everybody would do their best to have a big funeral, given the size of extended families around here. No wonder people are poor!" he added.

CHAPTER 22: FINDING GOD

Noise, cheers, confusion and even abuse, seemed normal at bus stations around this part of Africa. Everyone was after making a living. People came up with all kinds of ingenious ways of making money. Three foreigners, white no less, were bound to draw significant attention.

That day this was certainly the case. Young men were shouting at us from all directions. Often, we couldn't understand what they said. They would use their bus-station-English to call us. Some of what they said, only Philo could get. Even Philo was not familiar with all the languages around! In addition to the various people interested in our travel, all kinds of businesses were being pursued. Salesmen of everything from hair brushes, nail clippers, dried fish, sim-sim cakes, drinks, biscuits, and you-name-it, every knick-knack imaginable, was available and proposed to us. There were plenty of offers from all directions.

Philo considered himself responsible for leading us through the chaos, through the barrage of verbal abuse, and through the invitations to divert to this side or that. He had to keep guiding us so that we ended up in the right vehicle. As we ducked and weaved our way through, a fellow wearing a black suit grabbed Philo's hand. I thought he was a super-super high-pressure salesman. It turns out he was a friend of Philo, and that was his only sure way, in the crowd, of making sure he got Philo's attention.

Philo indeed gave his friend his full attention. Neither Richard nor I could understand a word. This friend was clearly very enthused. "Special church gathering tomorrow at his home. We are welcome," Philo interpreted for us. Philo's friend addressed us in Holima English. "Welcome to the fellowship at my home tomorrow at 9 a.m.," he added. We nodded. I wasn't sure what the plan was for the following day. I looked at Richard, who was looking at me.

"I guess so," I told Philo. Philo carried on talking in the local tongue.

"Let's get in that bus, it has lots of room," suggested Richard.

"But, if it has lots of room, and they'll wait to fill it, we'll end up waiting for ages before we begin our journey," Philo replied, strategizing as he was as to which was the right transport for us to use. The key for boarding a bus was to find one that was full, or almost full. Eventually we found our candidate. As we climbed in, Philo was repeating a certain word. Probably that was the price that we would pay—to make sure the price did not go up once we had sat on the bus, I thought. There must have been some order in the chaos. Philo handed over our money to what seemed to me a rather rough looking fellow. He took our money, and that of others, then handed out change. He was obviously sub-contracting. He then had to explain all the sums and who paid what to the bus's actual conductor. We waited five more minutes, enjoying the chaos all around as, finally, the driver boarded and off we went, crammed in as we were in the back, like sardines.

* * *

Later that evening, now at Philo's home, I asked him, "What was that fellow in the black suit inviting us to do?"

"Good question. I was just going to tell you." We were sat around a low table, each of us with a cup of tea in front of us. Tea in Holima, by default, has sugar added. It is also milky—although that is hardly new to Brits. What is unconventional for Brits, is that the tea is boiled with the tea leaves after the milk has been added. That does make sense though, Philo explained, because it ensures that milk is properly boiled. That was the kind of tea we were drinking in the dim light of a solar torch. For years, Philo had used paraffin lamps in his home. Then his household graduated to D-cell battery-powered LED torches, variously adapted for room lighting. Then it graduated to solar-powered lamps—each with its solar panel on the roof. He eventually installed a wired solar system using a twelve-volt deep cycling lead-acid battery to power LED lights.

"The person who spoke to me there at the bus station is called Anton. He's a member of a local church called 'Enchanted the Way'," Philo explained.

"A church called Enchanted. That sounds a bit mystical. And a bit dubious if you ask me," said Richard.

"Sure does," Philo and I said in unison, in one of those strange coincidences that sometimes happen in life. Both of us laughed as Richard goggled at us.

"We'll call it Ench for short," Philo added. "Anton is a member of Ench. I hadn't known before, but the church evidently has a meeting at a home near Anton's place."

"What kind of meeting?" I asked.

Philo wasn't too sure. "Some kind of crusade, I guess?"

"A crusade held at someone's home?" I reflected. "Shouldn't crusades be in a market square or something?" I also realized that there are many reasons people might want a crusade to be at their home. I am glad that Philo did not try and explain this time! There are depths of mystery and levels of mystery underlying the lives of Striden people that are very hard for Western people to grasp at all. I am certainly not sure that Richard would have understood had Philo spent a month of Sundays trying to explain what he himself barely grasped!

"You'll see, that is, you'll see if we go. What do you think?"

"Mum dragged me to church, years ago," Richard answered. "I want nothing to do with it now." His words had a way of finality about them: *That is it. No way whatsoever* .... To avoid clashing with Richard, we changed the subject of conversation. Even so, Richard remained particularly quiet. He hardly contributed, so that the conversation ended up being between Philo and myself. Can't even remember what it was about. Maybe the kinds of crops that people in the area were planting. In due course, one of the children staying with Philo came to tell us that the evening meal was ready. Philo, Richard, and I sat around the dinner table. Also around the table were five of Philo's boys. That was somehow incredible. For us it was a one-off. For Philo, such arrangement for mealtimes was very normal. Every evening at home, he sat around the dinner table with a group of five or six Holiman boys. The girls and women sat eating in the kitchen on the floor and on low stools. That's a way in which women show their love for the men.

I can't help but think that Richard was impressed by the devotion he observed around him. After eating we sat in a circle, this time with all the children and the housemother. They joined us, one at a time, after completing their duties, clearing the table, and so on. There we sat and we sang. Many, if not all, of the songs must have been unfamiliar to Richard. Very few were in English. Something, however, evidently spoke to Richard through that singing. Watching the children sing perhaps. Maybe it was the beat of the improvised drum (a twenty-litre plastic-drum). Something happened that evening. If I am not mistaken I even saw a glistening of tears in Richard's eyes. Perhaps, I thought, just perhaps his heart was softening. There is something wonderful about African children's singing. That night, I understand, God spoke to Richard. But Richard was still fighting his own battle.

***

"Do you mind breaking off just for a moment?" Julie said at that point. She went to visit the restroom. The shade of the tree had shifted considerably as we had been sitting there. We moved our chairs to make sure that we were going to stay in the shade. Some women walked by. They were heading for their homes, buckets of water on their heads. Always an incredible feature of African life that, I thought to myself. When Julie came back I asked her if I should carry on telling the story, or if she had had enough.

"Please carry on," she said, "the story you are telling is fascinating."

***

After we had finished that time with the children, when the three of us were left alone again, Richard said, "Let's go."

"Let's go what?" Philo asked. It was late at night, where did he want to go?

"To Ench tomorrow," Richard said, "that the fellow at the market invited us to."

"Are you sure you want to go?" asked Philo.

"If you chaps want to go, then I'm more than happy to join you," Richard said.

"Okay. It's not too far away, so let's leave at 10 a.m. We can easily walk there."

"But you said that Anton told you the meeting started at 9 a.m.," Richard asked, looking puzzled.

Philo looked a little bewildered. "That's why I said, let's leave at 10 a.m," Philo was apparently oblivious to the inherent contradiction in his words.

"Then, we'll be late!" Richard emphasized.

"I doubt it …. Oh, okay," Philo suddenly understood the issue. "You are thinking that Anton telling us that the meeting will start at 9 a.m. means that it will start at 9 a.m."

"All that concept of time is a bit confusing," Richard said.

"You mean 9 a.m. not being 9 a.m?" said Philo.

"Yes."

"I should have said 11 a.m.," Philo added.

"But what time did Anton tell you?"

Philo laughed. "Three o'clock," he answered. Now Richard really did look confused.

"Okay," I said. I was aware that when not using English, people gave the time differently from English time. That is, the clock in African languages in East Africa goes on biblical time, where midnight is 6 o'clock, so 9 a.m. is the 3rd hour, i.e. 3 o'clock.

"But when people say 3 o'clock, i.e. 9 a.m., they generally mean something like 11 a.m., so perhaps I should just have said 11 a.m.?"

"But what if Anton had known English and heard you saying 11 a.m. instead of 9 a.m.?" I asked.

"Well, that would have been a problem, because it would have looked like I was trying to postpone the meeting to 1 p.m., which would have been much too late for Anton's liking. I would have had to have said 11 a.m. to you after Anton had gone out of earshot."

"No wonder…. Wow! Indeed, language and translation are confusing!" I said.

"You mean," Richard said, "that whenever someone says the time using local languages, including Swahili, they adjust what they say to a twelve-hour clock, that is six hours out of sync with our clocks?"

"Yes," I said.

"That is amazing," he said, while looking duly amazed! "And you mean also, that people will say that a meeting will start at 9 a.m., i.e., 3 o'clock in their own language, when it will actually start two hours later? That's very confusing!"

* * *

The following morning it was as if we had a spring in our step as we set off for the gathering of Ench. It felt like we were three adventurers embarking on some maiden voyage of discovery, or setting out to push back frontiers! Little did I know at the time everything we would have to face that day.

What was to determine the tune of the rest of the day, began before we even reached the meeting place. I assume by coincidence, as I am not aware that Philo had planned it, we met up with Anton on our way to the gathering. Anton started walking with us. Then, as we were walking, and not actually very far from our destination, he suddenly recalled a certain sick person nearby.

"So and so is sick, Philo," he evidently told Philo. "Can we go and pray for them?" he added.

Philo thought about that question. I even saw him look at his watch. He turned to us. He said, pointing with his chin, "There is a sick man in the homestead over there. Anton suggests that we go and pray for him. What do you think?" Philo overseeing our program, there wasn't much we could say. We didn't know if we were late, or how late we were, or what was entailed in praying for someone who is sick. We nodded in agreement.

As Philo talked to Anton, acknowledging that we were ready to make the diversion, I heard Richard whispering a question in a low voice, "What good are prayers going to do for someone needing medical attention?" I was surprised that Richard would be so vocal in expressing such an opinion, even if he had the right to do so. Philo, it seemed, did not hear.

We filed into a small, dingy and very untidy hut. It was already hot in there, due to the iron sheets receiving the full force of the mid-morning sun. We didn't see anyone sick. "Come through," we heard a voice from the sleeping area of the hut.

I had been in huts like this before, but I had never graduated to a visit to the sleeping area. I didn't know what people's bedrooms were like around here. I was to learn that day. I assumed that for us to be invited into the sleeping area, the man concerned must be very sick. Otherwise, he would have come to us in the sitting room.

We entered the bedroom. Philo led the way, then Anton followed, then Richard, then me. Until our eyes adjusted, we could hardly see a thing. In due course, we observed that there was a bed of some sort against the back wall, but we couldn't see anyone in it. Instead, what came to my attention was a dishevelled blanket. Gradually as our eyes adjusted, we saw what appeared to be the skeleton of a man lying on the bed partially covered by the blanket. The skin of his gaunt face seemed to cover only bones. It was almost as if his whole body could be mistaken for a skeleton, so emaciated was he. Partly covered by that blanket, his feet stuck out at the end. His eyes were closed, and his face apparently permanently contorted as if he was crying in pain. Also, striking to me, was an extremely pungent smell. I wondered for how long this man had had his urine stored right there in the hut, or whether that bed had become his permanent toilet? Neither of the latter were very likely in fact. His wife was devoted and helping him and cleaning him, at least her testimony was to that effect. The smell was pungent, nevertheless. She sat, wearing a long red dress, poised on the edge of the bed near his head. Although rather short and skinny herself, her face was round. Seeing her, one could picture her in better days as a friendly, jolly, welcoming person. Looking after her husband in his failing health in this dank hut had no doubt taken its toll on her.

Glancing at Richard, I could only guess that this experience of visiting such a sick man in his village hut was creating deep culture shock in him. As soon as we had entered that bedroom, Anton indicated to Philo that he should pray aloud. Philo began to do so. People appreciated prayers in that part of the world that were noisy. Noisy prayers indicated a bold declaration of God's purpose and power at resolving the issue being addressed. Philo, standing as were the rest of us alongside the bed, proceeded with his prayer. He prayed in a language only a few words of which I could get. As he prayed, I was mystified, and then I guess horrified by another sound simultaneously coming from the other side of me. The person making that sound was Richard.

As Philo prayed, here is what Richard was saying: "Prayer is useless. What this man needs is not prayer, he needs help! Proper help. Can't you see that calling on some non-existent God isn't going to benefit him one bit. Someone around here needs to see sense, call a doctor, then diagnose and treat the fellow as per his malady." Then Richard went silent.

Philo was still praying at that point. Eventually, he finished.

"Amen," said Philo.

"Amen," said the rest of us, except for Richard.

Philo must have heard Richard's monologue. What on earth was he making of it, I asked myself? I started to wonder if there was going to be a fight! Richard seemed to be doing his best to upset Philo. I looked at Richard. From what I could see, given the dim light and the fact that his face was turned away, he was unmoved by Philo's prayer. His words were harsh and unrepentant. I looked at Anton's face. It was even more difficult to see his expression, but he appeared to be bewildered. Then there was Philo, from whom at any time I expected a string of expletives putting Richard in his place and condemning him for his crude blasphemy. Philo said nothing. That is—he said nothing about the situation regarding his tempestuous colleague Richard. He was talking with the sick man. He got out his Bible. That Bible was not in English. He was reading from it. Then, presumably, he expounded on what he read. Anton was nodding, apparently appreciating what was being said. The sick man's eye's flickered. Both he and his wife, perched on the bed beside him, seemed to be lapping up what Philo said. For a while, Richard was silent.

"What on earth are you doing, telling this man who needs help, fables about angels and a man you call Jesus?" said Richard, assuming he knew what Philo was saying. Philo stayed quiet, allowing Richard to complete his sentence. Then Philo said something else, apparently ignoring Richard's acid comment.

Angered through being ignored, Richard raised his voice higher. "Stop this stupid practice!" he almost shouted. Philo followed with a sentence of his own, his voice also appearing to be raised, but still seeming to ignore Richard's drift. Now Richard began a tirade. Some of what he said I shall not repeat. He attacked Philo for his folly in becoming a missionary. He attacked me for being Philo's friend. He attacked the church. He said the Bible was stupid. So, he went on, tirading … at an ever-rising pitch!

I stood absolutely flummoxed between the two men, as a few seconds into Richard's non-stop tirade, Philo began his own tirade! He was going as fast as was Richard, so fast that I could not get a word of what he was saying. He was anyway definitely not speaking English. Amazingly, Anton then started his tirade! Three tirades, each at high volume, by people in the same small room simultaneously! This continued in unison for a few minutes. Although I was doing nothing but listening, I found my whole body covered in sweat, so much so that my clothes were dripping! "What is going on?" I asked myself.

When Richard's tirade ended a few seconds later, Philo's ended a little while later, then so did Anton's. Richard walked out. Philo carried on talking to the man for another minute. He then asked me to pray for him. I did so—with Philo translating. We shook the hands of the man and his wife, and then the three of us walked out. We blinked as we emerged into the glaring sunshine.

As we walked out, there was Richard standing in the shade under a tree a few yards away looking towards us. Uncharacteristically, Philo let out a long wheeze as he walked; "pppp hhhh heee uuuuu uwwww www www."

Richard looked at him strangely. Philo was still wheezing as we walked away together. He turned around and waved goodbye to the lady of the house, now standing in her doorway. She was too poorly to walk with us. Philo waved, but said nothing. He was still wheezing, "pppp hhhhh hhee eeeee uuuuu uuuuu uuww wwww ww."

We carried on walking. Philo carried on wheezing! After two hundred yards, now well clear of the house, Philo couldn't help himself any more. He broke out into a fit of giggles! That's more than I expected from a man of over fifty. Whether I wanted to believe it or not, it was happening; Philo was engulfed in a violent fit of laughter! He almost fell over. Then his giggling infected the rest of us, until we were all giggling—including Richard. Four grown men, three white and one black, standing on the side of an African village path, engrossed in violent giggling!

* * *

"Is that really what happened?" Julie asked.

"Yes!" I said.

"Yes," Philo confirmed, "even if it was hard to believe. That is what happened." The memory of the event almost had Philo and me in giggles again. I composed myself and carried on.

* * *

We ended up sprawled on the ground in fits. Anton was the first to stop giggling and got his composure. Then Richard. Philo was the last.

"What was all that about?" I asked Philo. We had all been infected by Philo.

"Keep walking and I will tell you," Philo said.

"Tell us here!" I insisted.

"No. While we are walking away," he replied. We didn't have much choice as only Philo knew the secret we were wanting to hear about. Now that Philo might be very angry due to Richard's outbursts, we might have understood. But why the giggling?

As we walked, Philo explained.

"Richard, you are incredible. In the middle of my prayers you start blaspheming God. Wow! I didn't expect that even from you." However, Philo was still having trouble controlling his giggling. Judging from Richard's face, Richard was perplexed, frustrated and angry in one go. "I just kept praying. And you know what the old man and his wife thought you were doing?"

Richard looked by that point to be totally dumbstruck. "No," he said.

"They thought you were praying!" Philo exclaimed. Richard stood dead in his tracks. "Let's ask Anton," Philo suggested. Anton was having trouble following what was going on. Philo talked to him in his best Holiman English: "At the time when I was praying, Richard also prayed?" Philo asked him. We assumed that Anton understood what we said. He seemed to agree.

"Yes, Richard prayed," Anton replied. For the benefit of the Holimans, whose English was not too strong, Philo managed to turn Richard's aggressive tirade into a belligerent prayer session! Anton and the old couple assumed he was praying for the old man to be healed, as were Philo and Anton!

"So that's what you were laughing about," I said.

"I haven't finished," Philo said. I gave him a quizzical look. "Later when I was teaching and encouraging the old man," Philo added "Richard came back on again with a renewed vigor. So—I made out that I was translating. While Richard was busy criticizing prayer, and blaspheming as strongly as he could, that dear old couple thought you were a saint," Philo added, looking at Richard.

By the time we got to the location of the crusade, it was 10.45 a.m. Sure enough—nothing had yet started happening. People were milling around. There were enough people to give us a warm welcome. We were sat at a table in one of the houses in the homestead, and served with ample tea, bread, drop-scones and roasted ground nuts. The smiling ladies who served us were dressed in long skirts, and had their heads covered by carefully-tied cloths. This gave us time to continue to discuss what was happening around us and our responses to it. Richard was rather nonplussed by the interpretation that had been put on his words in the sick man's home! He felt rather outnumbered by Christians. "I am sure," he thought to himself, he told me later, "that had we been in England, where Christians are seen by some to be in the minority, then the boot would have been on the other foot."

* * *

"I wonder," Julie interrupted, "if Richard realized the general truth of the fact that even if he had true and important things to say, he could not communicate them there in Holima? That is a problem with clever English thinking—it does not translate. Even when millions of Africans spend decades learning English—it is still the church that grows more than secularism."

"Good point," I said. "The message about Jesus communicates much more easily and instantly, and in a more profound way, than do efforts at communication of so-called secular values."

* * *

The three of us were, in due course, left alone to continue with our own discussions. Then Richard spoke up. "Look folks. I just want to say some things. Firstly, I must say I don't blame Philo for laughing as he did when we emerged from the home of that sick old man. It was a classic. I wouldn't want him to feel in the least that by laughing he might have offended me. But now, what happened there has now really got me thinking." I was glad that Richard made that confession. I was intrigued as to where he was going now. What was he going to say, now that he had made his apology? "Seems I have a lot of apologizing to do, also for the way I went contrary to Philo's advice in my talking to Fred back there at the funeral," Richard added. "I am just beginning to see things after my three days here, that I had never seen before. Basically, I am seeing that things that I know or thought I 'knew' don't necessarily make sense in this context. In fact, they may not even exist! How can we in Britain be so sure of things that we know, if the same things are way beyond the comprehension of people who are flesh and blood like us, in a different part of the world? When we visited that sick man, I thought I had important things to say. What was happening made no sense to me, where I come from culturally. Yet my behavior was farcical! 'Sense' as I know it in the UK made no sense at all! This is forcing me to think very hard. I came here thinking that, as a European, I knew better ways of doing things and better ways of living than do Africans. Well—now I realize—that those ways aren't even comprehensible to them. Are we in Britain 'better' than are people in Holima, just because we think things that make no sense to them, while meanwhile they are thinking and doing things that make no sense to us? Although I must say—perish the thought! Are we Brits better, or not?"

"At the end of the day, only God can know that," I said.

"What!" Richard came straight to me on that. He didn't like people talking about God. "If there is a God, yes," he said after a pause.

"Let's reverse that," Philo suggested, "to say; that which makes that assessment, whatever or whoever, is God." Richard was quiet for a while. "So, because there's no rational basis for saying one way of life is absolutely better than another, in the absence of God, whoever or whatever he is, comparison is disqualified."

"That's right," I said. "Anyone comparing is drawing on a knowledge of God, whether they know it or not."

Philo added, "The problem in the UK is that UK people have outdated notions of superseded Christian explanations about God. When they reject such notions, they think then that God is not there at all. But if God is not there at all, that leaves us unable to say that any way of life is better than another. That means in effect, that whenever we suggest that one way of life is better than another, we are declaring belief in God."

"In effect then," Richard said, "the West coming to Africa and telling Africans what they are doing right or wrong, is rooted in an understanding of God that the West denies having."

"That is hypocritical," I said, "and misleading behavior. The West tells Africa what to do. But they conceal the foundations from which they are speaking, foundations that are firmly rooted in biblical Christian faith."

"It is alright for you, Philo," Richard added. "You've been working through these issues for years. And you are a declared believer. I went to church many years ago as a child—then ditched it. I did not like church the way we did it there in the UK."

"So, someone has to like something for it to be right?" I asked.

Philo went on to say the following: "The problem today, let's say, is that people think coming to Christ is an optional extra. It is not. It is the essence of life as we know it. When people pretend that it is not so, they end up telling us the same in Africa. A big difference is, that whereas European people have centuries of momentum of devoted Christian belief behind them, folks here in Africa don't have that same culture. This means that the need for Christ tends to be much clearer here. In your face if you like."

"Tell you what," Richard added, looking at Philo, "you need to share some of these insights you have acquired with people in Europe."

"That's a thought," Philo responded! He looked at me. It is something we had talked about in recent weeks—and at some length. Now Richard—the arch-enemy of all that Philo was doing—was suggesting the same! We did not tell him that his idea was not original. I think both of us were realizing that we were receiving confirmation of plans for a trip to the West.

"In the meantime," Richard asked, "do I have nothing to say in Africa?"

I responded "No," at the same time as Philo said "Yes." We all three laughed.

"Okay you go first," Philo said to me.

"Well, there's something here that seems to illustrate our problem," I said. "In European English, a negative answer would be affirmative of your question. In African English, a positive answer would be affirmative. That may be the total of my 'disagreement' with Philo."

"What are you on about?" Richard asked.

Philo responded, "If you ask, *do I have nothing to say?* then in England, if someone wants to agree with you they'll say no, meaning no, you are right indeed you have nothing to say. Here in Holima someone wanting to agree with you will say yes, i.e., yes, you are right, indeed you have nothing to say. So, in this case, the meaning of *no* in England is the same as the meaning of *yes* in Holima."

"Wow, this gets more complicated every moment," Richard grimaced.

"So then Philo, tell us," I added, "do you think Richard has anything to say in Africa?"

"Yes," Philo replied.

"Okay. Please explain," I said to Philo.

"We had already discussed the fact that there is no ultimately legitimate basis for evaluative comparison between cultures without recourse to understanding God," Philo said. "That implies that of course there is such a legitimate basis for evaluative comparison providing someone is being guided by God. This is traditionally the role of the prophet. The prophet declares that God says X, Y, Z, and the fact that God declares something is the basis for the legitimacy of his words. Therefore, Richard has something to say to folks in Africa, in so far as he is able to connect with God, and to receive words from God."

"Okay, fair enough," I said, "and I agree with you. But the second question pertains to the language that Richard will use in communicating whatever insights he has that he wants to share. How can God, except through the gift of tongues, give Richard insights into a way of life that uses a language he does not understand? That is—if God wants to use the intelligence of a person, rather than bypass it and just give him words to say that he himself may not understand?"

"You mean like words in another tongue that have no translation that Paul talks about?" Philo asked.

"Yes!"

"I think I am starting to follow you," Richard told me. "Carry on."

"Okay, let's take an example. In the UK, I may be given a word from God to say that men should pay more attention to loving their wives. That would be on the basis, presumably, that UK men are paying too little attention to their wives. Does it follow that men in Africa are paying too little attention to their wives in the same way? Presumably not. What exactly is meant by *pay attention* anyway? In the UK, there may be an understanding of that. But that understanding may well not carry over to Africa. Then what of polygamy? If a man has more wives, should he pay more attention to all of them? A polygamous household can run on very different dynamics than monogamous households after all. Because of the option of polygamy, monogamous households in Africa tend to operate in a way that would allow room for an additional wife. Then there is the massive question of the interpretation of the term 'love.' In the UK and other European nations, understandings of this term arise very much from the Christian message and the Bible taught over many centuries. It is to do with the sacrificial self-giving of oneself for others. Of course, that may be just a small part of European people's total understanding of love. The point is though—that whatever African term is used to interpret love may have very different meanings to the British-English equivalent. So then, how can a prophet, when he says that men should love their wives to British people, be at all sure how he will be understood in Africa?"

"Ah, so," Richard came in, "actually a prophet is a translator."

"As we saw in radical terms earlier today," Philo added.

At that point, a lady came and spoke to Philo. "We are welcome to join folks outside in the tent," Philo told us. "They want to start their meeting."

"Look," Richard said, "we won't understand what is going on. How will you help us?"

"I can try and translate, or at least summarize for you."

"So, if people will anyway expect us to be listening to your whispered interpretations, then instead of just translating what the person says, you should give us a commentary, and respond to our questions," Richard said.

"We can try that," Philo responded.

Moving out, we found a group of about fifty people gathered under the canvas. The bishop and his colleagues were there. The bishop was a large man. Not particularly old, probably somewhere in his early fifties, and dressed in flowing, brightly-colored robes, he had a warm affectionate face but with somewhat piercing eyes. Sitting alongside him were similarly clothed men on either side. All of them were dressed in dark suits. Their shoes were polished to a tee. It was an impressive sight, to see those young men looking so sharp and so alert in preparation for our joint gathering.

Philo went to talk to the bishop. He had arranged for chairs to be set up for us next to where he was sitting. Philo explained that he would be doing whispered interpretation. Hence, he suggested that we sat at a less prominent place, so as not to be a distraction. That was agreed, and our chairs were relocated.

By the time we sat, people had begun singing. Philo sat between the two of us. Around us were green fields and trees. We could hear birds when the gathered crowd under the tarpaulin wasn't singing. There were probably, in due course, one hundred or more people in the tent. The majority were women, dressed in long dresses and head-scarves, as had been the ladies who had served us our second breakfast. Apart from the canvas under which people were sitting, houses with rusty iron roofs surrounded the periphery of the homestead, which occupied perhaps a third of an acre.

"That singing is amazing," Richard whispered. "These people seem to believe whatever it is they are saying."

The men leading the meeting were sharp, and co-ordinated. Already two languages were being used. Philo told us they were the Striden and Swahili languages. Men sat segregated from women. Probably they had decided it of their own accord.

"Why do men sit separate from the women?" Richard asked me. I signalled to Philo, and he answered him. He could have explained that in many ways. He said simply and frankly, that people are there to worship God. They do not want to be distracted by either sexual temptations, or issues, like wondering, "Where is my wife?"

"Many folks in most UK churches would find that wrong," Richard informed me. I knew that. Richard's comments reminded me of my time with Martin many years before, when Philo first came to Holima.

"Who is the pompous fellow wearing the bright clothes in the middle?" Richard asked.

"What makes you think he is pompous?"

"You have to be pretty pompous to wear clothes like that in a crowd."

"Or brave," Philo said. "Would you dress like that?" he asked Richard.

"No way!" he said.

"You're scared?" Philo asked.

Richard laughed. He had not thought about it that way before. This bishop looked brighter than the pope. I was struck by Philo's analysis. Just like Richard, I would not have wanted to dress like that. It would not have been far off, either, to say I was scared! Someone dressing like that is a marked man. Just imagine someone coming and saying, "We're going to shoot all Christians." Others might pretend that they weren't Christians, but only here through curiosity. The man in the robes would get shot!

"People here have great respect for what we might in England called priestly robes," Philo said. "Presumably so did other people around the world at one time, or we wouldn't have the same traditions in the Catholic, Orthodox and other churches. Wearing priestly garb may appear pompous in some ways. In another way, it is pure dedication and commitment."

Philo hadn't said who he was, so Richard asked again. "But who is he?"

"Oh, sorry. I didn't say," Philo responded. "That is the bishop."

"Tell me, Philo," I asked, "when you look at those pastors and the people in the congregation, they seem to be very dedicated. I mean—they seem to be so enthusiastic and totally committed. You know them. At least you know them better than we do. Is that correct? Are they so dedicated? Or is it just an appearance? Are they putting on a show?"

As we continued our whispered conversation, trying to understand what was going on, the men in front of us were speaking, and the congregation sat quietly, attentively listening.

Philo laughed at my question. I guess it wasn't easy to answer. The preacher was then totally invested in his message; he made many gestures, and in the heat of the day that made him sweat profusely. His translator vigorously imitated his every move. The crowds sitting there, especially the women, seemed to follow every articulation and gesticulation with care and attention. They frequently declared "Amen" in unison. This was no sleepy Sunday morning service in a UK church, with people looking at their watches to make sure things weren't going over time. These people seemed to be totally committed, and incredibly focused.

"Hang on a minute," Philo said, and he went to the front. The other translator stepped aside. Philo took over. For a while, he translated into that other language, whatever it was. Then he summarized into English for us. He had obviously been called to the front for that purpose. "We welcome the visitors … especially Philo who we all know … but also his two colleagues who have come with him today … we feel very privileged to have them in our midst … Philo will introduce them to us." At this point, Philo took over speaking in English while the other person translated. He introduced us. Then he translated for each one of us in turn as we stood up, and announced our names and background. In due course Philo re-joined us. The others carried on as before.

"Here's the response I can give you, Dave," Philo said, speaking to myself and Richard simultaneously. "People are as committed and dedicated as they appear. It is something very impressive, and very much to be learned from. It comes from something amazing that God is doing in their hearts. They also know, more than we Brits, what it is like to live without God. They do not have all the social safety-nets that we have, which have been put into place by our Christian predecessors. They are emerging from a society dominated by witchcraft fears. A Christian gathering is to them a wonderful experience. Let's say it is a breakthrough experience—resolving numerous issues that used to trouble them before. Jesus, thus, is very important to them, and they are very committed to him.

"I suppose I can also add," Philo went on, "that does not mean they are not human. Don't think these people are some kind of giants. They are very human, and as liable to human failings as are we. Do remember also that they are African. While I can I think, helpfully say, using English, that they are very committed and devoted—such commitment and devotion does not turn them into Brits. And we should not expect it. That is to say—if we try to understand what we think we are seeing according to what we perceive as Brits, then we will be wrong. Even the very term 'commitment' might be misleading; are they committed? Whatever it means in (British) English to be committed, they do not know about. So, yes, they are very committed, in a Holiman way."

"This is an interesting and helpful way of putting it," said Richard.

"Very often," I interjected, "we have assumed that once someone becomes a Christian, he should become like us British or French or American Christians. You are saying that need not be the case at all, Philo, right?"

"Right!"

Richard was nodding pensively.

The meeting carried on. Philo would not translate everything. The translation work was extremely tiring. He kept us up with the gist of what was going on. An additional thing he told us was that this church was truly indigenous. That is to say—it had no foreign missionaries, bosses, or donors. People guiding the church, and making the decisions about it, were entirely local.

The bishop himself, in due course, stood up. By this time, it was around 1 p.m. The crowd did not seem to notice the time go by. Neither did we.

Two hours at this service went by very quickly! The bishop spoke for about forty minutes. He spoke about deliverance from oppressive powers. Philo explained that in the worldview of people around us here, life was all about overcoming powers that were oppressing you. That is, success in life was believed to be actioned by hitting the bad, rather than by building the good.

Philo's words might have seemed a little empty for a while—but not for long! We were about to get a live demonstration of just what he meant. We were about to discover that, whether it was saving people from their problems and illnesses, or if it was to help them achieve socio-economic development, as it would seem, both were considered to happen through the overcoming of untoward spirits of their forefathers!

Although neither Richard nor I could understand the language, we both became aware of a build-up in levels of what is in British English called "emotional tension." I looked at Richard. At that moment, he was looking at me. Then his eyes went back to the congregation in front of us. The tone of the bishop's voice was changing. He was speaking more quickly. The translator into that other language (presumably Swahili) was having trouble keeping up with him. Suddenly, one of the women in the congregation started crying. Then a man left his chair and rushed to the front, in the space between the congregation and the leaders. In no time at all, almost everyone was responding to the bishop's message in this way. Moments later, the whole congregation was on their knees, bowed to the ground, crying loudly! Most people had moved to the front. The empty space that had been left between the preacher and the other leaders, and the chairs of the congregants, was filled with people kneeling and crying loudly. When I say "loudly," I mean: very loudly. As they cried, tears flowed from the eyes of many. They cried, and cried, and cried in loud voices. If Philo hadn't looked so unperturbed, we might have been panicking. What on earth was going on in front of us?

The leaders at the front, including the bishop, seemed totally unperturbed by the chaos and din happening in front of them. They were beginning to respond to it. Many had raised their hands heavenwards, and were engaged in fervent prayer. Gradually, the ten or so men doing so, the leaders who had been at the front, moved amongst the crowd of people who were on their knees. As they did so, they touched the heads of those concerned. Although there was a predominance of women, many men were also amongst the crowd of people knelt low, crying loudly. The noise continued, it seemed, unabated probably for five minutes. Then gradually they all went back to their seats. They sat down again calmly. Once they had calmed down, one of the leaders of the service said something else. Philo didn't translate. I guess we didn't think to ask him to do so, so taken up were we by what was going on in front of us.

Then many members of the congregation began singing. Some, however, went right back to where they had been minutes before, back onto their knees, and back to crying loudly. The first time everyone came forward. This time they seemed to be only those who faced terrible issues, I thought. The leaders at the front went back to praying for them. This time, also, it seemed they prayed with a renewed gusto. Some of the singers moved further forward. They were clapping loudly as they sung. Those praying were moving their hands from head to head, blessing those knelt in front of them. Some of the people being prayed for stood up and joined the singing crowd, presumably singing to God and searching for his mercy. Two of the ladies who were kneeling, fell. They fell from their knees onto the ground almost simultaneously, perhaps just a second or two between them. They were a few metres apart. They began convulsing and writhing on the ground. Another lady rushed to one of them to cover her legs with a cloth, presumably so that the men attending would not be distracted by seeing her legs.

By this time, we had realized what was going on. Demons were being prayed out of these women. The smartly-dressed men were pointing their fingers at the women's faces while shouting loudly for the demons to come out. Sometimes their fingers came very close to touching the ladies' faces. One of the women appeared to want to vomit. We assumed that she was trying to vomit out her demon. The other was more engaged in rolling around on the ground, thus her dress was now filthy. Suddenly, the one rolling on the ground sprang up. I saw Richard starting. He started moving towards her, as if to go and help the other men to stop her from running away. He stopped himself, and sat down again. Three men quickly grabbed hold of her arms. Doing so, they wrestled her back onto the ground. They continued their noisy prayers. Another five minutes elapsed, before peace finally returned to the congregation. Everyone returned to sit quietly back in their seats. That included the two women, who by now seemed to feel that the demons had been successfully removed from them.

In due course, a ten-minute sojourn was announced. This gave us opportunity to turn to Philo. "Now you have seen exorcisms in action," Philo told us.

I had some inkling of what was going to happen. I think the whole experience was entirely new for Richard.

"What was troubling those women?" Richard asked Philo.

"Ancestors."

"What do you mean, ancestors?"

"Long story," Philo said. "People have troubles. I guess we all know that, all around the world. Here troubles are largely believed to be caused by what we could, in English terms, call 'ancestors.' That is, perhaps way back in a family's history, something happened. Perhaps someone did something bad, like killing somebody in cold blood, incest, or whatever it was. That bad act, the nature of which is no longer known, is held responsible for the family's misfortune to date. That's why *families' fortunes* differ, and it is considered the source of people's problems. That kind of 'generational curse' is almost insurmountable by conventional means. The coming of the good news of Jesus, combined with the kind of prosperity brought by the white men, the early colonialists and missionaries, and now even people like you and me, has given people real hope. Hope, that is, that somehow, they may be able to overcome those things that have troubled them for generations. In Europe, we feel that we have individual problems, over here these problems are interpreted in a large context, referred to as family and ancestors: it is more embraced collectively. It is the hope in Christ that makes people so determined."

"You mean, our example is what they are aspiring to?" Richard asked.

"Yes, partly at least."

After the recess, we came back to order. The bishop was still the one speaking. He motioned to Philo to come up to where he was standing. This time it seems he wanted Philo to translate into English. Philo translated for us. This appeared to be something that the bishop was particularly proud of. "Our church," he said, "takes economic development very seriously." The gist of the message was that Ench, through its recognition and dealing with ancestral spirits in such an overt way, had uncovered secrets to progress, that Philo translated into 'socio-economic development.' Now they were to build on their discoveries to provide their members, and their anticipated growing membership, with material prosperity of a kind, greater than that provided by any other competing church.

The day finished well. We enjoyed ongoing fellowship with people in Ench over a good meal, after the event was formally closed. Everyone there very much appreciated what Philo was doing in the community.

We found that everywhere we went—people were very supportive of Philo. Not because of anything that he did. Philo had no big projects. He had not done anything mega, at least that he had told us about. So, what did they appreciate him for? In short: one could say, for loving them, that is, for accepting them for who they were, for coming on board, for identifying with them in non-pretentious ways, for walking with them, and talking to them, and for doing all of that over a long period.

That's what struck me about the way they treated Philo.

CHAPTER 23: LIFE, MONEY, EXORCISM

That evening, back at Philo's home, we had the opportunity to dissect the day's events.

"You said that church was totally self-funded?" Richard asked Philo.

"I don't know where they get their money. Who knows—they might get some money from the UK somehow. But—they run their own shop," Philo replied.

"What I am gathering," Richard went on, "is that doing so is not so common?"

"That's right," I chipped in. "It's a sensitive area, though. No one says that they are working with a church that is not indigenously rooted. All foreign missionaries claim to be working with truly indigenous churches. Of course they do! Then of course they have to convince their supporters of the same. Many Western people working with African churches have to make out that the church is functioning independently of their finance, or they'd be accused of generating dependency! But they still find ways to give. Many people would, as a result, want to claim that the kind of indigenous church we saw today was not particularly exceptional."

"So, who is right then?" Richard added.

"There's a litmus test," Philo said. "I think it is quite simple; if you want to know if people will keep their Christian activities even if you aren't around, then be as if you weren't around."

"Huh?"

"Europeans have an obsession with money," Philo said. "It's like they cannot come to Africa, without spending money on something, or someone, or everything, or everyone. It's like they can't visit African people without getting involved in running a project for them! Such projects invariably require foreign funds, so making African people financially dependent. Many African people don't mind being clients to a white community. That's their system—you praise the patron; he gives you money. But, what about relating to African people without giving them money? Those kinds of relationships are these days almost totally absent."

"Another thing I couldn't help but notice," Richard said, "was the orientation of the church to the driving away of demons. That is, to cleansing."

"People are in prisons that Europe generally does not even recognize," I added.

"Exorcism used to be practiced in Europe," Philo came in, "then for some reason it stopped. Now people look back on all that with disdain. Here in Holima such disdain does not exist. People want help to have evil spirits removed. Otherwise they are bound by them. How to communicate the advisability of exorcism in Europe that rejects it outright? However, the good part of it is, that it is, in Africa, a community action. People take charge of each other's demons."

"So, exorcism, in the European world, goes underground," I added, "but here it is done very openly."

"We were told, according to my understanding of your translation, that 'exorcism' is the gateway to development. I am beginning to see how that makes sense. If we start off with people who are imprisoned by their traditional beliefs, they need release from those beliefs, and that's what the 'exorcism' provides," Richard added.

We paused. Tea was being brought for us. The children who brought it were slightly nervous of these white people, but polite.

"It's like shame," I said. "People are afraid of shame. It's shameful! So, once someone has done certain things that could cause shame, they're frightened."

"Like revenge porn?" Richard added.

"What do you mean by that?" Philo asked.

"In the UK nowadays, people post revealing images of others on the internet as a means of revenge, especially on an ex-girlfriend. That is a very big issue. The person feels ashamed of their nakedness being exposed to the public, but there's nothing they can do about it, because it's there posted on the net for everyone to see. While people are free to post any picture they want to publicly, that has become an irresolvable problem. If a means could be found to release shamed people from that prison, they would jump at it!"

"That's a good illustration," Philo went on. "Exorcism is that kind of release. Remember also, that it's all very consequential, because in the African tradition the wrong thing that you did has become a shameful part of your identity, it brings you misfortune."

"Or that your forefather did," I added.

"Yes," said Philo.

"But the same is the case for revenge-porn," Richard interrupted. "Once that picture is on the web, you can't tell who might have downloaded a copy. The person who has been shamed can feel embarrassed even to go for an interview for a job. And indeed, businesses nowadays look for your name on the internet to check your reputation. Misdemeanors or innuendos are in the public realm. It's a terrible situation to be in."

"That's the kind of thing from which people in that church were getting release," Richard said.

"This is so ironic," I said. "The West has been busy telling African people that spirits don't exist. Now we are suggesting that the elimination of the same troublesome spirits could be the key to African development!"

"And you are saying that the same spirits are causing the pain connected to internet revenge and internet porn!" Richard added.

I paused, then added, "Spirits, then, in a sense, are those ancient issues that are still bringing people problems today."

"That is also the way people talk," Philo came in. "That is to say, people will talk of *kuong mag anyuola*. We could translate that into English as *curse of the family*, or *generational curse*. The point is that such a curse goes down a family line from generation to generation. In the past people in the West have concentrated on asking if such a curse is real. They have tried to convince people that it is not real, that physical and mental diseases are linked to genetics. That obviates the need to get rid of it. They should have realized that it is as real as it is in people's heads, and that is pretty real!"

"Saying that something is not real is a bit silly, or a bit of a cop out," I said.

"Yes, when the problems it is causing people are evidently very real."

"This has brought us right back to our major theme of language," Richard said. "Because you," he said, referring to Philo, "have learned the languages, you can follow what people are saying. Following through translation would have been hopeless, for a start, because people get tired of translating into English. Secondly, also, because it is applied to all the wrong categories. When you hear the language, and you begin to grasp when terms are used, and how and in what contexts, then you can begin to understand from the inside where people are actually at in their lives." To my surprise, Richard concluded: "I used to think you were wrong to draw closely alongside the African people in the way you do. I also used to think that you were a racist for what you wrote about them. Now I see that I was wrong. You were only telling the truth, and truth that badly needed to be told. Your way of getting to be a part of the indigenous, is right."

Well, I had to smile, Richard was speaking like a convert.

CHAPTER 24: DRUMBEATS

As we drank tea, Philo left us to go into the kitchen where the ladies were busy preparing supper. Richard and I remained alone. Richard was checking something on his phone. I started reading a chapter of the Gospel of Luke. I guess I wasn't concentrating very much because some of the conversation happening in the kitchen was echoing in my head. Essentially what I picked up was *"kik ... dhi ... liel."* Those were easy Striden terms to learn. *Kik*—don't. *Dhi*—go. *Liel*—funeral. Philo was discussing with the ladies. They were saying *"kik dhi liel."* Philo wasn't disagreeing. They seemed to be discussing pros and cons. I did wonder—what was that about? Which funeral should one (who?) not go to? When? Why?

When Philo returned, we took advantage of the countryside around to go for a stroll before it got dark. This was to be our last night at Philo's home. His home is very African. He doesn't like having Europeans stay there too long. I think most of them don't want to stay too long either. Philo lives amid children. There's not much by way of privacy. There's certainly not much by way of luxury. Not even a decent sofa. Everything seems a bit thrown together. Philo had told me years before; he had to make an effort to be slack in his way of running things at home. To fit into the village scene, in order to live closely with peasant farmers, he needs to live in obvious poverty! Not pretentiously, but by forcing himself to accept circumstances which in Britain would be unacceptable.

It works though—Philo had already had children for over fifteen years by that time. Typically, he tells me, they have one leave every year or so, and a new one comes in. It means that the average length of stay for a child is twelve years—that's pretty stable. The children are very polite and very friendly, as well as being good at making room for guests.

Philo had explained to me once, it is not bad for a missionary to invest into a community, even using money from overseas. What he recommends though is: don't invest your money into the people with whom you will have your key relationships. Doing the latter makes it hard for people you work with in ministry to be honest with you. Typically, though, those are people you want to be honest. If you are at the same time their boss, then they can be pleasing you to make sure the money keeps flowing. In Philo's case, though, you could hardly say he was tight, not generous, or not caring, given that he had twelve children staying with him. The fact that he rode a bicycle, so didn't need to cover vehicle expenses, plus the fact that his village house was cheap to rent, left him with money out of his missionary stipend with which to keep the children.

Given the generally dense population in the area, Philo's home is in quite a pleasant spot. One does not have to walk far to enter a wooded area which includes a lot of diverse tree species. Quite a menagerie for a naturalist! Hence, we could have a good stroll. At the same time, although I valued staying at Philo's place, I was also looking forward to being back in my own home the following night.

That evening I had agreed to share the message with the children. I took the message from Luke's Gospel. Philo translated. I noticed that Richard was particularly attentive. He was clearly asking himself again what all this Christian stuff was about. He had seen his friend turn down a very high-paid job, wife, and children, choosing instead to give his life to live in this community in Holima. It was difficult to find anyone not committed to Christianity doing that. It came from his faith in Christ.

After we had finished dinner and remained chatting, we unexpectedly heard the beat of a drum nearby. It was evidently very close, so that the rhythm of the drum was loud and clear. The mellow, hollow, resonating sound easily penetrated the protracted silence of the tropical night. Outside, there was just a sliver of a moon to create ghostly shadows out of trees. There were a few distant sounds—a cow mooing somewhere, some cicadas, some children talking in low voices in bed, then through all that came another sound, a very distinct and very clear, very African drumbeat.

"What's going on?" Richard asked. The housemother sat with us, getting what she could out of our conversation in English.

"What? The drum?" Philo answered. "It's a drum." Philo added.

"Ha, ha," said Richard. The sound probably reminded him, as it did me, of Tarzan movies, or some past television viewing when we were children. The drumbeat came back again, just for twenty seconds, then stopped again. Then three drums in unison beat to a rhythm, becoming easily audible. The sound of the three drums began to feel creepy. It's like we had finally arrived in the "real Africa." Something mysterious was going on, and late at night.

"What's happening?" Richard asked again.

"A funeral," Philo said.

Richard looked puzzled. "What, now? How near?" he asked.

"Funerals, go on for days," Philo reminded Richard. We sat still and listened, as the three drums continued to roll. "They are only warming up," Philo told us. At that moment, the conversation I had overheard going on in the kitchen came back to my mind: "don't go to the funeral!" Wow! I wondered if this was the funeral mentioned that we should not be going to. Maybe the drums were calling on spirits that could end up haunting us. I said nothing. You could sense the way Richard was being drawn by that drumbeat. It was a post-modern drumbeat, I thought to myself.

Richard liked African music. I was wondering—would Richard ask the question? It seems Philo was asking himself the same thing. I noticed his shoulders move up and down as if to say, "We may have no choice," as he looked at the housemother. Richard wouldn't have seen that. His eyes were closed, he enjoyed the beat. I wasn't about to volunteer to go out to have a cultural experience in the middle of the night. But I couldn't put it past Richard. It turns out that Richard was thinking what we all seemed to fear. Seconds later, he said the fateful three words "Can we go?"

As he spoke, I saw the housemother move back in her chair just a fraction.

"Hmm," said Philo.

* * *

As I was developing my story for Julie, I saw her jump when a child came in and spoke to Philo. She was obviously captivated by the story.

"Lunch is ready," Philo told us.

"What, now?" Julie said, once the child had moved out of earshot.

"We must go, as the hot food is sitting on the table," Philo said.

"So, when are we going to hear the rest of the story?" Julie asked. "I'm fascinated," she added. "I really want to know all the things that happened that turned Richard around."

"I don't know, Dave," Philo said to me, "Time is getting on. I think you have to get back tonight?"

"Yes, we do."

"You should tell Julie the rest tonight at your place," Philo said.

"No!" Julie protested. "It's much better told when you are around," she added, looking at Philo.

Philo laughed. "Dave's the great story-teller," Philo said.

We agreed to break the story off there. We went and enjoyed some very good food. *Ugali* was on the table. That's the classic African staple, this time made from maize, but it can also be made of other cereals like sorghum or cassava. Knowing that visitors often struggle with ugali, rice was also on the table. The other "staple" was *chapatis*, made from wheat flour, carefully kneaded and mixed with layers of oil before being cooked in oil like flat pancakes. Cabbage was one of the vegetables. So-called *sukuma wiki* was the other. *Sukuma wiki*, literally translated back into English, means something like "push the week." *Sukuma wiki* was made from kale, but so called because it's the cheap vegetable that can be acquired every day, and makes the poor-man's week go by. Striden people, of course, are excellent at cooking tilapia (a fish from the local lake). There was also fried beef, and boiled and fried chicken, as well as eggs. Oranges were available for desert. Then, having a time of fellowship with the children reminded us of the things that we had just heard about Richard's time there.

I tried to convince Philo to come with us to Deja. He wouldn't budge. "You go and tell Julie the rest of the story, once you've arrived in Deja," he said.

"Will you though?" Julie asked me

"Yes, when we get home. We'll sit, no TV. I'll tell you the rest of the story," I agreed.

We said goodbye to Philo. That night I continued telling the story just to my sister Julie, without Philo around, in my house back in town.

* * *

So, Richard had asked, "Can we go?" I knew that a prior conversation in the kitchen had indicated that we shouldn't go. I did not know why. Richard didn't know about that. Philo had yet to speak.

"Well," said Philo, a little hesitantly, although Richard might not have noticed it, "I guess we could." I didn't see any resistance in the eyes of the housemother. She was slim and slight in build. One could say she was a very practical mother. She always seemed to have a wise word for the children at the right time. She realized that she would not be able to give a good reason for us not to go. Richard's clear declaration of intent, unprompted by anyone else, seemed to be a sufficient reason for her not to block us.

"Is it far?" Richard asked, oblivious to the conversations that had been going on regarding his simple request.

"Not far. Not far at all in fact," Philo answered.

* * *

"Why did the housemother and Philo think they might want to block your going?" Julie asked me.

"I did not know at the time, but they were wary that there might be fighting at the funeral. And that our presence could aggravate it," I said.

"Fighting! Why?"

"Tell you later," I responded. "You said you wanted the rest of the story, not a lot of additional explanation?" I reminded her.

"Fair enough!"

* * *

So, Philo turned to me and asked if I was interested in going to the funeral.

"I've never been at a funeral before, where people beat drums in the middle of the night," Richard said.

"Then you haven't lived!" replied Philo.

"We'll lock the doors," the housemother said, "but Philo has a key, so you can let yourselves in when you come back," she added, as I understood her. Or did she say, "If you come back?" I asked myself.

At the time, the drums weren't beating. Indeed, it wasn't far to the funeral. Two minutes of walking from Philo's home, and we had arrived. We found a homestead dimly lit by a few incandescent bulbs. A generator was humming in the background. There was mud underfoot. Groups of people were sitting on plastic chairs and on benches in different parts of the homestead. The veranda to the house at the top, the parental home, I assumed, was lit, and seemed to be a focus of attention. We made our way directly, guided by Philo, to that veranda. We found that it was the location of the coffin, outside the house at the top of the homestead. The first thing we had to do was to pray, standing at the coffin. Not sure whether we were praying for the person who had died, or for family members. Philo led our prayer.

As we were moving away from the coffin, three young men approached us. "Come this way," I guess they said, and they took us to where there were some seats. They were wearing long prayer-robes, with red crosses stitched into them. They were friendly, but firm. The oldest was tall, perhaps six feet, and seemed to walk with a stoop. The other two might have been just about fourteen, their faces still juvenile, pre-puberty, from what we could see in the dim light offered by the scattered bulbs. A funny thing then happened. After we had sat there for a while, some other young men came and took us away. This time they were wearing suits. They were of roughly equal height, and of a similar age, probably about twenty. One of them spoke to us in English. They were also very friendly, but perhaps a little agitated. Their shoes were caked with mud. They took us to some other seats across the other side of the homestead. Some minutes later, two of the initial three young men came to where we were, and took us back to where we had sat originally. Then we were taken back to the second place. This went on about three times, for six consecutive moves! Something was going on.

"Why do we keep getting taken back and fore?" Richard asked Philo eventually.

"This is a divided funeral," Philo explained.

"Whatever does that mean?" Richard asked.

"Long story," Philo said.

"Well, you'd better tell us before we get dizzy," Richard responded, sarcastically.

"There are at least two parts to this story," Philo continued. "Maybe the first thing you need to know is that there was a funeral right here not so long ago, perhaps eight months ago. It was the wife of the deceased who passed away on that occasion. I tell you this does not happen often, and you shouldn't expect to see any tonight, but a couple of white people turned up unexpectedly at that funeral. That couple turned out to be new to Holima. They had come to some poor people to help. They gave out a lot of money."

"Okay. Got it," Richard responded, although I think not really knowing what Philo was driving at.

"The other thing you have to realize is that the mother of the deceased is a very active member of one church, while the deceased himself worshipped at another church. Hence, we have two churches represented here tonight, not just one."

"Oh," I said.

"Now, one problem is," Philo went on, "that the two churches are not very much in agreement. The other is that—based on prior experience, they anticipate that if they get white visitors like us, someone is likely to win a jackpot! They are strategizing on how to make sure that if you decide to give a lot of money you will give it to them, and not the other church. Hence we are being moved back and fore."

"Okay. So, every time we shift we are going from the claimed territory of one church to that of another?" Richard asked.

"That's right," Philo said. "The reason they are so concerned is because we have white skin. So, they expect that suddenly one or other of us is going to make a generous contribution towards whatever church succeeds in hosting us. Now they ought not to think that way, because I am here and they know me. But they remain very wary about the tendency of unknown white people like you to be unexpectedly and unpredictably very generous."

"So we were being bandied back and fore to see who would get our money," I said, not sure whether I ought to laugh or cry.

"That's right," Philo said. Then he added a phrase that struck me, and remains with me very much today; "and it is the fault of white people for being so unpredictably generous."

I had thought at times about generosity being always a good thing. But what if it resulted in jealous competition for white patrons as was happening in this case? That made me think of a parent and their children. Parents should be careful that the way they give things to their children does not cause disputes, division, or jealousy. The system in Africa is not parent-child, but it is a rather similar patron-client. Most donors refuse the idea that they are patrons. They do not want to see themselves as patrons dealing with clients. They like to think of themselves as partners. But—I think, say what they like—they are likely to be perceived as patrons or potential patrons—then the situation can cause problems!

Our seating situation eventually stabilized. That back and fore did, though, help us to realize something that was going on. There were two competing churches at this funeral. We did not realize, although Philo probably did, that we were not just going to sit there and then go home. More was still going to happen that night at this funeral. People were asked to sit facing one direction. Two men stood up facing them. One of them wore brightly-colored robes. The other wore a suit. The one wearing the robes represented the church that liked to wear robes. The one wearing a suit represented the church that thought it was more important to wear suits than it was to wear robes.

The man wearing the yellow robe and a white sash said something. Then the man in the suit also said something. "Okay," I thought, "the man in the suit is translating for the man wearing robes." They carried on going back and fore. As they carried on, I began to hear a hubbub of dissent from the crowd.

"What on earth was going on?" I thought. "Are the people murmuring against these their leaders?" I looked at Richard. He was looking as perplexed as I was. I looked at Philo. He seemed to realize what was going on.

I whispered to him "What's going on?"

"They're not translating," he said. "Each one is thinking that the other is translating for him, while both are speaking and saying different things! I don't know how long this can go on."

As we carried on watching, the hubbub grew greater. Eventually one of the men stopped. He spoke to his colleague "You should be translating!" he said (I guess). I suppose his colleague said the same back to him. They stood there arguing, maybe for a minute. Then one of the men, the one in the suit, marched off. He gestured with his arm, after which about twenty people out of the gathered group followed him. They took their chairs with them. They set up shop at the far end of the homestead. A few more followed suit later.

Now I could see why there was a risk of a fight. We could be fought over, that was one danger. The churches were not agreeing with one another. Philo indicated that we should stay where we were. Another man stood up to translate for our speaker. Over across the homestead the suited man was talking. There was another meeting going on at the same time as ours! They had by that point asked one of their own people to translate for their pastor. Fortunately, I thought to myself, no one at this funeral had any loudspeakers! These were often used at funerals. Then one group might have aggravated the other by drowning them out using their loudspeaker. Or if both groups had loudspeakers … so much the worse! The whole thing could have been a crazy hubbub.

"I say we should stay here, because that church over there is more like the one we were at today," Philo said. "This one is a little different." In the background, we heard the noise of the other meeting going on simultaneously with ours. "According to them, we over here are unclean," Philo explained. I did wonder why that might be, but didn't ask anything straight away. I thought we'd probably find out sooner or later.

I was glad to discover some minutes later that the group we were with was the one with the drums. Previously, when we'd heard them from home, the drummers had just been practicing. Now we were to hear the real thing. The drums started rolling. Three young men each had a drum slung around their neck by a cord. In one hand, they held their drumstick. With the other hand, they used their palm to thud the other side of the drum, giving them essentially two sounds with which to produce a rhythmic melody. Singers would begin leading in a song, then the drummers would follow. From a distance, quite likely people would only be able to hear the beat of the drum that would travel much further than the voice of the singers. The drums were sufficiently powerful that we could feel our internal organs vibrating to the beat. The reverberations from the drums seemed to penetrate deep into our bodies. I wondered whether the beat of the drums would help people with heart conditions, as I am sure the vessels of my heart are rarely made to vibrate as much as they were that day! This was an African heartbeat, communal, arising from the beating of drums, late at night.

As we watched, the crowd surrounding the men beating the drums stood up. We stood with them. I could see Philo rocking to the beat of the drums. Richard stood still like a rock. I was more like Richard. We weren't as used to this as Philo apparently was. It was quite something to witness—the drums beaten so aggressively, combined with the crowd, particularly the women, seeming to have endless energy for dancing. We began to see, even in the cool of the night, streams of sweat pouring off the drummers' faces. Their clothes became soaked through with sweat. I looked again at Philo. None of this seemed to faze him, although he was glancing periodically in our direction, keeping an eye on us. I guess this is because he anticipated what was likely to happen next, and knew that we were going to be shocked by it.

The dancers seemed to get very carried away by and with the beating of the drum. Many of the women were jumping up and down aggressively to the beat, their white dresses flying as their breasts bounced. Then one of the women raised her arms above her head. She was still jumping rhythmically. She spun around a couple of times, then carried on dancing. Then she repeated the same manoeuvre. This time, however, she spun around more often, and seemed to keep on spinning. She began to fall sideways in one direction. In response to her falling, one of the women near her bent her body at the hips. She laid her body with outstretched arms like a wall alongside the spinning lady. Thus, she could stop her from falling too far to one side. She used her arms to further restrict the movement of the lady who was spinning. This enabled her to spin continuously without falling into anyone, although it was hard to imagine how she was not getting a lot dizzier than she seemed to be. Her arms were stretched out horizontally as she spun. The drums kept beating at the same ceaseless, aggressive pace.

The lady supporting her spinning colleague was beginning to have a difficult time. I looked across at Philo. This seemed to be run-of-the-mill for him. Nothing new here, said his eyes. I looked at Richard. It seemed to me like he couldn't believe what was happening before his eyes. Suddenly the spinner lurched into our direction. Richard started, and jumped to make room for her. Philo also shifted. A couple of women grabbed their colleague to stop her from falling onto us. I was shocked, and I think so was Richard. Not so Philo. I gradually realized though, that for the ladies in this church, not only was this not shocking, not only was it normal, but it was also what they wanted to happen! That realization amazed me. Why did they want to behave like this?

When the lady lurched in another direction, the answer to my question began to emerge. She grabbed the hand of a colleague. She proceeded to drag her colleague, willingly, to the outside of our circle. Then she came back and carried on spinning. Moments later she repeated the exercise with another lady, then with a young man. In between times, she would go back to spinning. The people who had been removed all shifted to one side. Once there, they would stamp their foot while clapping and shouting into the night air. After having done that for a minute or two, they would re-join the rest of the crowd, and then carry on dancing. The drums, of course, carried on beating continuously.

The next thing the first spinning lady did, was to move to where the leader of the worship was. She came clasping another lady by her waist, pulling her to the front. Both knelt there in front. She proceeded to tell the lady she'd pulled along something which I doubt even Philo could hear, it was said so quickly and quietly. Both stood again. All this carried on for some time. In due course, the beat of the drums changed. A while later, they were quiet. Soon after that, the lady (who had been prophesying) was kneeling in front of the men who were leading the service. While on her knees, she sat on her haunches, bent forwards, her arms lifted straight up behind her. With her arms, it was just as if she was going to come out of a butterfly stroke in a swimming pool. While she kept talking, this position seemed to indicate that her time of prophesying was over, Philo told me later. The man at the front raised his hand in front of her, and said some words confirming the same. Sure enough, she stood up and re-joined the other women, as if nothing had happened.

CHAPTER 25: THE *ROHO*

These were the activities that marked the lively climax of all that the church did that evening. They had opportunities after that for people to share their dreams. An interpreter was on hand to tell them the meaning of what they had dreamt. Many dreams, Philo told us, pointed to impending death. If the impending death and its nature is known, then people can be advised on how to avoid it. Usually the latter is done by a prayer of some sort. These were all elements of the churches', known as *Roho* churches, regular Sunday services. Here they were brought to the funeral. (*Roho*, an East African term, originates in Arabic. It is widely taken as a translation of the English term "spirit.")

After these various activities, it was already well past midnight. Then teaching ensued. Philo told us two things about the teaching of these churches. One, it was hard to understand. This, Philo explained, was because it drew deeply on the living contexts of the people. These were, Philo told us, extremely complex. Such complexity was rooted in endless traditions, sometimes laws, which had come down from the past to contemporary generations. Two, it was often very pertinent, sharp, and strongly contextualized. For Philo, the teaching from the Bible given by those indigenous *Roho* churches, was some of the best available: true Christian contextualization!

As we sat, the *Roho* church we were with continued teaching. Philo was given an opportunity to share, which he did for about five minutes, using the Striden language. Everyone seemed to appreciate what he was sharing. Across the way meanwhile, the other church (which seemed to be of a more Pentecostal style) was also teaching, with intermittent singing. They perhaps had the liveliest preachers. Certainly, the noisiest ones! It was sad to think that the two churches had to operate separately, independently, and in competition. It was even more sad to think that missionaries, i.e., well-meaning but over-naively-generous white people from the West, had unknowingly through over-generosity on their prior visit, aggravated that situation. This particularly troubled Richard.

While we sat listening to the two separate services going on, Richard commented, "If there is one thing I have been enlightened to here, it is how problematic it can be for foreign missionaries to be generous. That is not to say that generosity itself is wrong. But when, and to whom, and how to give. If missionaries come fresh to Africa, how are they supposed to know how to give and to whom? They must be guided by someone. Then they must take the advice they are given seriously. That is—they do not have the required knowledge to be discerning. Hence, who they will give to will be determined by who can capture them. So then, enormous efforts can be made at 'capturing' a white person coming."

I understood, following what Richard was whispering to me.

"That makes a missionary sound like an animal being preyed upon by lions and tigers!" Richard commented. "Is that really what a missionary wants to be? Then also—what the predators are after is not the gospel at all. If I was a missionary, then I think I would prefer people to see me as such, as someone bringing the gospel, not just money."

"But how?" I said, "Missionaries have such a reputation for generosity. Then, when new ones come, they perpetuate the same reputation. Very often they have money to bring, and that is a big part of their agenda. That may even be their whole agenda! They want to help financially. Everything else they do—even building relationships—can be with that aim in mind."

Richard added, "Now that I am here, I understand, it can seem really quite silly!" We were both quiet on the issue for a while.

Meanwhile Philo was busy listening to what was being said by the people in front of us, that we could not understand.

About 1.40 a.m., Richard suggested to Philo that we go home. Philo agreed. We set off back to the house. As we left, our hosts extended a warm welcome to us to the following day's ceremony. As we walked, I said to Philo, "Richard and I have been talking about the money thing."

"Oh," Philo responded.

It was certainly nice and cool walking at night. Not like in the sun during the day.

"Thinking about how those other white people created division between the churches, really made us feel ashamed," Richard said. "How can our people be doing that to African Christians? We now see that coming here with money to offer to African Christians can be really divisive and destructive," he added.

"What is crazy also," I added, "is that our colleagues do not realize the damage they are doing!"

"Better not to have any money at all," Richard said.

"What do you think, Philo?" I asked him.

"I'm glad you have seen this issue," Philo said, glancing at Richard, but also looking at me. "That is more than some. Many Europeans come and go without realizing what is going on. What to do about it—the kind of changes that are needed are often outside of the radar screen of European people concerned. They just don't get it! They perceive that a little money can go a long way here. It is tempting to give without thinking. Their excuse is that the Bible promotes generosity. Well, yes it does, but just as a parent must be discerning as to what they give to their children, we should make it clear that giving in Africa shouldn't be applied unthinkingly. There are many better ways of expressing love than giving money."

We arrived back at the house. We found a cup of tea waiting for us. That was a pleasant surprise. As we sat, Philo said, "In my view this issue is very complex, and can be looked at from many different angles. I think there is a kind of simple solution. This simple solution transfers the problem of unequal wealth, that we have seen can so trouble the Africans, back onto us. That is—*we need missionaries whose ministries are not built on outside money*. We need some such missionaries. We need more such missionaries. They can be enabled to do things and to work in ways that others can't. Then a big requirement which is currently very difficult for European missionaries and development workers—those few or many should be listened to and not condemned by other missionaries."

Philo was speaking from first-hand experience. Many missionaries preferred the security offered by their identity as a conduit of funds. African people rarely argue with them—they need the money. Both sides can easily end up not liking the vulnerable missionary—the one who does ministry on the back of local resources, as we had just done, and as Philo does. Fellow missionaries feel unsettled by such a challenging life-style testimony. This deception was running much deeper though, and we were realizing it increasingly. There were several substantial injustices going on, even in the name of mission.

I got a phone-call at 8 a.m. the following morning. I was needed back at work at 2 p.m. An urgent situation had arisen. I had to get back to Deja earlier than had been anticipated.

Breakfast was the final opportunity for the three of us to discuss what had happened over the last two or three days. Richard was at this point thoroughly disoriented and reoriented! He seemed to have gone through a paradigm shift. He had ditched almost all the understandings he had come with just three days earlier. He was thoroughly enamored by the case that Philo was making for missionary vulnerability. That is to say that some missionaries—and more than was currently the case—should use local languages and local resources in key ministry. Richard had already seen, in just about three days, all too many laughable disasters that arose if those principles were not followed.

Richard and I did have some questions for Philo about the previous evening's experience. Particularly about the *Roho* church.

"Perhaps an important thing to realize," Philo told us in response to some of our questions, "is that some of what we saw in the *Roho* church last night is in common to pretty much all African churches that are not obliged, typically through financial dependency, to do things the European way. In that sense, what we saw was a genuine expression of 'where is the African's heart?' That is to say—if we leave African Christians to their own devices, then they are led in certain ways. They are led, the evidence indicates, differently to ways in which Europeans are led. In this sense, if you go to indigenous churches like the *Roho* churches, you get the truth. You see something of what many African churches might be doing if it was not for missionary control from the outside."

"Wow, that's quite something to say," Richard stated. "You mean the others are hiding the truth?" he added.

"Well not so much hiding the truth, although sometimes they are. But— living pragmatically in a way that works. People who do things in European ways draw crowds. They bring benefits like having relationships with wealthy people and organizations. Bottom line— money. There are a lot of benefits to churches who fall in line with the European ways of doing things. Those benefits are not to be scoffed at. Unfortunately, that also means that there are dependencies going on and being perpetrated. Dependency on European resources is one of these. Dependency on unfamiliar ways of thinking is another."

"What do you mean by dependency on unfamiliar ways of thinking?"

"I mean," Philo said, "that if financial incentives to doing things in the European ways were withdrawn, then churches would change their way of doing things. Yes, they would move towards resembling the *Roho* church more closely."

"That's interesting," muttered Richard.

"A big issue raised last night, or was it this morning," Philo went on, "regards people's relationships to their predecessors. Since colonial days it is as if Europeans have been trying to disconnect African people from their past, including their ancestors. Many things have contributed to this effort."

"Like what?" I asked, although I had a pretty good idea of some of the things Philo was going to say.

"Lots of things. Trying to replace people's languages with English, trying to appropriate them into our European or American educational systems, condemning the way they relate to their dead, are just a few."

Richard nodded. Then he said, "What do you mean by condemning the way they relate to their dead?"

"These people relate to their dead through what we would, in English, call spirits."

"That was what was going on overnight. The lady who spun around — that was quite an impressive physical achievement."

"She was connecting with people in that gathering, dead people, that is. It indicated that she had the power that the people were seeking to draw from, to get insight that would help their lives."

"Frankly, what they were doing seemed crazy," Richard said. "If you are taking them seriously — that means you are crazy with them, Philo," he added.

Philo didn't immediately add to Richard's observation. It is like he wanted it to sink in. Maybe he was gathering his thoughts. Then with a deep sigh, he shrugged and continued as if nothing had happened. "Some people pretty much write them off, for that kind of reason," Philo said eventually about the *Roho* churches. "It's like they have a mental block, they can't get it, instead of seeing sense and taking on things like science, they continue to believe in the ability of their dead to communicate with them. I find that deeply troubling." Then Philo added, "That is why I reach out to them with the gospel. They are people who God loves. I believe that no-one is beyond the pale for the gospel." Philo took another breath; he was sharing from deep in his heart. He was revealing something more of the essence of his ministry. Others would not have touched these indigenous churches with a barge pole. Philo was right in there, relating to them. That was not just last night. He related to them constantly. Some might condemn Philo for getting so close to such movements. He himself had said—to some of the more Pentecostal churches, they are unclean. Philo saw himself as sharing the love of Christ with them.

"Once you get close to people," Philo shared, "you find that you are no longer sharing from a position of strength, but of weakness and vulnerability. They know what they are doing and how and why. And they do it well. You, as an outsider know less, and are less able. You appear weaker. What you are left with—is sharing Jesus with people, telling them about Christ, demonstrating your own faith through what you share."

"That sounds incredible," Richard said.

"It's killing me!" said Philo. That was a strong phrase. It startled both of us. We saw tears welling up in Philo's eyes. "People in the West hate it."

"I'm sorry for the ways I used to attack you, Philo," Richard said.

"That's alright," Philo responded. "But it was only the tip of an iceberg. It is everywhere. It is massive. We have intelligent men here, fully functional, leading their families and leading their churches. Missionaries despise them. Somehow, with the best intentions in the world, they ignore them. They consider them as dinosaurs. But they are people like you and me. They are just as alive as you and me. They are thinking people. They are intelligent people. They are people whom God loves. But if you get close to them, the West can hate you for it."

I did not have to ask Philo to explain more. Richard had seen what Philo was referring to. That is—a whole civilization being smashed into the ground. Last night, some of that civilization had put on a display for us.

"God loves all people," Philo went on. "He loves them—starting with who they are. He is interested in them. He cares about them. He desires to be known by them more and more. I believe that. Powerful mission won't cut the mustard," Philo said. "I am not saying there is no room for powerful mission. But there needs to be room also for mission that reaches the heart of the people. Mission is not primarily about telling people about a superior language called English. Mission is not about telling people how super and powerful we are, and how much money we have. Rather—mission is vulnerable, where the white man is no longer the big hero riding in on a black horse to rescue everyone, but a partner in discovery. A place where God is the only hero."

"I hear you," Richard said. And this time, he meant it.

* * *

Philo did forward some emails to me that I kept. They were between Richard and him. The first one was written by Richard:

Dear Philo,

I'm back home. Greetings from my family. I was very glad to get back to them. They are well.

I cannot forget all the things we went through together, dear friend. My week away from home has turned me around! My wife is still incredulous that someone can change so radically and so quickly. Yesterday, I went to visit my local pastor. I did not want days to go by without my opening up to him about my change of heart. I rejected Jesus in my youth. I see now, that was out of naivety. I desire to serve God. I am a new creation.

I apologize, Philo, profoundly, for the negative things that I used to say and write to you. I was wrong. I was a fool. I know I have already apologized to you verbally. Now I also want to put it into writing. Forgive me, Philo.

Philo—keep doing what you are doing. We are in prayer for you.

Richard

Hi Richard,

Great to hear that you got back safely and are at home and well. Greetings to your wife and family.

Your apologies are wholeheartedly accepted. You are totally forgiven.

Think of it this way: you did help me formulate what was in my heart. Something new—many of the issues that we discussed continue to press on me. I feel strongly that I ought to share them more widely. I am thinking of making a trip to the USA, and perhaps Germany and the UK to share the word. That should be for three months, starting in ten months' time.

Hope we will be able to meet then.

Philo

Hi Philo,

Wonderful news—that you are seeking to share the word.

I am glad you are going to endeavor to share the word on the importance of vulnerability in mission. I don't give you much cause for hope though, Philo. Remember how stubborn I was? There are a lot of people like that. It took me four days to turn around. That was under your constant tutelage, and with you there on the ground. I don't know how you will convince people in America—who are very set in their ways.

That is not to say you shouldn't try. I am right behind you. I herald your efforts.

Yours in Christ,

Richard

A week later Richard wrote again.

Philo,

You should do it! That is—you should make your trip and share the word on vulnerable mission. I think it is important that you do so. I have shared the same with my pastor. He agrees. We will pray for you regularly. You have something important to say. Take the word out there.

Next time you are in the UK do come to visit me, and do visit my new church also, and tell them what you are doing.

Yours,

Richard

Part III

Exposure

CHAPTER 26: A TRIUMPHANT ARRIVAL!

"Richard may think it's a good idea to travel to the West, but I am not so sure," Philo was saying to himself. Philo was committed to Africa, not to America!

* * *

"Where is the girl who combines beauty with character?" Philo would ask himself. That is: "Character, and a potentially strong commitment to serving God amongst African people." European girls came and went. Few seemed to meet the criteria. Then came a student on internship from a university in Vancouver. It transpired that although she had never been there herself, her father had been a Bible translator in Papua New Guinea. Her name was Norah.

"I am not even sure I have the wherewithal to impress a European girl anymore," Philo thought. "Was she serious, or was this a one-off trip to add to her résumé? In the West, the talk was all about sexual equality. Could some women be as keen to commit themselves to the gospel cause as men do? Might Norah be one of them? With that 'breeding' in Bible translation, surely she seemed a strong candidate? Might Norah be the woman for me?" Philo asked himself.

From what I heard also, Norah was, of all the young women who came to Africa, one of the more conscientious ones. She was serious. She wanted to know and fulfil God's will. This was her first time to travel so far from her homeland. It certainly was the adventure of a lifetime. Some girls, as some boys, don't notice the cultural differences around them. Norah did notice. They hit her between the eyes, it seems. Although mature enough not to show it, a shock, of the nature of *culture shock*, became her daily diet while in Holima. Norah was below average height for a woman. She bore herself confidently, and had an attractive figure.

A girl facing so many shocks of the unknown, seeks for someone who can help her better understand. He might even be a knight in shining armor. Perhaps that is how Philo appeared to her? Having been around longer than everyone else, knowing local languages, being academically highly qualified, being British, made him rather exotic. They say girls have crushes on older men, but Philo wasn't that much older than Norah.

Philo approached me on this issue. He phoned me. That's not an ideal medium for a deep conversation. I told him straight; leave her alone. "But she's so genuine!" was his exact response, if I remember rightly. I can certainly see that the idea of serving in mission as a married couple is very attractive. No matter how rough things are on the field, providing your relationship is strong, to go home to fall into the arms of a loving spouse who is longing to hear your stories, and a good meal on the table! Hmmm. That sounds good!

How to get her alone is, of course, always a question. "Let's invite her for a tour of the mission station," Philo thought. (Philo was at the time teaching theology two-days weekly with some American missionary colleagues.) That's a pretty innocent kind of thing to do. Providing he planned it right, they could be just the two of them. It worked!

"Here is the chapel," Philo told her. He explained something about the history of the place. Then he asked, "Would you be my girlfriend?"

"Yes," was her response. Philo knew what he had to do next. That would not have been the convention in North America.

"It must not be known," he told Norah. "People here don't court," he emphasized. Thankfully, Norah was ready for a few more culture shocks, and certainly ready to acknowledge Philo's superior knowledge of these issues, overwhelmed as she was that such a dedicated servant of God should have an interest in her. That approach certainly didn't indicate that he was about to drag her into premarital sex, so that was reassuring for her.

"Courting" in the West, UK and Canada certainly included getting to know a girl long before you propose to her. This supposed, for Christians at least who did not go along with sex before marriage, that you could enjoy a girl's company, and perhaps holding her hand as you walked, without being drawn into closer physical contact.

Mila's teaching came to Philo's mind. Mila sought to help British Christian young people to know how much petting was allowed before one had crossed the line premarriage, so that what one was doing was inappropriate before God. As Philo recalled, holding hands with your girlfriend in public was definitely allowed. Kissing, he was sure, was allowed. But what about here in Holima, in Africa? Philo knew that should people see a man walking holding the hand of a woman, they would quickly assume her to be a slut, or a prostitute.

I have observed a number of things myself. On my observation, in this African context, it seemed impossible for an African man and woman who feel affection for one another to be alone together without their engaging in full sexual intercourse. Petting, it seemed, invariably led to something more. Philo had told me similar things. Of the relationships he and I had known of, that had been influenced by the freedom of European culture, a Christian boy and girl spending time alone together always resulted in pregnancy.

"We need to, and can, communicate," Philo told Norah straight off, "but we can't *go out* in a Western way."

Philo enjoyed some days with a Canadian girlfriend, even though he never touched her, bar a handshake. Unfortunately, it wasn't to last.

"I'm going back to Canada," she told him. "You aren't going to follow me there are you?"

Philo had clearly told her about his commitment to Africa, poor fellow! He needed a slave, not a wife, I thought to myself. I was reflecting on the apostle Paul's self-description. It seems though, that to be the slave of a slave, perhaps a role for a wife for Philo, would be worse than to be a slave! I couldn't see it happening for Philo.

Then, Philo thought, "If I plan a trip to North America, then just possibly, that might convince her that I am serious?"

What this all demonstrated was that Philo's heart ached for a relationship, that was, after all, natural. Other men had wives to keep them company, so why not Philo? Perhaps that is why Philo sometimes comes across as stoic—his work required him to deny himself many of what were, to others, normal pleasures.

I wanted to tell Philo, "Look, are you really serious, giving the strength of your commitment to what you are doing in Holima?" I doubted whether such a move was going to budge the girl anyway. Although, it was intriguing to me that God might use such a scenario to get Philo to the USA!

* * *

A few weeks later, an email arrived from Philo: "Dave, if I go to Europe and the USA to promote vulnerable mission, will you join me?"

I knew that this question was coming. I had to admit that we did seem to work well together.

"Are you serious, or are you just chasing a girl?" I wrote back to Philo.

"Well, both, perhaps," he said, "but yes, I am serious."

"There is only one way it might work. I am due to spend three weeks with my mother in the USA next October. I don't know when you were planning on making your trip. I might be able to take some time out from Mum to spend with you then." October was, at the time, ten months away.

"Prayerfully considering it," Philo responded.

A few days later, I got an email from my sister Julie. "Dave. Philo has asked if I could join him when he makes a trip to the USA. He is thinking about next October. He said you might be joining him."

I responded to Julie, "I am planning to visit Mum in October next year. That's why Philo is looking at that month. I told him I might be able to take some time out from visiting Mum."

"What do you think?" she asked me. "Should I accept to join Philo?"

"That's up to you," I answered.

"I know," she said, "but what do you think?"

I thought about it. To have a woman around is always good, I thought. Philo knows Julie, and he likes her. "If Derek has no problem with it, then come along and join the party!" I certainly didn't expect her husband, Derek, to have a problem. Philo often spoke well to me about Derek. He was my relative, but perhaps more Philo's friend than mine. Derek had appreciated Philo enough to release Julie to visit him before, even though he himself on that occasion had not been able to make it.

Sure enough, an email also came from Richard. Philo is efficient! "Philo has invited me to consider joining him for a trip to the USA next October," he wrote, "but I am not sure that you will be able to cope with me. Before, I was very against Philo. Now I am very pro-Philo! It seems I am a bit like the apostle Paul: I start off by persecuting the Christians, then once converted, I'm 100% gung-ho! Maybe I'll come across as just too strongly in favor? If Philo has invited you, and you can make it, for goodness sake do your best to be there," Richard continued. I wrote back to Richard explaining my situation. He did not write again, so I could only infer that he assumed I would be accompanying Philo.

***

It was my experience as well as Philo's that it is hard for Holiman people not to notice when a white man is around. Walking around one invariably hears comments. Some only hear the comments when made in English. Philo would hear them also when made in Swahili or in Striden. Sometimes people just say *Whiteman*. A favorite equivalent in Holiman language is *mzungu*. Very often the white man is marked out by being greeted, when a fellow African might just be ignored. Someone may greet a fellow African with a regular vernacular greeting, or with silence. The chances are, though, that a white man would be asked, "How are you?" Crowds of children can run up to a foreigner, just to greet him in that way, in what they perceive to be his own language.

"Constantly having people shout at you because you are white gets wearing," Philo confided in me. I knew exactly what he meant. "The very morning I was heading for the airport it happened," he said to me later. "I was cycling. It was early—perhaps 7.30 a.m. I ended up passing several homes in a row. The children in one home would run up to me shouting at me. They then alerted the children in the next home who alerted the children in the next home, and so it went on. That happened for a few hundred yards worth of homes!" Children were probably the worst culprits.

Westerners coming on short-term visits love it when little children ran up to them with great beaming faces. I remember when I'd have an African colleague, they'd chastise me when greeted in this way if I didn't respond. That is for the first hour. After a while African colleagues would realize that a white person was a marked man. Children would ignore black men, but run screaming up to a white man. Once they'd realized, African colleagues would understand why I chose to ignore such mobs of screaming children, to discourage them from such behavior.

They did it though, because they were told to do so. I have met mothers as they walked towards me, and heard them say to their children, "Greet him in English because he is a Whiteman. Say to him 'How are you?'" Occasionally, I have tried to discourage mothers from such racism. I am not sure that they have ever understood me. At least, the practice continues.

Being greeted in English was common. Philo tells me that often, even when he was deep in African villages, people would say to him, with their voices expressing shock, disbelief and incredulity; "You know Striden?" or, "You know Swahili?" They would say this as if they were the only person ever to make such a comment. As if Philo did not know what languages he knew. The fact that one couldn't blame people for making comments like that didn't always make it easy to take the constant barrage of remarks. Unfortunately, most times local people were correct—white people are generally ignorant of indigenous languages.

* * *

"Hello, is this Dave?" said a female voice over the phone. It was 2.50 a.m.! I recognized the voice. It was Julie.

"What time is it?" I asked her.

"Sorry!"

"What's up?"

"It's Philo," she said. "I can't find him anywhere."

"Where are you, Julie?"

"Seattle!"

I was gradually getting my bearings. "You haven't seen Philo?" I remembered that they were to meet there that day.

"No. No sign of him. But his flight is in. I even managed to find out that he was on the flight. But no sign of him where we were to meet. I am wondering what on earth has happened, so I'm calling you in case you know anything?"

"I think he left yesterday," I said, "but then you know that if he has arrived. I haven't got a clue what might have happened."

At that point Julie allowed me to go back to sleep. There wasn't much I could do to help in Seattle, after all.

Julie, meanwhile, was tearing her hair out. Their host had come to the airport to pick them up, but no sign of Philo. She apologized to the fellow, also called *Philo* as it happened, who had come to pick them up. Philo-the-driver was of medium build, perhaps with some Latino blood in him. Probably the most striking aspect of his appearance was the way his receding hairline left a bushel of hair isolated by bald areas all around, above his forehead. That bushel of hair was like a reed-island in an East African Lake, Julie thought to herself. But now what to do? The airport seemed to be filling. How could they spot Philo? He had not yet got an American phone line. His Holiman-lines weren't responding.

Then an announcement came over the loudspeaker system; "Anyone missing a man thought to be called Andy aged about thirty, of medium height wearing red pants and a blue jacket, please go immediately to the airport medical service." Why he should be called Andy, neither Julie nor Philo-the-driver gave a second thought. Julie's heart started beating like a steam-engine on overdrive.

"Where's the airport medical service?" she asked the person selling peanuts and snacks a few yards away. He pointed. Julie and Philo-the-driver ran in that direction. Well, they didn't run very fast. Julie couldn't, but they went as fast as they could, elbowing their way through the crowds. They found a blue door. Written on the door were the words; "Medical access only." In no time, they had barged their way in.

The medics in the room jumped in shock, then recovered their composure.

"We've come to find the injured man described on the announcement," Julie exclaimed, extremely flustered. The medics were for a moment awed by her Scottish accent. Moments later they took her behind a curtain. Philo-the-driver also walked in. A man was laid there covered by a sheet. Julie was by this point shaking all over. Philo-the-driver was puffing.

"Take a seat," said the medic. They sat. Their world seemed to have collapsed around them.

A police officer also standing alongside the corpse stated in a firm voice, "This man was hit by a taxi crossing the road as he left the terminal. We have confirmed his name. He is Andrew Balovitch, a Russian citizen, just arrived in Seattle from Ecuador." Julie and Philo-the-driver were very still. "Andrew Balovitch, a Russian from Ecuador," Julie said to herself. Then they both registered—it couldn't be Philo!

"Let me see him," she insisted, just to make sure. They uncovered the face of a man with a large mustache. It was not Philo.

Julie became overcome by multiple emotions. It was hardly good news that this Russian man had just died, whoever he was, after a flight from

Ecuador. At the same time, she was elated that the dead man was not Philo. At the same time also, she was asking herself—then where is Philo? It was as if her head was rent into three pieces. Julie collapsed into a chair. A cascade of tears poured out of her eyes. She was exhausted.

Philo-the-driver took over. "She shouldn't be getting excited in her state," he said. The medics had by this time helped Julie onto another bed, and were attending to her. "We are looking for a visitor. A Brit who has just arrived in Seattle from Holima," Philo-the-driver explained to the police officer, a typical long-nosed American with the poise of someone who has been in the military.

"One moment," he answered.

Philo-the-driver overheard the police officer talk over the phone. "The man arrested for disrupting the peace, what is his name?"

Philo-the-driver heard the voice on the other end; "Philo, a Brit from Holima." Philo-the-driver couldn't believe it.

"Philo arrested, for disturbing the peace! They'd already mistaken him for a dead man. Now Philo the missionary was accused of being a terrorist!" he thought to himself.

"That seems to be him anyway," he thought. "There can't be that many Philos around, especially if the man just came from Holima."

"Where is he?"

"In police custody."

"Where?"

"Police Station, which is on …."

Before he could finish his sentence, Julie cried out in pain.

"The police officer and I looked at each other in shock," Philo-the-driver told Julie later.

"Ambulance!" said the officer.

At that moment one of the medics came alongside us. He gave one look at Julie and shouted, "Call an ambulance!" Within three minutes an airport ambulance had arrived at the back door, and two minutes later Julie and Philo-the-driver were being rushed to one of the city hospitals.

"It looks like it's going to be a breech," the medic whispered to Philo-the-driver, "but I don't want Julie to be worried."

"For her not to be worried," Philo-the-driver exclaimed later, "and here she was being rushed through the streets of Seattle in an ambulance, sirens wailing at full volume!"

Amazingly, Julie managed to give Philo-the-driver her phone as the ambulance momentarily halted.

"Call Dave Candomble, and tell him to Google *Seattle Police* and try to rescue Philo," she told him. She was still concerned for Philo, and had obviously overheard the conversation between Philo-the-driver and the police officer.

It was 3.30 a.m. in Deja. A call came from Julie's number. I did not recognize the voice. I could hear noisy ambulance sirens.

A male voice told me, "Julie is about to give birth. We're on our way to hospital in an ambulance. Find the number for Seattle Police Department. Call them. Philo has been arrested for disturbing the peace. Must go."

The phone was cut off.

"Philo's been arrested for disturbing the peace!" I exclaimed to myself. How on earth and what on earth. I didn't understand. How can Philo, a missionary in Africa of all things, be arrested within an hour or two of arriving in Seattle to visit a Christian university, for disturbing the peace? And in the meantime—Julie was about to give birth!"

"I told her not to go," I thought to myself, but she was too stubborn. She did not even tell Philo she was pregnant in case he would advise her not to join him in the USA.

Julie was probably in hospital, presumably receiving adequate attention, having finally got pregnant 20 years after her wedding! But what about Philo? Being held by the police! I jumped out of bed. I would have to go to work tired, I realized. I soon had the computer on, and got a phone number for the Seattle Police Department. The phone rang for about 30 seconds, then a lady picked it up. I started explaining what I understood of the situation.

She stopped me about a minute into my diatribe. "Police procedure will require you to submit a query in writing. Please make sure you include full information, including name and details of the defendant. Write to this email address with the following code given in the subject box."

Her voice disappeared. Instead, a six-digit number appended by two letters was repeated again, and again, and again, with an email address. I should send the email, then I would phone back as early as fifteen minutes later, quoting the same code. I followed the instructions. Twenty minutes later I was back on the phone. I was passed on to an Inspector Roble.

"Good evening, Dave," the inspector said. "We are holding your friend, Philo, here at the police station for disturbing the peace. Please note that this phone call is being recorded. Please let me know if you have anything relevant to say regarding Philo's case."

"What happened?"

Here is my summary of what officer Roble told me. Philo was found in the middle of a gang of African Americans. The African Americans concerned were charged with various offences, mostly to do with drug smuggling. At the time they were arrested, they were engaged in a raucous argument. Philo seemed to have provoked them somehow. The group was accusing him of making racist comments. "Our research has revealed that he is a missionary in Holima. Are you in Holima, and are you personally known to him?" asked the inspector.

My mind, by that point was racing. I couldn't believe that within an hour of his touching down in the USA, Philo had got involved with a drug-smuggling ring! I certainly know Philo well enough to be able to vouch for the fact that Philo was not involved in such activities. But how come he had got embroiled in such an issue? Of all the people at the airport, why Philo?

"Philo is a good and long-time friend of mine. I can personally vouch for his character. I am certain that whatever he was involved in has been a result of some naive misunderstanding," I said to Inspector Robles.

As I spoke, we seemed to lose network. I was on a mobile phone, and this was a common problem when at my home. I could hear nothing. I put the phone down, and tried again. "Hello," said a lady's voice.

"I want to continue my conversation with Inspector Roble," I said.

"I'll put you through," she told me.

At that moment, I noticed a smell. I realized my mistake. Not for the first time, I accidentally locked the cat into my room overnight. The cat had pooed in my room. I had to put up with the smell as I talked on the phone. I pushed the door ajar with my foot.

Seconds later the familiar male voice said, "Inspector Roble." I apologized for having got cut off, and told him of my network situation. He communicated having understood.

I reiterated my explanation: "Philo is a good and long-time friend of mine and I can personally vouch for his character. I am certain that whatever he has got involved in has been a result of some naive misunderstanding," I repeated.

"Make your case clearly," said Inspector Roble. "My colleague Inspector Davies is here with me. We are listening carefully to what you are saying. We are close to charging Philo with being a part of a smuggling network. Once so charged, the case must go to court."

Was I under pressure! "What to say?" I thought. There was only one thing I could think of. "The reason Philo mistakenly got involved with that gang was probably because seeing black people, and because he himself lives with black people, he became more familiar with them than would every other white European at the airport," I surmised. "Philo's entire adopted family is African. He loves Africans." I explained this over the phone. Then I added, "Philo is, you know, used to engaging in types of discourse in Holima that could be considered racist in the USA." My mind continued at 200% of maximum speed as I said that. "That's what can save us!" I assured myself. It suddenly became very clear to me that what I said was exactly what happened on the other side of the world there in Seattle airport: Philo's being accustomed to interacting with blacks made him over-familiar with the black men he met at the airport. That over-familiarity was misunderstood by them, which then got him into trouble with the police who thought he was part of the group.

At that point Inspector Davies raised her voice. That was when I discovered that Inspector Davies was a woman, and judging from her accent, that she was African American. I pictured her, rightly or wrongly, as about forty years old, plump, and with a round face. "Philo seems to be a racist," she said, I think. I worked hard to get her accent.

"Philo is a victim of racism!" I responded. This was incredible, that I should be having such a conversation with two Seattle Police Officers at 4.30 in the morning, while in my house in Deja, Africa!

"What do you mean, *Philo is a victim of racism*?" Inspector Roble came through.

"Philo is white, isn't he?" Inspector Davies added.

"Yes, he's white," I responded. Then I realized that the Seattle police force generally considered racism to be against blacks. They did not know that a reverse kind of racism might be happening too. I didn't know much about the Seattle police, so I had to try a bit of a shot into the dark.

"When Philo and I move around in Holima, it is very common for people to shout *Whiteman*! at us. Children especially do that. When they do it, no one tells them to stop. The Holiman people are extremely racist. I don't mean that they mean it badly. When they see a white person, though, people constantly comment when you are around. I hear them do that in English. Philo also hears when they do it in African languages. People talk about you, and laugh at you."

"One accusation made against Philo is that he didn't speak to those black men in English," Inspector Roble said, "as if he assumed them to be ignorant and uneducated. I am afraid that should you be right and Philo is not a drug smuggler, we will still be forced to prosecute him for racist behavior."

In far-away Seattle, Philo seemed to have landed in a boiling cauldron! Could I provide a quick defense of his apparent racist comments to get him off the hook and avoid masses of court proceedings?

"You people who accuse others of being racist are the bad ones," I said. I heard a wheeze from a female inspector.

"You know what your racist legislation does?" I said. "It elevates white Europeans. In America, and not only in America but also in European countries, everyone has to be treated the same. As if they are white. Do you realize that you have exported the same policy to Africa? Do you realize that in Africa as well, everyone has to be treated like they are a white European?" No one responded when I paused. "Things in Africa are therefore reversed," I said. "For you, it is racist to assume someone does not know people's languages. In Africa, it is racist to assume that someone does know the indigenous language. For you, it is racist to think that blacks are stupid. In Africa—it seems almost everyone assumes whites to be more intelligent than blacks. Not to do so would be considered," I hesitated as I searched for a word, "at least, strange."

I paused. I heard nothing for a few seconds. Then Inspector Robles said, "You mean that Philo should be excused from being accused of being racist, because he lives in Holima, where everyone is racist, so racism is the norm?"

"Yes!" I said. "You might think it is racism to think that a black man one meets in America doesn't know English," I said. "If you reverse that, then it would be racist to think that a white man does not know Swahili. I tell you though, my experience tells me that 100% of East Africans will assume that a white person does not know Swahili. You people's efforts in the West at doing away with racism are making a serious mess over here!" I reiterated, to drive my point home. I was just hoping that the case I was making might somehow rescue Philo from a long drawn out court case in the US!

Inspector Davies chipped in. "Allow me to clarify what I think you are saying David," she said. "If indeed Philo behaved in a way that could, in the US, be considered to be racist, that would be because of his living for many years in the African community in Holima. Philo had been in the US for just one hour when this incident arose. What you are also saying is that legislation that seeks to counter racism in the US, generates and perpetuates racism in Africa?"

"Yes!" I said enthusiastically, glad that she had understood.

"I don't get it," said Inspector Robles.

"It is clear to me," said Inspector Davies, in her thick African American accent. "I must admit it is something I had never thought about in this way. David has really opened my eyes," she added.

"I therefore plead on Philo's behalf that he be released without charge," I added. I continued to overhear conversation between the two inspectors.

"I think the case is already clear that Philo is not a drug smuggler," said Inspector Davies to her colleague. "The case that David has just made to excuse racist behavior on Philo's part is also extremely convincing." It appears the inspectors were unaware that I was still overhearing.

I coughed. Inspector Roble came back on to me. "Dave. Thanks for what you have told us. I will put you over to our assistant. Please make sure you give her an email address. Give us two hours. If you have not heard within two hours, then I suggest you seek the help of a professional lawyer. If we manage to waive all charges, that will happen very quickly, and we will make sure that you have an email to that effect at the very latest," the inspector paused as he made his calculations in his head, "by 6.30 a.m. your time. Good day."

The female voice of someone who obviously knew nothing of the issues in hand came onto the phone. She asked for my email address and phone contact. I gave her the information she requested. She called off.

The inspector seemed very serious when he'd talked about the lawyer. Within two hours I could be finding myself entrenched in a complicated court case in the US, with Philo in the accused box! Potential charges against Philo all sounded very serious.

An email came into my inbox at 6.15 a.m. It was from the Seattle police. Philo was exonerated. No charges were being brought. At the instant the email dropped into my inbox, Philo was discharged with an informal apology from Inspector Davies herself, in person.

CHAPTER 27: THE CULTURE OF FOOTBALL

While waiting to find out if Philo was going to be incarcerated, a plethora of news reports was coming from a medical centre in Seattle. "Looks like a breech birth," was the first report given by Philo-the-driver.

Fifteen minutes later, it was "Breech birth confirmed. Caesarean. Please pray."

Some minutes later. "No caesarean. Julie in coma. Please pray."

Then came news of Philo's release. That was a relief to people, although if Julie was in a coma, she could hardly have received that news.

"Baby in incubator. Mother still in coma," was the next news. I was reluctant to call Julie's husband. It was about 2.30 a.m. in the UK. Eventually, I did call him. Derek was a very conscientious man. He was an excellent listener, and often had deep insights on life. He also liked to do things right, making me think that his decision to let Julie go to the USA at this late stage in her pregnancy, probably caused him a lot of agony. I very much valued having Derek as my brother-in-law. He was tallish, thin, and had large feet—so much so that, Julie had remarked to me in the past that getting shoes for him often proved difficult. "I am on the next flight to the USA," he said. He was to fly from Manchester airport four hours later. I caught him ten minutes before he was to leave the house, he told me. That was not a long conversation.

Then came a call from Philo. "You won't believe what has happened," he said, "I ended up getting …."

I interrupted him at that point. "I know what happened," I said, "I got you out!" Philo was quiet. He obviously didn't expect me to know so much.

"Do you have any idea where Julie is, or the university driver who they tell me is called Philo?" Philo asked. "I can't for the life of me work out how to find them. The university people say the driver has gone to a local hospital. But then, what about Julie?"

"Julie has had a breech birth, almost had to have a caesarean."

"What! She was pregnant?"

"Yes. I realize that you didn't know. I suggested she go to see Mum. Mum is dying, Philo. I knew she was pregnant. She shouldn't have flown. The only thing I can think is that she got permission on the basis that she wanted to see her dying mother."

"I'm going to the hospital. Which one?" Philo asked. I told him.

* * *

Two days later I had brought my trip forward because of Julie's emergency. Philo and I were together at Western University in Seattle. I had seen Mum. I had visited Julie. Mum was in a hospice. Julie was recovering, her baby boy, also called Philo, was out of the incubator and in her arms. Probably in for another night, Julie was still racking up the hospital bill.

"Julie put her baby at risk on my behalf, then still called him Philo. You have been an enormous friend to me for a long-time, Dave. Now I feel like family—like you are my uncle! I guess that makes Julie my mum. What can be more valuable than an extra mum? So, what on earth did you tell the police to get me out of custody?" Philo enquired.

We were together with Will who was originally from Georgia, and was the department head for missions and development at the university, and his wife Debbie. Will had been our main contact there. He had certainly not expected his visitors to arrive in such a flurry of excitement. Will struck me as a typical Bible-belt Christian, totally committed to Christ and his work, probably with a reformed belief. He could be a little introverted. He appreciated company, but was also keen to analyze every word one said to him in great depth. Aged about forty-five, Will retained a head of relatively bushy hair. When he gave me a strange look, I filled him in.

"As soon as I got the report, I realized that what happened to you was something that we had often discussed in the past. You know how we had talked about the issues of race?" I asked.

"Okay, yes," Philo said. "You will need to explain that to Will here," he added. Instead, I asked Philo to give his account of what had happened.

This is what Philo said. "I was walking towards the place where we had agreed to meet Julie. That is where we were going to get picked up. I was contented and happy, not a care in the world. As I was walking along, I came across four black men. When I saw them, I felt at home. After all—Africa is probably where I feel more at home than anywhere else. So, I greeted them. In error, I greeted them as if they were Holimans. I greeted them in Striden! When they heard my greeting, their faces turned angry. I did not understand why. I guess I assumed they were acting as someone in Holima might. Pretend anger! They talked to me. Well—one of them did. He used Ebonics—a very broad African American accent. I repeated what he'd said in English that I understood. I think they said, 'Why you not talk to us English?' From thereon they started shouting and pointing fingers at me. I guess the basis of it was—I was being accused of being a racist. 'You think we are primitive African so don't know English?' they said, or words to that effect. Suddenly I was surrounded by those men shouting at me and pointing at me. This was a busy part of the airport, so we were obstructing the flow of people. Before long we were a crowd of ten as others joined in, either to appease or to stoke and aggravate the situation.

"Before long, airport security was onto the case. I said nothing further after I'd repeated the sentence of greeting above. The action happened all around me. There seemed to be nothing I could do to stop it. By the time the police came, I was still in the middle, and there was a group of black men angrily pointing their finger at me. I guess the police had no choice but to assume me guilty of something, so I was arrested."

"You know, the way the West is trying to avoid being racist is creating problems for everyone else?" I said, looking at Will.

Will sat up straight on hearing that. "What do you mean?" he said, "That's a new one on me."

"The West is talking of racial equality," Philo said, "but they less often think equality with what." There was quiet for a while.

"Well, in our case, we want to take foreigners as being equal to us Americans," Will said.

"Right. That's it!" Philo said. "Thanks for being so clear and explicit. That's exactly it. So, Americans are the standard against which everyone else is measured."

"I didn't quite mean that!" Will said, trying to defend himself.

"Yes, you did though," Philo said.

"Hmm," Will grunted.

"If a foreigner comes to the US, the idea is that he be treated the same as the people he finds already living here," Dave said. "So, for example—one expects people in America to know English. If you were to assume, based on someone's skin color, that they did not know English, well wouldn't that be considered racist?"

"Yes, very much so," Will agreed.

"If that is the case, then what should countries in Africa do to keep the same standard?" Philo asked.

"Well, they should also insist on treating everyone as if they know the national language, regardless of their skin color," Will responded. As he did so, I noticed his forehead folded up just a fraction. I don't know if Philo did.

"Which language?" Philo asked.

"Well, their language," Will said.

"Which is their language?" Philo asked.

"Well, in the case of Holima, English."

"Really?" I asked.

"Well, no," said Will.

"Yes and no?" Philo said. "Yes, because we've made it so. But, not really. Why and how have we made it so? By applying our notions of racism to their country," Philo added. "So, it just kind of so happens that whether you are in America or in Holima, the non-racist thing to do is to assume that someone you are talking to knows English. If they don't, then one should be surprised."

Will was obviously having to think hard about that one. He had always assumed, it appeared, that not-being-racist was simply a good thing. He had not really thought about the standard according to which racist behavior was to be assessed.

"So then in the US the 'normal' person is he who knows the native language, English. In Holima, then, the 'normal' person is the one who knows the foreign language, English. That's hardly fair, is it?" Philo said.

"In Holima, it should be assumed that everyone knows the local language, like Swahili," Will suggested.

"Nice idea," I said.

"What proportion of whites in Holima do you reckon know Swahili fluently?" I asked Philo. "About 0.01%!" he answered.

I had a sense of revulsion well up in me. I suppressed it. It was revulsion at Europeans' habit of dominating people, and not even knowing that they are doing it.

Philo came in. "This thing really hurts me," he said. "I don't want to sound brash or condemning. I am thinking of my children at home. The language policy in Holima has them really struggle to do the simplest things. They are often at school 7 a.m. to after 5 p.m. Then you ask them a simple question like, 'what is a quarter of two hundred?' and they don't have a clue. But it's not their fault!"

"So then," Will's wife Debbie asked, (this is the only comment she made through the whole conversation) "if the president speaks to the nation which language does he use? Surely that could indicate what is the real Holiman language." Debbie, on my assessment, was a very attractive woman, sporting a head of long, flowing brown hair. Probably just a little too plump to be a model, but she was the kind of lady whom one might have imagined could have been on the catwalk in a fashion parade in her younger years. She was careful to play "second fiddle" to Will, something that gave me the impression that she was both the most intelligent and the most out-going of the two of them.

"Hang on a moment," Philo said. "Who is important, people with money, or people without money?"

"Those with money," I suggested.

"Holima, as a country, is dependent on foreign charity, yes?" Philo added.

"Yes," Will agreed.

"So the important people are the foreigners. When the President speaks, he may seem to be addressing Holimans, but the people he is trying to impress are the foreigners. So, he frequently uses English."

"Hmm," Will murmured.

I think Philo knew this wasn't an entirely new topic for Will, but also for the sake of his wife Debbie, he added, "That doesn't actually only apply to presidential speeches. It also applies to parliament, to large-scale business, to the entire educational system—all those things are set up to please foreigners. And foreigners are taken in. That is—often they believe what Holimans (and the same applies to almost all African countries) say as if they are Europeans. It is as if all cultural differences have disappeared. Then they give funds on the back of what they believe to be the case according to Africans' use of English. They don't even see anything wrong with doing so!"

"So explain what you said to the police officer, who was it, Inspector Robles?" Philo asked.

"I told him that in much of Africa, white people can be seen as very special indeed, even if they are ignorant," I said. "They have brought almost all the wealth and knowledge that Africa has since emerging from their prior so-called primitive way of life. I don't know if it is because they respect, despise, love or fear them—but a white man is always treated differently. In some ways he gets preferential treatment. He gets looked at, talked about, called *Whiteman*, shouted at, pointed at, laughed at, jeered, and mocked. That's the treatment that Philo is used to getting in Holima. He did not see it as untoward to reverse that a tiny bit in the US. He forgot that what happens all the time to white people in Holima, must not happen to blacks in America. Therefore, Philo was deserving lenience. Thankfully, lenience is what he got."

"Wow. That was a complicated and serious situation," Philo said, reflecting on it, after a thirty-second pause.

Debbie meanwhile took advantage of our pause in the conversation to invite us to share in a light meal. We sat in front of an impressive spread. Amongst the choices were numerous salads and dressings. This was a foreign world to Philo. The Holiman diet he knew never included salads or dressings. Philo appreciated salads when he came to America, he assured me. The crops he grows are primarily maize and beans. That's like everyone else in his village. Sometimes some kale, some groundnuts, some sweet potatoes, tomatoes, onions and fruit like pawpaw. The daily diet for many people in Holima is maize and kale.

"So, what should be done about all this?" Will asked. "Listen, dear," he added to his wife, encouraging her to stay in the conversation rather than head back to the kitchen.

"Many of the answers, I know, are provocative ones," Philo said. "One thing would be to stop prohibiting racism."

"That's pretty provocative," Will said, while letting out a wheeze through the gaps between his teeth.

"Stop modeling race on white Europeans!" Philo added. "Okay. Something slightly less radical. How about encouraging some Europeans, say Americans, to try to understand other people?"

Will looked a bit taken aback by that comment. "You realize that to prohibit racism is to say that I don't care what you are actually like? Any difference between you and me and your people and my people I take as unfortunate and temporary. I will ignore such differences. I will treat you as if you are the same as me."

"That sounds like a gross distortion of the Biblical command *'Treat others as you'd have them treat you,'*" I said.

"Right," Philo said. "Laws that seek to prohibit racism are misinterpretations of biblical teachings."

"Even in secular society?" Will objected.

"Is there such a thing as a secular society? What is a secular society?" Philo jumped in. "So," Philo added, "we need to be able to seek to understand and even compensate for difference. Not just to steam-roller differences as is currently happening."

"Come on," Will said, "that's rather harsh."

"Harsh or not," Philo said, "it's true."

"I believe Philo," I said. "I've heard him before. Hear him out."

"Are you suggesting that even missionaries going to Africa are not actually wanting to understand the people they are reaching?" Will asked.

"We have already estimated that only 0.01% of white visitors in Africa know any African language fluently," Philo responded. "Or do you expect to get to know people while using your own language with them?"

I realized that this was basically impossible, because Philo had explained it to me before. I'm not sure if Will realized as much. "Remember also," I interrupted, "that usually African people do not want you to understand them. Remember that their true selves are considered an anomaly, primitive, misguided, uneducated, backwards, primal. They know that foreigners will look down their noses at them, if they discover their true character. It's easier just to keep up a pretence. Not only easier—also more lucrative. Better learn English and learn to imitate how the white man speaks it. Then you get friends, donors, money, prestige, degrees, blah, blah, blah."

"Okay, okay, okay," said Will. "How then does one get to understand the African as he is?"

"Use his language," Philo responded, "and don't buy him."

At that point Will's teenage son came into the room. The topic of conversation turned to water polo. He wanted to play water polo. He had not expected Philo to know how to play the game. "I've played a lot of water polo," Philo assured him. The two of them engaged in animated conversation. Although—while Philo had evidently once played water polo, Will's son knew more than did Philo.

Later Will said something to me that he obviously did not want Philo to hear. "Deep in my bones I think Philo is right," he said, "but he is too right. He comes out with truths that might obliterate someone else's lifetime's work in five seconds! Most of the people I know about cannot cope with that. Philo is too hot to talk to Americans!"

Philo remained oblivious of that short conversation. As we left Will that day, I overheard him say the following to Will: "You know the missing ingredient, Will?" Will turned and looked at him. "It is Jesus. We have swamped Jesus in English and in development. Jesus speaks powerfully into the issues we are addressing." There was no opportunity on this occasion for Philo to explain his point.

"I'm just very glad that the Seattle police dropped all charges against you," Will concluded.

As if to drive his point home, about Philo being too hot for Americans, Will called me that night. "Are you with Philo?" he asked.

"No," I said.

"Look, Philo has important things to say. But you can't let him loose on Americans. They'll, they'll, I don't know what, someone might end up hitting the poor fellow," Will told me. Now, Will might have been exaggerating. Americans aren't known for mobbing and beating up people. But, I got his point, and his point gave me cause for concern. How much was Philo going to aggravate the Americans he spoke to?

* * *

The following day was free of planned activities.

"What is the latest on Julie?" Philo asked.

"She's making an amazing recovery," I told him.

"I do feel bad that my crisis put her through a lot of stress. Maybe that is why she almost had to have a caesarean and the baby ended up a breech! I only hope the baby is healthy. Poor fella," Philo added.

"We've got some students come to meet you," Will said.

"Oh?" Philo responded, "Do they want to know about mission?"

"Perhaps," said Will, "but that might not be their main interest."

"So what are they interested in?" Philo asked.

"Meeting a Brit!" he was told. "We have, believe it or not, a British society here at the university."

"Made up of Brits?"

"Yes," was the response. It was about fifteen minutes later that three lads came to us. They all seemed to be about twenty. One, obviously a Liverpudlian, called Bill, who was very talkative, and two apparently from the East End of London. Bill, an engineering student, had a complexion that made you think perhaps he was from the Middle East or India. The other two lads, amazingly enough, both had red hair. It transpired that they were non-identical twins. All three had very conspicuous British accents. We were often told in East Africa that British people spoke through their noses. This was somehow particularly noticeable now that we were with them in the north-west of the US.

"Do you know who we are?" asked one of the red-haired lads, called Rod, looking at Philo. The name of the other one, I can't even remember. Philo confessed that he didn't have a clue. "Our dad supervised you for your PhD in the UK," Rod said. Philo made out that he recalled his supervisor for his PhD having twin lads, although I am not actually sure that he had. We did the inevitable talk about Britain.

Some minutes later, Will piped up "Let's watch a football match."

"Sounds good to me," Philo said. I agreed. That would give our brains a rest. It would help us to recover from the recent stresses. The three lads were keen to join us. They liked sport and valued cultural experiences. I went with Philo to see my mother early in the day. By late morning we were through. Mum was stable, but not well. We all joined Will, and went to the match.

"That's the strangest football match I've ever seen!" Bill told us a few hours later. We were sat having a cup of tea afterwards, in a restaurant. This time, to Philo's chagrin especially, the tea was not hot and milky as he generally liked it. There was no milk in sight, and there was ice in the tea. When he asked whether hot tea with milk was available, at first the girl did not understand. The notion that tea might be hot seemed to be strange to her. She had trouble with Philo's accent. Eventually she walked off with Philo's glass, that had ice from top to bottom. She came back with ice filling only the top few inches. When she put the glass down, she did not even look at him in the face. She had removed some of the ice, and added more tea. What more could we expect her to do? Philo wasn't too impressed, but had to make do. The waitress had gone.

I put two and two together. I realized that none of the three lads we were with, all being new to the USA, had expected that the match we were going to see was an American football match. The three lads drank water. They told us they needed to get off very soon. We had taken much longer than they had anticipated.

"I'm not surprised that you found the match strange," I said.

"Why, I don't know what was strange about it?" Will said. I laughed. "Have you ever been to the UK?" I asked Will.

"No."

"Then that's why I would guess you didn't find that football match at all strange." Will looked bewildered for a moment. Then he realized what was going on.

"Okay. Got it," he said.

"Do your matches always go on so long?" Rod asked Will.

"That was a short match," Will responded. It had taken two and a half hours. Others easily take four hours. What to Rod was long, for Will was short!

"You folks can't talk straight over a game of football," I said.

"Uh?" Rod responded.

"If that was football, and if that's what you play in America, then there's no doubt in my mind that British football is better than American football," Bill said.

Will became a little tense on hearing that. "How do you expect me to respond to that?"

"If it goes on for hours and hours, don't you get bored with it?" Rod asked, as his twin brother nodded. I am not sure whether the lads were being intentionally provocative, or just talking out of naive ignorance.

"No," Will said.

Rod explained, he was thinking that a football match that could go on indeterminately would disrupt everything else in life. You couldn't know, for example, which bus you'd take home. "How do you arrange your transport home if you don't know when a match is going to end?" Rod asked.

Will was confused now. Americans all drive their own cars. Many of them had never ever boarded a bus or a train. He did not know what Rod or the other lads were talking about. Their heads were stuck in a British context.

"You need to tell him about soccer. That's the American name for the sport you are calling football," I told Philo.

"In soccer, that's the proper football, we use a round ball, well, spherical actually, and we kick it," Rod responded, before Philo had a chance to.

Will, whose exposure to the UK and soccer enthusiasts seemed to be minimal, was not impressed. Much of the thrill of American football arose exactly because the ball is oval, not spherical, making the way it bounces unpredictable. To have a spherical ball would knock out most of the thrill of playing," he surmised. As for kicking the ball—well the Americans can kick it too!

"People who go to see American football," Will said, "want to witness aggression."

"You mean violence, people running in to each other?" Bill replied.

"They don't run into each other, they tackle," said Will.

"Look, we really must go," Rod said. "Don't take us too seriously; we enjoyed the match," he added diplomatically. The three lads said their farewells, and were gone.

"We're going to join some of your seminars," they told Philo as they went.

"This conversation is interesting, although perhaps becoming laughable. A farce!" I exclaimed after the lads had gone.

We sat quietly for a while. Everyone was enjoying their drink. I assumed Philo was enjoying his iced tea! Then Philo made a comment: "If we can't sensibly compare each different country's view of football, what chance do we have of enlightening people about Africa?" Will had lived for several years in Korea, but he had never set foot in Africa. How could Philo possibly enlighten him about Africa? How could he possibly enlighten Philo about what life is like in Korea?

"Very good point," I said. "Our descriptions of varieties of football seem to presuppose more than they describe."

"That's it," Philo said. "When Rod tries to describe soccer to Will, Will is struggling to appreciate what he is being told. It seems to him that he is attacking American football and is doing so out of ignorance. So, let's imagine," I added, "that soccer is like Africa and American football is like America. How on earth are Africa and America going to understand each other?" That question had us all thinking quietly for a few seconds.

Our conversation turned to the question of—who is best qualified to enlighten the American about the nature of soccer? We discussed two options: Is it Philo, the Brit, who probably knows soccer inside out? Or is it me, because I am an American? I've known American football since my youth. I used to play it. I've even been trained in it. Then subsequently I moved to the UK, and lived there for a few years. Am I better qualified to enlighten Will?

"Common sense would seem to say," Philo suggested, as Will and I were listening attentively "that I, or probably any of those three lads, would be the best equipped to tell Will about soccer. After all—we know the game inside out. But there is a problem. That problem is that we do not know American football." Philo paused. "We could also go further than that though," he added, "even in so far as I do know American football. I've just been to see a match after all—but I do not know it as Americans know it. I know American football as a Brit might know it. That's quite different to the way an American, like Will or Dave, might know it."

I realized that was why the Brits' comments to Will tended to be at cross-purposes. After a while I added, "In order to communicate the nature of soccer effectively to an American, it seems to be more important to know American football, and to know it as an American knows it, than it is to know soccer well!"

"To communicate effectively," Philo added.

"You are making some interesting points," Will said.

"Look," Philo added, "Are the points we are making primarily interesting, or are they also important?"

"Important in what sense?"

"Okay, let me repeat a little for emphasis. Then I will tell you what I mean by important," Philo said. "If I tell you, as the lads just attempted to do about American football in relation to soccer, you get upset, and you do not understand. Dave is the one who can help you to better understand."

"Hmmm," Will muttered, indicating that he was following.

"Also, I and the lads almost certainly are soccer men. I was born and raised on it. Dave knows it relatively little. Now let's think about international and intercultural relations. Let's think about who can most helpfully and most effectively explain what Africa is like to Americans. Is it a European who has been to Africa but knows relatively little about Africa? Or is it an African, who knows Africa well, but does not know much about America?"

"It is an African of course," Will said. "Only an African, born and bred in an African community who entered Africa head-first and not feet first, can be expected to know Africa. That's why we have employed Africans on the staff of our university. We want to ensure that our students get a good international flavour, and that they can hear about Africa from the horse's mouth."

"Slow down a bit," I said. Philo was looking towards me for support. "Will, are you sure that you have understood Philo properly? He is not talking about who has a better knowledge of Africa. That would be the African, born and bred there, as it would be Philo who knows about soccer, born and bred in England. The question Philo is addressing regards someone's ability to *explain* or *communicate about* something. Presumably, someone with a lesser knowledge of something can nevertheless be more able to communicate about it. After all, a nuclear engineer capable of running a complex atomic power plant may not be the best person to teach principles of nuclear physics to college students."

Will appeared to be puzzled, defensive, and angry all in one go! Fortunately, he forced those emotions to subside, and resorted to a face that expressed openness to listen some more. "Okay. So, the question even for our students may not be who knows Africa the best, but who can best communicate to them what Africa is. Is this what you are suggesting?"

"Right," Philo came in. "The most important quality for someone wanting to articulate Africa to Americans could be their knowledge not of Africa, but of America!"

This was coming to be an interesting discussion.

"Frankly, there is an infinite number of ways of communicating or describing Africa. Therefore, from when he first opens his mouth, someone teaching about Africa is making an evaluative judgment: out of all the plethora of things he could say, what will he say?"

"What do you mean by a 'plethora of things?'" Will asked Philo.

Philo explained with reference to his PhD thesis: "After I had failed my first viva for my PhD," Philo said, "my examiners advised me to include a section that was descriptive of the place I lived in and the people I worked with. I baulked at that suggestion. I told them, in not so many words, that it was a stupid suggestion, because of the sheer number of descriptions that I could have included. By my next viva, which I can say gratefully, I passed, they told me that my descriptive section was a waste of time!"

"Philo's told me about that before," I came in. "Yes, there are countless ways of describing Africa: you can talk about the cut of African people's hair, their GDP, their language, the soil type, the climate, their uptake of mobile-phone technology, their sexuality, how they respond when provoked, their taboos, things they eat or do not eat, how beautiful or ugly they are, whether their home landscape is hilly or flat … ad infinitum, ad nauseam!"

"Okay, I get it," said Will. "So then, if we bring in an African to talk about Africa, he either must make a choice out of an infinite number of options even regarding where to start, or we tell him where to start. In the latter situation, he is no longer speaking freely out of his knowledge of Africa, but following some European agenda about how Africa ought to be articulated."

"That's right," I said. "What you require from someone who will tell your students about Africa is a response to a discourse that is going on in America; and that requires a knowledge of America. Hence, we can even say as before, that for such a person, their knowledge of America is more important than is their knowledge of Africa."

"In order to know what to say to you, as an American football fan, about soccer," Philo came back in, "I needed to know American football. Even more importantly, I needed to know how you comprehend American football. Talking about the color of the bootlaces of soccer players will interest no one in the UK. For all I know that may be an issue in the US."

"Hmmm, I don't think so," Will responded.

"Okay, but you get my point?" Philo asked.

"Yes, I do," Will replied.

"So then," Philo went on, "the most important thing in communicating about Africa to Americans is not knowledge of Africa, it is one's knowledge of America!"

"That's quite a conclusion," Will said with a smile. We were all quiet for a while as Will seemed to be thinking. "I think it is also a right conclusion," Will added a few moments later.

"If that is the right conclusion," Philo went on," then why do you have African-born people on your staff to talk about Africa?"

"It may be a right conclusion," Will added, "but it is also a very radical conclusion!"

"It is," I agreed.

"I can add another thing," Philo said. "From my experience, African universities do not employ Americans to talk to their students about the West. That's because the African view of the West is one understood by Africans. It is a view that Americans typically do not get at all!"

At that point, Will was flummoxed. He did not know what to add.

"Expecting Africans to be the authoritative informers to the West about Africa has been a big, big mistake," I said, "and we have seen why."

"That practice is killing Africa!" Philo added.

"Why is it killing Africa?" Will interrupted, trying to defend his case.

"Because it is adding constant misinformation. African people expected to enlighten the West do not know how to communicate. Secondly, because it prevents other people from being taken seriously," Philo said.

"What do you mean it prevents other people from being taken seriously?" Will asked.

"If native-born Africans are taken as the authorities on Africa, then other people's views and articulation are, by implication, not taken seriously," Philo responded. "Things have to come from the mouth of an African, and that is silly," he added.

"If that's silly," Will said, now with considerable emotion in his voice, "then it is also silly for white people like you to go to teach Africans!" Will might have thought he was striking a mortal blow there, but Philo shrugged his shoulders.

"You are right," he said.

At this point, Will was angry. "Then why are you there teaching the Africans?" he countered.

I knew that Philo hated what was happening now. I was also sad deep down. "Why do people have to get angry like this?" I asked myself. People can be very amicable and claim to be very, very open-minded, until something comes that they find threatening. But the nature of discussion that crossed between Africa and America tended to be threatening. Threatening that is, of people's securities. It was tempting to avoid this kind of confrontation, just to say nothing, and talk about the weather. Then misunderstandings would just continue. People should listen instead of getting angry ....

"I am not, I am trying to teach Americans," Philo retorted, "if they are ready to listen."

"Bathroom break," I said. "Don't say anything till I've come back," I added. When I got back, it seems Will and Philo had followed my suggestion.

"If I want to know about Africa, then I'd rather learn from an African than from you," Will said. The bathroom break had not cooled him down very much. "I need to get home. I think it is time we went back to the university. I can drop you at your room."

Driving back to the university was a hair-raising two-mile experience. Will didn't say a word the whole trip. So, neither did Philo or me or Will's wife, Debbie. We cowered—trusting that no obstacle was going to come our way and interrupt our journey. Trusting the same also for our ongoing relationship with Will! We were trusting that the police wouldn't catch up with us for speeding. Will dropped us off.

We were back alone at our digs. Well, not alone. There was Julie and a crying baby Philo! Julie was proving amazing. A baby three days old. She'd had a difficult breech birth. Yet she was determined not to miss more action than she needed to. Moments later, her husband, Derek, appeared. He had come to collect Julie and the baby. Julie had waved her wand over our flat, filling the fridge, and rendering it all incredibly clean.

"How did it go with Will?" Julie asked. Derek sat with us, also listening intently.

"You can't take Philo anywhere!" I said. "Him and those British lads have upset Will. I think we might be booking the next flight home!" Philo was giving that nonchalant look. He did not know what to say.

"What happened, Philo?" Julie asked him.

"Americans like to think that they can think out of the box," Philo said, "but it seems I am not only taking them out of the box, but across the ocean. For all of the wonderful American character—perhaps that is more than they can cope with? Dave, this is crazy" Philo added. "Why, why, why do people get so upset over what we tell them? This is driving me crazy, and it's just so, so, so, sad. Sometimes it seems there is no point. We've lived in Africa. Why? To find out what's happening. For whose benefit? Not only ours. Not ours at all. For the Kingdom of God. For everyone. We take years to learn things, through the school of hard knocks, we travel thousands of miles at great expense to share the word. Then when you tell people something important, instead of listening, they get angry." Philo grabbed his Bible, and went to sit in a chair in the corner of the room. It was as if he was going to look for God's help with this issue. Philo builds up strong convictions over what he must share with Americans about Africa, to overcome difficulties and improve relationships. Why does this make some people so angry?

I left Philo to sit for a while. Then I went up to him, and I told him straight. "Don't shut up. Keep telling them. Sometimes people need to hear what they don't want to hear."

Philo looked up and responded, "You know, you are telling me to be a prophet. People never seemed to like prophets very much when they were around. Just read the Old Testament to find out. Later when they were dead and gone, they were declared to have been prophets of God."

Derek chipped in and said the same. "Someone has to have the guts to say what you are saying, Philo. You've got to say it. If people don't like it—then that's the cross you bear." Julie didn't say anything right then. She did write a note though. She left it on Philo's bed for him to find later. This is what she wrote:

Philo,

We stand with you.

You have an important message.

Share it.

Julie x

---

* * *

Will dropped Debbie off at a church fellowship, then went home incensed. If he'd have had a cat, he would have swiped it. Being alone in his house, he sat in front of the TV. All the while he was thinking, "Who is this Philo? Some kind of proud oaf!" Nothing from the TV went in. He was waiting for his wife, Debbie, to come home. Then he could unload on her. It was 9 p.m. and she was still not back. Then he heard the garage door open. Debbie walked in with a cheerful grin on her face. She had in the meanwhile taken their children to spend the night at a friend's. When Debbie found the TV on—she became wary. It was not common for her husband to be brain-dead in front of the TV of an evening. (Of course, Philo and I did not know all this that was happening at the time. Will and Debbie filled me in later.)

"Have you eaten?" Debbie asked Will.

"Yes," he said. She got him a drink from the fridge. "Turn the TV off," Will told her. Their remote was broken. She turned it off at the set. Will immediately launched into his tirade.

"Philo is turning out impossible!" he told Debbie.

"Oh?" said Debbie in a way that she trusted would encourage Will to talk some more.

"We had some long conversations today after the football match. Philo seems intent on attacking America," Will said.

"He says America has things to learn from Africa?" Debbie interjected.

"Yes, it's terrible!" Will responded.

"Did you hear what I said?" Debbie broke in again.

"Yes. What?"

"I said that Philo says 'you have things to learn from Africa,' and then you responded: 'it is terrible.'"

"Is that what you said? Is that how I responded?"

"Yes! Well, do you still go along with that statement?"

"What do you mean, dear?" Will asked his wife, by now a little confused.

"You said it was terrible that we have things to learn from Africa. Most of the time, I hear you say the opposite, that we have a lot to learn from Africa, so what's changed?"

"Yes of course we have things to learn from Africa," Will reiterated Debbie's words, "but from Africans. Not from people like Philo. He's one of us. Except he is worse."

"So, Will," Debbie went on, addressing her husband by his name to make sure he was hearing her clearly. "You should learn from Africans. Philo should learn from Africans. But neither of you should learn from each other about Africans?"

"Of course," Will responded, "for goodness sake that is why we employ Africans on our university academic staff. We have students go on field trips and internships. Some go all the way to Africa. We have books in the library written by Africans. What does Philo know?"

Debbie had clearly thought much about this through following earlier conversations. "So, according to your reckoning, you here in Seattle with African books and a few Africans on staff are too knowledgeable to listen to the likes of Philo—who has lived right there in an African village for nearly thirty years, and who speaks their language with them, daily? Sounds to me like you are too proud to learn from anyone who is not African. There is something else I have been thinking about," Debbie went on, not actually giving Will a chance to answer her question. "That is—how do universities in the US get their African staff, and where do they come from?"

Will by this time was enjoying realizing yet again that his wife was one of the most intelligent women in Washington State!

"They come from Africa." Will got a quick response in before Debbie could carry on.

"I know that," Debbie answered him, "but what I mean is ...."

"Yes?"

"On what basis are they employed by the university? This question has been troubling me for a few months. What I am asking is—do they, in choosing to come to teach here, reject other similarly lucrative career opportunities, or does this end up being their only option?"

"What on earth do you mean, Debbie? You sound like a scrutineer, whatever that is."

"Let's look at you and your American colleagues at the university. You have made career choices on the basis of personal conviction. In most, if not all cases, the choice to teach at a university, such as this one, meant turning down better-paid alternative employment."

"You can say that again!"

"Hence, you are here to fulfil a calling and not primarily for the money."

"Fair enough."

"Can the same be said of the African faculty you have talked about?"

Will started to see where his wife was going with her questions. He thought about it. "The African faculty have all been teachers at African theological institutions. They came here for further study. Some of those who were found to be bright, were taken onto staff."

"So, when they came onto staff, did they have equally lucrative alternative career options?"

"No," said Will. "Their alternative was to go back to Africa, where employment opportunities, salaries, and opportunities for bettering themselves would have been much lower. What you are implying, and unfortunately, I think rightly so, is that the kinds of Africans we get onto staff at European theological institutions tend to be those who are most apt at pleasing Europeans. Yes, of course you are right, if they were not so, they would not be here in the first place."

"I suspect that they have to spend years and years learning English, then come here, many of them to become yes-men," said Debbie. "The reason you are reacting against Philo is because he is threatening that comfortable status quo. You can dominate Africans, but it is not so easy for you to dominate Philo when he speaks the truth—because he is a fellow European! Philo has spent thirty years acquiring a voice at great personal cost, in a way that none of us have deigned to do. He has not married, his children are African orphans, his annual income is a small fraction of ours—we should listen to him!"

CHAPTER 28: HEADS ON

Will did not take his wife's advice lightly. He respected her greatly, and he respected what she said. She had made a good point. He had begun to see much the same thing himself—when he realized that his frustrations had got the better of him. Now Debbie had explained things clearly and comprehensibly. Will had much re-thinking to do.

Will was a good friend to the vice-chancellor of the university. The circumstances seemed to warrant paying him a visit. When he phoned him the following morning, the vice-chancellor, Kevin, said he'd be free at 10.30 a.m.

At 10.32 a.m., Will knocked on his door. Kevin welcomed him in.

Kevin, unlike some vice-chancellors, was very approachable. He was the kind of vice-chancellor who would at times sit at mealtimes with students. He was a bit of a prankster—he had been known to pick up a broom to sweep the hallway outside his office when he was expecting an important visitor. That humor had not always been appreciated. Some people despised Kevin, originally an ex-Canadian military, for these kinds of antics.

"Kevin," Will said, after turning down an offer of a cup of coffee, "there is something here that I think warrants your attention."

"What would that be?" Kevin said.

"I guess you know that we have a visitor called Philo with us for this week?"

"Yes," said Kevin. "I believe he is taking a few classes in the Africa department and the missions department."

"That's right," Will responded. Will paused. Then he went on: "He is on to something. I think you should hear him yourself. Perhaps even with the senate that, I understand, meets tomorrow. He keeps, apparently innocently, coming out with perspectives that seem to undermine a lot of what we do. He undermines things, then gives a clear justification for the ways in which he has undermined them."

"It would be very unusual to invite a visitor like that to address the senate of the university," Kevin said. Obviously, in the ongoing conversation, Will convinced him.

That evening we were to be engaged in one of the strangest and most unexpected conversations I have ever had in my life. The following day was a potential opportunity for the senate of the university to give audience to Philo. Members were informed of that possibility to give feedback if they wanted to. Kevin was to decide on whether to invite Philo the following morning. Philo, for the time being, knew nothing about that plan. Nor did I.

The phone rang later that evening. The two of us were in our guest room at the university. "Hello, Dave speaking," I said, after picking up the phone. There was a woman on the line.

"I want to talk to you about Philo, and about tomorrow's meeting," the voice said.

"Philo is here with me listening in. I am Dave," I confirmed.

"It's about the meeting tomorrow," she said.

"Oh," I said, looking at Philo. "I didn't know that there was to be a meeting tomorrow. What meeting?" I asked.

"Between Philo and the university senate," she replied.

"Okay," I said, trying to sound as if I was not totally perplexed. Philo flinched. He sat up straight in his chair. This was also news for him. No one had told him that he was to meet the senate the following day. The voice on the phone appeared to be ignorant of the fact that Dave and Philo might not yet have known about the meeting. She assumed that Philo and Dave were fully informed.

"I am calling to warn you," said the voice on the phone, "to be careful of what you say."

"Excuse me. You haven't told us who you are?" I interrupted.

"Professor Nancy, a member of the senate of Western University, in Seattle," she enlightened me. I swallowed. I tried to recollect having heard the name before. I think she was a prominent member of the local business community, as well as being a professor in the university. I couldn't remember what she was professor of.

Professor Nancy carried on by repeating what she had already said. "I am calling to warn you to be careful of what you say."

She seemed a little hesitant as to how to go on, so I asked her; "What do you mean, professor?"

"You may not be aware that we have, in this university, worked very hard at cultivating our donors. We are very close to clinching very significant amounts of money. That money will go towards projects to be overseen by university staff, to promote essential services to poor communities in different parts of the world. I am telling you that donors do like to look at the minutes of the senate meetings. If they find anything contrary, that could be bad news for those projects, and it could be bad news for the whole university."

We were in the ironic situation in which Philo was being warned about what to say or not to say in a meeting before he had been officially invited to it!

Nancy paused for a while. "It could be especially bad news, of course. for those poor communities that stand to lose the services they have been anticipating. That's the crux of the matter, and I hope Philo bears that in mind as he waxes lyrical in front of the senate. Good day," she added. Then her voice disappeared.

I looked at Philo. "Seems this is where the rubber hits the road," Philo said to me.

"Hmm."

"Let's put the matter to prayer," he suggested. We did—both of us prayed, there and then, for wisdom and for guidance. When we had finished praying, we heard something that was very unusual in those days. Something that used to happen in the 1970s and 1980s. Someone walked past our room outside with a ghetto blaster! It was playing a song. The song was admonishing the people who were using the temple as a means of making money. It was describing how Jesus overturned their tables and chased them out of the temple. We had received the answer to our prayers.

* * *

Philo told me he was due to take a class at 11 a.m. the following morning. We reasoned that if the senate were going to invite him, it would be then, instead of that class, so that they knew he would be available. Sure enough, around 8.55 a.m., a courier brought a sealed letter from the vice-chancellor's office. I was sitting at my computer. Philo was writing some notes in preparation for his anticipated class. There was a knock at the door. The courier had obviously been given specific instructions. He was to hand us the letter, make sure we read it, then to verbally make the same request as was stated in the letter, receive a response, communicate it to the senate, then give us a ride to the meeting to get there by 11 a.m. The letter specified that the senate was looking forward to an audience with Philo. He needed not be concerned about making a formal presentation, as they would ask him to respond to their questions. They were looking forward to hearing answers that came from his heart.

"This is beginning to be more like an exercise in espionage than in giving a set of lectures!" Philo commented.

"Whatever else your message is doing," I said, "it is having an impact!"

"What on earth are they going to want to hear from me?" Philo asked, rhetorically. "They have my books …."

We had some time to kill, so we sat for a while. "Have you been following Holima news on the internet?" Philo asked me. I hadn't.

"Tell me about it," I said.

"Storm clouds are gathering," he said, ominously.

"Meaning what?"

"The next election might be a dodgy one, from what I am hearing," Philo told me. "Politics is already very hot, and the election is still far away …," he added, "but I am concerned." I told him I would be checking news on the internet more thoroughly from then on. I did. That election was to majorly interfere with all of our plans and activities.

At 10.45 a.m. the courier knocked on our door. He was obviously a good time-keeper. He was of Indian extraction, and spoke with a strange Indian version of an American accent. He was brisk and efficient, as would befit the uniform he wore. We went down into his vehicle, a pickup, as it happened. He took us the half mile or so to the vice-chancellor's office. We spent three minutes or so sitting on a comfortable settee outside, before the door opened and we were ushered in.

In the room, eight people sat around a large table with a shiny brown surface. All around the white-painted walls were pictures of groups of students, presumably going back to the founding of the university. Except, that is, for one side of the room. That side was lined with four large windows that gave an incredible view over a wooded scene. Although past its best, some of the tapestry of that year's fall colors was still visible. Especially noticeable at the far end of the room was a large clock, funnily enough a square one, apparently made of a reflective metal that could have been gold, or copper. There were two spare seats remaining at our end of that rather imposing-looking boardroom table. The vice-chancellor signalled that we should sit. A drink of water was set before us. A coffee percolator was standing on one of the side tables. One of the members of the senate indicated that we could help ourselves at any time. As he said that, the door opened. Will came in. He sat in a chair alongside the senate table, obviously invited into the room just for this session.

* * *

The vice-chancellor, Kevin, began speaking. He thanked us for coming. He explained that the groundswell of interest arising from Philo's and my visit had reached his ears. Will, especially, had encouraged him to hear what we were sharing, from the horse's mouth. He decided to give the senate opportunity to do the same. "I will ask three simple questions," Kevin said, addressing Philo. "Please answer those questions. I am afraid that your answers must be short. That process should take ten minutes. Then we will have another fifteen minutes for discussion." All present seemed to be very attentive.

"First question," Kevin said, "and please answer briefly," he added. "If a people already know English, why address them in their own language?"

I was grateful for that question. So many people never get beyond this. They think, well they know, that once English is known somewhere, then there is no longer any point in using anything but English. I could imagine Philo faltering, and not wanting to anger more people. I looked at him, and gave him what I hope was a look of assurance, encouraging him to be courageous. He caught my look.

"A brief answer—and given the time constraints I can only answer the question in part—" Philo spoke clearly and plainly, "is because the missionary and development worker needs ears. He needs to hear responses to intervention, some of which local people will not translate. Secondly, even when they use English, the categories people imply through words in English can only be understood if one grasps the relationship between the English that people use and their indigenous language."

"Second question," Kevin said. "An institution such as ours has raised funds to help provide basic services to the poor in other parts of the world. Philo is encouraging missionaries and development workers not to use funds. What should we do?"

I glanced at Nancy. She was around fifty-five years old. Her confidence levels indicated that she was indeed a prominent community leader as well as a university professor. Although she was glaring at Philo at the time, I got the impression that her "glaring" was motivated by her genuine concern that the right thing should be done. Professor Nancy's head bobbed up and down slightly, especially when she was listening attentively. Perhaps she had been the prime person responsible for raising the funds being referred to? She saw her enormous efforts might be thrown to the wind! This was a more difficult question than the first. Not that it was more difficult to answer as such. It was difficult because answers could be just too threatening. Professor Nancy was now certainly a case in point for Philo.

"I am not going to comment directly on use of money or otherwise. We all know that Jesus chased the money changers out of the Temple," Philo said. At that point Professor Nancy took a deep breath. "I do suggest that we need some missionaries-cum-development workers who base their relationships with majority world nationals on something other than financial and linguistic superiority. The latter I believe to be the biblical model."

"Thank you for being brief," Kevin said. "Third question. What is the future of European mission in Africa?"

This question took Philo longer to think about. This is what he eventually said in response to it: "Bible translators have had an excellent focus bringing God's word to people in their own language. We should take that as a foundation to build on. Some will object that there are too many language groups in Africa. We Europeans don't have to learn all of them. But we can start somewhere. Neighboring language groups do learn from one another."

"So instead of doing our thing, you mean we could be a part of doing their thing?" Kevin reflected.

"Yes, let's volunteer to join in doing their thing," and then Philo added, slightly ominously, "and at their pace."

Because of Philo's succinctness, only nine minutes had elapsed. Kevin indicated that the floor was now open for questions. One of the board members, who I later heard was a large business entrepreneur, coughed. He was called Sam. He was short and stocky, and sported a splendid moustache.

"We approach a community. They themselves say they prefer to use English as the medium of communication. Should we discount their preference?" Sam asked.

"You approach a people and ask them whether they would prefer an option that you could fulfil (English) to one that you could apparently not fulfil (speak to them in their own language), which one will they opt for? If we are the powerful ones with the resources, then we are the ones who should change that dynamic. Give people a choice. Will they prefer their better-known heart language, or an outsider's language they have been taught by foreigners? Remove money from the equation," Philo emphasized the last point.

"How do you remove money from the equation?" Sam asked.

"There's your challenge," Philo said. "Can the great Western nations ever not be known for their money? If not, what kind of greatness is that? What kind of Christian mission is that?" Philo's challenge was left hanging.

At this point Professor Nancy raised her voice. "Philo," she said. "Would you deny a poor African community the access to water that we could give them?"

"Are Africans so stupid that they cannot get water for themselves?" Philo responded.

Professor Nancy's face turned purple. "You tell me," she said. "You live in Africa."

"I appreciate that the question as to whether Africans are too stupid to get their own water is not a question that Americans want to ask," Philo said, feeling himself to be fighting a street battle with racism. "I submit that there are reasons which disallow some African communities access to water. These reasons might justify some extensive research. Unless, that is, America is going to take responsibility for plumbing throughout the continent? When I say take responsibility, I don't mean a project with a five-year horizon, I just mean *full responsibility*. The kind of responsibility political leaders in America have for their own constituencies. Anything less could be construed as interfering."

Professor Nancy appeared to be a bit undone by Philo's responses. "So, tell us—just where does the African brain fall short?" she asked.

"In which African language do you want me to tell you?" Philo responded. I gasped! I'm not sure if my gasping was noticed. I am not sure that all of the senate got Philo there. I felt that I did understand him clearly: use English, and African people will seem to fall short. Use an African language (as used in respect to its indigenous context), and European people will fall short. I hoped that Professor Nancy understood Philo there.

"Why should we listen to you?" Sam asked his second question.

I was looking into Philo's eyes when Sam asked his question. Suddenly Philo's eyes welled up with tears, he seemed to rock, then he sat down. He put his head down—almost between his legs. He started sobbing. "Will you excuse me?" he said, although it was hard to make out his words, he was so overcome with emotion. Philo walked out of the door. I followed him. The others remained sat where they were. Philo was sitting on one of the chairs outside the office. I sat down beside him.

"You alright?" I asked. He didn't respond. I guess he couldn't; he was too choked up.

"I appreciate what the senate is doing asking frank open questions, but I couldn't cope," Philo croaked.

"It's okay," I told him. Philo sat for about five minutes. Kevin had, in the meantime, come out. After five minutes, Philo stood up and was ready to walk back into the boardroom.

"I'm fallible and human like the rest of you," Philo responded," but I'll give you a challenge," he added. "Find another European who speaks an African mother tongue fluently on a regular basis, and see if he (or she) says the same things I do."

I could see members of the senate thinking, did they know any Europeans who regularly used an African mother tongue? It seems they drew a blank. Then, in my own mind at least they were thinking; "Why do we need to hear a European who knows an African mother tongue. What's wrong with listening to an African who regularly uses an African mother tongue?"

"You might be asking why a European who knows an African language should be privileged over an African who knows English?" Philo asked. He was evidently assuming what I was! "Africans are a collective people. They tend to close ranks. In brief—for most Africans, not to be pleasing Europeans is to put too much of their livelihood on the line, and those of their families—who have mostly become grossly dependent on European charity, such as the provision of water mentioned by Professor Nancy." Philo paused. "More generally," he added, "the best translators are those most familiar with the world of their hearers. Will can confirm that."

"What's that got to do with me?" Will piped up, apparently having wanted to keep out of the conversation.

"Remember the soccer and the American football?" I said to him.

"Oh! Yes I do," he said.

"What's that about?" Kevin inquired.

"Oh," Will said. "We watched a game of football with Dave and Philo. It was interesting. Of the three of us, I know only football. Dave here is an American, but he also knows something of soccer. Philo, as a Brit, knows soccer much better than does Dave. We concluded that the best person to help me to understand soccer was my fellow American."

"On the same basis, the best person to communicate Africa to the West is an American who knows Africa and not an African who knows America," Philo added. Some queries followed from different members of the senate, after which most seemed to grasp this key point.

The vice-chancellor shared his heartfelt thanks for Philo's and my time at the university in general, and specifically for the input we had given to the senate. We were allowed to leave to permit the senate to go on with their meeting.

Round the corner from the boardroom was a small room with chairs. "Let's collapse here for a while," Philo said. We sat. We took a cup of coffee each—Philo's decaffeinated.

"That was tough," Philo said.

"Yes, it was," I agreed.

"You know who I'm thinking about?" Philo asked. It seems at the time we were both led in the same direction. Of course, Philo expected me to say no, but I thought I did know who he was thinking about.

"Yes," I said. Philo gave me a surprised, quizzical look.

"Who?" he asked.

"Joseph," I said.

"How did you know?" he responded.

"I was obviously right," I replied.

"Yes," he said. "Amazing." After a pause, adding "Do you think that's right?"

"Yes, I do." I said.

"Tell me how?" he asked.

"We are talking about Joseph whose account is given in Genesis 37–50, if I get you right?"

"Right on," Philo confirmed.

"Joseph telling God's truth to people who didn't want to hear it made him very unpopular, so much so that his own brothers hated him, and sold him into slavery. Joseph remained faithful to God to such an extent that he ended up the prime minister of Egypt. From that position, by saving food in years of plenty, he was able to save the lives of millions of people (lots anyway), including the lives of those who had wanted to kill him but instead sold him into slavery," I said.

"You've got it Dave," Philo responded. "Do you think that's a good analogy?" he added.

"Joseph's brothers hated him for telling the truth. You had better carry on telling the truth," I said to Philo. "Who knows whether that might not end up saving millions of people?"

CHAPTER 29: SMALL MIRACLES

When we got back to our accommodation, Julie was there. "How's Mum?" Philo asked.

"Not too well," she said. "Doped up on morphine, she's in the hospice. Derek is with her right now. Her thinking is still pretty clear most of the time, but bodily, she is deteriorating very fast indeed." I was due to spend time with her that evening. In fact, for the following two days, I was hoping to spend a lot of time with Mum. So, I was going to leave Philo to complete his teaching engagements at the university by himself.

I tried to pack some stuff. As I did so, I noticed that Philo had gone to pick up baby Philo. He sat rocking and talking to the baby. Not sure baby Philo understood! Philo had a lot of time for children. Back in Holima, Philo's life was all about children. Many men like to put their feet up and watch the football of an evening. When Philo was at home, he would tell me, he spent many long evening hours chatting with the children. Now here in the USA he had fallen in love with Julie's baby.

Before I had gone anywhere, Julie made an announcement. "There was a phone call from Ryan," Julie told us.

"Ryan who?" Philo asked.

"Ryan, you know, for the conference," she answered. Indeed, the conference was just three days away. We were having occasional conversations with Ryan about different things. I wasn't surprised that he called, looking for me, or more likely for Philo.

"There's some amazing news," said Julie.

"What?" I asked, "Tell us!"

"No, I won't," she said.

"Go on!" Philo added.

"Secret," she said.

"You mean you know this news Ryan told you, but you won't tell us?" I threatened to pick Julie up and drop her off the veranda!

"Don't do it," she said. "I'll tell you." But when I sat down again she still didn't tell us! "I would have told you by now," she said, "if my brother wasn't such a big bully!"

At that moment, the baby cried. Julie went and suckled him. He became quiet again.

Julie had prepared a light lunch. "If you don't tell us, then I won't eat," Philo said to Julie.

"Best kept secret," was her response.

"Okay, don't tell and I'll throw your food into the bin," Philo threatened her again.

"You throw my food into the bin, baby goes hungry, cries more, your fault, you suckle the baby," Julie said to Philo. I guess Philo realized that would be hard, so he acquiesced and started eating, leaving Julie's lunch just where he found it.

"Meeting a success?" Julie asked Philo.

"Yes," he said, "I think so."

"They paid attention!"

"Hmmm."

"You startled Will when you called him to give evidence!" I said.

"It did—he didn't know he had already become a convert," Philo said laughing, "helping us give evidence in court!"

"Most senate members didn't say much," I said.

"Did you see the purple colour though on Professor Nancy's face!" Philo commented.

"Who?" said Julie suddenly.

"What do you mean, who?" Philo asked her.

"Who went purple?" she said.

"Professor Nancy," I said.

"Oh! She was at the meeting?"

"Yes, you know her?"

"Secret," she said.

Philo said, "Obviously, Professor Nancy has something to do with your secret. When did Ryan say he'd call?"

"2.30 p.m., when he's out of a meeting."

"Okay. It is 1.40 p.m. now. Fifty minutes and your secret is out. The fact that Professor Nancy is part of your secret does intrigue me! What do you think, Dave?" Philo added, looking at me, "Do you think we've converted her?"

"Judging by the particular tinge of purple on her face during the meeting, I shouldn't say so," I replied. We all laughed. Julie laughed more knowingly it seemed, than the rest of us!

"What did Julie know about Professor Nancy?" I was asking myself.

"Did I ever tell you," Julie said at that point, "that a group of us have started up a ladies' fellowship in Scotland?"

"No," I said. "I didn't know about that!"

"There are a lot of very depressed and discouraged women in Scotland," Julie added.

"Hmmm," Philo exclaimed.

"You two have been part of my inspiration," she added. "We are calling it 'Joseph's wives.'"

"Why Joseph's wives?" I asked.

"Because Joseph refused to try to quench his depression through fornication. Joseph went through some great difficulties. Through them all—he believed God had greater things in mind, and he did—he used Joseph to save all the people in Egypt." Philo and I looked at each other. I don't think Julie noticed.

"That is excellent," Philo said to Julie, "and very encouraging to find that God has given you a heart to do that kind of work!"

At 2.50 p.m. the phone rang. It was a lady's voice. "I'd like to speak to Dave or Philo," she said.

"Dave speaking."

"Two things Ryan asked me to tell you," she said. "I'm his PA, Cynthia. First, and this will amaze you. A private media company will cover the conference for the purposes of producing a documentary to be made available on YouTube and, if possible, broadcast on TV."

"Who, wha …, why …, ho …," I stammered over the phone.

"If you want to know why or who—ask someone called Richard," she said.

"That's amazing," I said. When I thought more about it, I wasn't so sure. Did we want the event televised? It looked like we had little choice—Richard seems to have just arranged this for us off his own bat. I thought that must be the secret Julie had been referring to! Surely Cynthia didn't have more news to add?

"There's something else. Ryan said to let you know that one person has registered and paid in full for twenty-one people to attend the conference," Cynthia added.

"You hear that, Philo?" I asked him. "Twenty-one people registered by one person!"

"Why?" I asked Cynthia.

"We don't know," Cynthia said. "The lady who registered all twenty-one seems to be with you in Washington State," she added. "She is called Nancy. She works right there at the university."

"Professor Nancy!" Philo and I said in unison, as we both looked sideways at Julie who was wearing a broad grin.

"She has registered twenty-one people!" Philo added, amazed. "Ask her who the twenty people are, assuming she's the one!"

I asked. "Big people," said Cynthia. "The list reads like an honours list of key mission fundraisers in North America."

"It seems Nancy has influence," I said to Philo. "That has boosted conference attendance to an anticipated eighty people," Cynthia said. "Ryan did say to tell you though—re-check your notes. Cross your t's and dot your i's. The calibre of people coming has raised this to the level of a key strategic event. I'm afraid Ryan is unlikely to have time to talk to you today," Cynthia added. "Anything else I can tell you at this point?"

We had nothing. She called off.

"That is incredible!" Philo said. "Has Julie gone?" he added.

"Yes, looks like she went," I said. "Julie has bounced back amazingly. Don't know why she went without saying goodbye. Good job Derek's around for her. You must be chuffed at her calling her baby Philo?"

"Very, very chuffed indeed," Philo said. "Julie has a heart of gold. Tell you what though," Philo added, "we need to call Richard."

"He won't be in bed?" I asked.

"Not yet," Philo said. Three minutes later we were on the phone with Richard.

"Yes, I did it," he conceded. "I put up the fee money. They're not going to do it for free. I thought word needs to get out there, even if I am not going to be at the conference myself."

That night, I think I can speak on behalf of Philo as well, our heads were so full, neither of us was going to sleep quickly. I think Philo was still chuffed at having a baby called after him. Then we were full of thoughts regarding the upcoming conference.

I went to see Mum the following day. I told her all about what had been happening. I think she was glad, and she understood, though she could not speak. The smile on her face seemed to be one of incredulity. Whether she was only really happy about baby Philo, or whether she was also pleased about the growing prospects for our conference though, I could not tell.

The next few days were filled, for me at least, with a kind of pensive expectancy. I am very grateful to Julie that she agreed to stay with Mum, and let her enjoy the baby, thus releasing me to attend the conference. I had been very much hoping to attend. By the time we went, the anticipated attendance had risen to 150. That's not a phenomenal number, but the calibre of people who we were now anticipating was beyond what were initially our wildest dreams.

* * *

A couple of days later, and there we were in Pennsylvania. The entrance hall to the conference site, PATS (Pennsylvania Theological Seminary), was a buzz of activity as registrants arrived and began to find their way around.

Philo invited me to join the meeting of the committee at the time of the opening of the conference. One issue was particularly notable in our discussions.

Ryan gave an opening report. He was tall, imposing somehow in appearance, with Irish blood, of which he was proud. He was a mission's tutor at PATS.

"Many of you will know that about two days ago the registration for our conference was boosted by a total of twenty-one people, all of whom registered simultaneously, and whose conference fees were promptly covered by one payment out of one bank account. The key person responsible for this group seems to have been Professor Nancy, coming from the same university in Washington State where Philo and Dave have just been. The twenty-one-people concerned are all, we can say, key leaders in mission and development organizations here in the US. Their coming has no doubt contributed to the general flush of late applicants we have had since. Registrations over the past two days bring our total conference attendance to an anticipated number of about 150 people. The facilities are adequate for that number. This represents approximately a doubling of original expectations regarding attendance levels.

"Of particular interest, and perhaps concern, is that the group of twenty-one have not come without their agenda," Ryan added.

At that point, I could hear various people in our circle drawing breath. "Did people join conference *en masse* to determine, at the last minute, the direction or content of the event?" I asked myself. A low-level of murmuring ensued, as Ryan paused to allow what he was saying to sink in.

"Dave and Philo have already briefly shared with me the content of a meeting they had with the senate of Western University in Washington State. Apparently radically opposed to their input, and a member of the senate, was the same Professor Nancy who is leading the entourage of twenty-one," Ryan went on. "This group of twenty-one have not come to learn from or to benefit from our agenda, but to oppose it." Ryan looked around to assess the responses to that of those looking at him.

Philo piped up, "That's fine. We welcome her. This conference is open to everyone. I am just a bit surprised that they should attempt to so swamp a conference with contrary views."

Ryan pulled a pile of papers off the desk beside him. He handed them around. There was a letter written by Nancy and counter-signed by a total of, I counted carefully, a total of twenty-one signatures. Ryan stayed quiet to allow us all to read the letter. The key paragraph in the letter read as follows:

> We are extremely concerned that the vulnerable style of missions and development work that you are advocating at this conference is contrary to American interests. We are concerned also that it is contrary to the interests of the majority world. Many, if not all, of the signatories to this letter, are heavily involved in the raising of funds that are to benefit members of poor communities around the world. We perceive that Philo and those who are working with him are endangering our fund-raising strategies. Therefore, they are endangering the livelihoods and future hope of billions of our less well-off brothers and sisters around the world.

The proposal addressed to us members of the organizing committee regarding the direction the conference should take was contained in the next paragraph:

> We therefore propose, seeking your amicable approval for this suggestion, that appropriate forums be included in the conference, not only for the purposes of hearing what is being proposed, but also for a re-examination of its basic principles. We congenially suggest that space be made within the program, so that there can be open discussion and presentations of views that are contrary to the main agenda. We think this is of vital importance to safeguard the interests and progress of numerous people and numerous institutions concerned for the poor.

From where I sat, I glanced at Philo. He was laughing. His eyes expressed disbelief. If I am not mistaken, I saw him pinch himself. I looked at Ryan. He was also looking at Philo. Ryan was shaking his head in a slow rhythmic motion. At that moment, a lady entered the door pushing a trolley of drinks and refreshments for us. Ryan announced a tea break. Our laughing and silent incredulity turned into an aggressive hubbub of conversations as members of our group endeavored to come to terms with, and to grapple with, the scenario we were now facing. Ryan let us carry on our discussions. The clinking of cups, saucers, spoons, and rustling of candy papers ran on simultaneously with intense deliberation as people shared their amazement at the turn of events.

About fifteen minutes later, Ryan chose a coffee cup to act as a bell and a spoon as clanger. We went back to our places, most of us clutching a cup of some sort.

Debate went back and forth—how should we change our program, if at all? How to adapt it for good television viewing? How to accommodate the desire of Nancy's group to bring our agenda to its knees? We all agreed that Nancy's coming with her group of twenty-one was doing us a great favor.

"What is intended by saying there should be space for open discussion and presentation of contrary views?" Philo asked.

"People are free to speak freely at a conference," Ryan shared.

"But should they be allowed to hijack the agenda?" I asked.

All sat quiet for perhaps ten seconds. Then Ryan said what we were probably all thinking. "With their money, you mean?" he asked.

"Can that happen? Surely not!" Philo asked.

"Yes, it can," said Ryan. Ryan had apparently thought ahead on that one. "When the theme of a conference is somehow related to poverty. Well—there are two ways to overcome poverty. One is to encourage, by some means, people to help themselves, perhaps by being industrious, using initiative, innovating, working hard. The second is by giving them money."

"The latter results in dependency and certainly not sustainability," I added.

"But it is a very tempting way to go. Once money is offered, whether or not it will be in people's long-term best interests—that is almost certainly the way they'll go."

"So that is why," Philo asked, "you say that conferences held in poor countries attended by wealthy Westerners often cannot work? The money is just too irresistible?"

"Yes, that's it," said Ryan. "The main agenda of the poor becomes pleasing potential donors. Anyone who suggests anything to the contrary may be politely listened to, or publicly disparaged, but either way their contrary agenda is not welcome, as it might put donor money at risk."

I could see Philo trying to process these thoughts from Ryan.

"The same issue extends to discussion by indigenous people," Ryan added. "In secret, they can be honest, but whenever their discussion is formal, and can be interpreted to the ears of the donors present, they will be very careful of what they say and how they say it."

"So you mean a lot of the big conferences arranged in poor countries to address poverty, actually curtail the real agendas in this way?" Philo added.

"I am afraid so," said Ryan. "It is also very difficult to get around this issue. And it is really sad."

"Sad?" said Philo.

"Yes, sad." Ryan reiterated.

"Why sad?" Philo asked. "You obviously know more about conferences than I do."

"It is sad because it is so misleading. Wealthy Westerners come from such conferences thinking that they have heard the truth, when actually they have been presented with ploys angling at their money."

"Wow!" Philo said. "But we are not in the poor world here," he added. "We are in the USA."

"You are right of course Philo," Ryan said, "but …." Then he paused.

"It only takes the pressure of two or three or even one or two people from the majority world to swing a whole conference. Western people will defer to such people as having superior knowledge, not realizing that, frankly, they are obliged to speak in such a way as to ensure that donor offers continue."

"Obliged!" I exclaimed.

"Actually, that makes sense, Dave," Philo came in. He was trying to follow Ryan's argument.

"'Obliged,' for example, through family pressure—hospital bills to pay and children's need for school fees. Remember that many majority world cultures are communal and not individualistic. People function according to the demands of their community, and they really often have no choice."

I grunted.

"I am trying to follow you," Philo said to Ryan, with the rest of us overhearing, "and I can see that in a conference even in the USA, once the donor agenda is given traction, everything else can go to the wind. Also—that it can take the presence of only one or two majority world nationals to bring about the shift."

"That's it," said Ryan.

"But then," Philo asked, "What should we do?"

"The solution is easy but hard," Ryan said, puzzlingly. "First, for our conference, I think if Nancy and her entourage are coming, so be it—it's an open conference, we pray for God to lead. Also—there are some majority world nationals who will speak up against donors. Let's hope we have someone of that ilk."

"Okay," said Philo.

"More generally though," Ryan added, "dependency is a big trap. Many global conferences are arranged by, and funded by, big donors. What chance then of having an agenda that does not play ball with donors? So, we need conferences that are *not* arranged by big donors."

"Yes, that's the next problem. So then—you need conferences which donors or their agents do not attend."

At that point Philo laughed. "How are you going to keep donors and their agendas away?" he asked.

"Think about it," Ryan said.

"I'm trying," said Philo, "but it defeats me." Philo looked across at me. I didn't know either what Ryan was driving at.

"Language," said Ryan.

"Language?" Philo repeated.

"Yes. Use a language that donors don't get!" Ryan said.

We were all quiet. "What about translations?" I asked.

Philo looked at me nodding.

"This is a tough one," Ryan added, "but translation must be disallowed."

"Disallowed!" Philo exclaimed, laughing again. "But we have so many scholars in the West desperate to hear what majority world theologians and leaders are saying," he added.

"That's why it's difficult," Ryan added.

"So, those very scholars who are trying to learn from the majority world are the very ones who are the problem!" I exclaimed. Ryan gave me an affirming look. "So, the way forward is conferences not sponsored by wealthy Western (or Western-leaning) donors that *must* be in people's indigenous languages, and for which there must *not* be translation!" I exclaimed.

"Well I never …," said Philo.

"Look," said Ryan, "this is a planning meeting for our conference."

"Yes, yes," said Philo, "but this discussion has been very enlightening."

"I agree. Let's go on with our conference planning," I said.

As we talked, I couldn't help but think that Nancy was probably largely unaware of what we had just discussed. At the same time, she would be aware that her interest was also giving our conference a great boost. Just the fact that her group had come, and how they had come, added enormous prestige to our event. I loved her desire for openness and truth that had her do what she did.

"Drawing together contributions from various members of the group," Ryan said, "I propose the following." I noticed that everyone was attentive. "Both Nancy and her group and the television crew have come to share in our event that we have organized according to our requirements. We welcome them all. I do agree, however, with those who have suggested that we make some changes. Especially, that we open the door to a great showdown, or as I said earlier, battle of Armageddon. I suggest that there be a plenary session to be given a total of three hours for Friday night, 6 p.m. to 9 p.m. That can be held in PATS' great hall. We can even invite outsiders to the conference to join us for that evening for a small fee." Positive murmurs and light applause indicated a general approval of Ryan's plan.

"The program for that Friday evening is what we still need to work on," Ryan added, "Any suggestions?"

"Okay. Here're some thoughts," I said. "We have a total of three hours for Friday night, yes?"

"Yes," the others agreed.

"So, let's give Philo and Deborah half an hour each to present. Then we break for twenty minutes. In that twenty minutes for refreshments, let's solicit questions. Then we have three quarters of an hour of questions and answers."

"Who will chair that?" Ryan asked.

"Find someone," I suggested. Then after the question and answer session, we pause for ten minutes. Then, somehow," I added, "we try to pull all the loose ends together."

"Who will sum up?" Ryan asked. "That is—who will pull the loose ends together?" Minds were working on this, but no one spoke.

"I tell you my thought," Ryan added.

"Hmm?"

"What about if after another ten-minute break, let's say there might be thirty minutes or so left, as we'll probably go over somewhere. Let's say we all leave the platform and ask Nancy's people to finish as they see fit. That seems a Christian thing to do."

"That's interesting," Philo said. "The last word is often the loudest, and the one people remember. You are suggesting giving them the last word?"

"Yes!" I said.

"Do we tell them that's what we'll do?" someone asked.

"Look," Ryan said, not really answering the question, but contributing in a different way. "Let's not tell them. We know what we'll do though. It will be important to finish the evening on one page, not divided on some issue. When there is half an hour left, we'll give them fifteen minutes to give their final reflections. If they think that the last fifteen minutes is for us to bulldoze them back, then let them think that. But let's instead give over the last fifteen minutes for worship, thanksgiving and prayer."

Everyone was quiet for a while. Then Ryan said, "Everyone in favor of the program outline as we have discussed it raise their hands." Nine hands went straight up. The tenth hand was up within the following few seconds. It looked like we were decided.

"One thing though," I said.

"Yes?"

"Tell them about our plan for the last half hour. They take fifteen minutes, then prayer and worship. That's better."

"Let's leave that for the executive committee to decide," Ryan suggested. "The point though is—and we hope the televised version of this event will get this clearly—we are not trying to win an argument or put anyone else down. We're still all in it together. We are one in Christ."

"Before we close out," I said, "I need to tell you that my mother remains very sick. As a result, if I get any news of her deterioration, I might need to back out at a moment's notice. All your prayers for my Mum would be much appreciated."

"We also heard that your sister recently had a difficult birth," someone added.

"I doubt they'll be coming to the conference?" someone else asked.

"As well as the baby, Julie is looking after Mum," I said.

* * *

The day arrived. One hundred and fifty plus people filed into the PATS great hall. At 6.05 p.m. a hush fell over the hall. Ryan stepped up to the microphone. "For two days we have been enjoying seminars and workshops, lectures and panel discussions. The feedback I have been getting verbally has been very good," he said.

"Not entirely," I thought to myself. Some conference attendees were not pleased with the proceedings. Sad to say—some were struggling to understand what Philo and Deborah were saying. In some ways, I was not surprised and could hardly blame them, especially given the strong donor presence at our conference. It was my long-term experience of Africa while interacting with Philo that had helped me to understand. How could I expect them to get what Philo was at after just two days of conference? The context-dependence of the message that we were trying to communicate at this conference was making progress, at times, painfully slowly. It made it very hard to convince people who were not capable or willing to take a contextual view.

"Before we invite our first speaker for this evening we want to pray for them both. Following a special request, I am going to ask Professor Nancy to come up to the front to offer that prayer, and then to invite Philo," Ryan went on.

When Ryan said Professor Nancy, I almost jumped out of my seat. That was not a part of the plan! Why was he asking her? "Would she pray for Philo and Deborah, or curse them?" I asked myself. I managed to stay stuck to my seat so as not to make a scene. I was not the only person surprised by the choice of person to pray. Professor Nancy stood up and went to the front.

"Before I pray, I would like to say …." Nancy started speaking carefully into the microphone.

As she was speaking, Philo was beside me, looking rather nervous. I was really paying attention to Professor Nancy, and the amazing things she was relating (given the original reason for her having come to the conference), but seeing Philo out of the corner of my eye. Philo didn't really need anyone to come up to him, and give him a warm greeting as he was seconds from giving his presentation. That didn't deter an oldish American man with plentiful grey hair from approaching him, and whispering to him while Professor Nancy spoke. I looked at that older man, then I looked back at Professor Nancy. Then I looked back at him again. He looked familiar. I registered! It was Bruce, the same Bruce who had visited us years before when we were in Zambia. The pastor with the loud voice. He was whispering something to Philo. Philo was disconcerted, I think, as he was preparing himself to stand and speak.

Bruce came to me and whispered, "Good to see you fellows again," he said. "You remember me?"

"Yes, Zambia!" I whispered back.

"Good work!" he said, then he walked off again. Bruce had obviously heard of our conference, and come to attend the final event, the battle of Armageddon!

Here is what Nancy went on to say: "Something has happened that I never expected. I came to this event to knock sense into anyone who'd deign to be convinced by the things that Philo is sharing. Instead, I find myself seeing more of the sense of what Philo is trying to say. Hence, I am especially keen to hear Philo tonight, and privileged to pray that the Lord give him an exceptional eloquence." Nancy prayed along the lines of her statement. She shook Philo's hand as they passed, with him going to the microphone as she was returning to her place. Professor Nancy smiled. The hall was hushed. Differences in opinion at the conference had not been hard to detect. Many by that time knew that Professor Nancy had come to oppose the central thrust of the conference. While perhaps not convinced, she seemed to have been at least moved.

"Now here's my paper," Philo said.

"I am not one of those people who wanted to be a missionary when I was five or six years old," Philo said. "Not at all. That might have been the last thing on my mind at the time. But I was challenged while studying at an agricultural college. I asked myself, 'What am I going to do with my life? Am I going to use it for myself? Or am I going to give it to God, and to other people?' Implicit in that question was the sub-question, 'Would my life be of any value to anyone for me to give it out anyway?' By faith, I believed that it could be. In the end, I believe under God's guidance, I committed myself to working for God in the poor world. In those days, we still used to call it the Third World."

"I was twenty-three years old at the time. It was October 1987. I was doing teacher training, after finishing my undergraduate degree in agriculture. There was something peculiar about my calling. It was the kind of calling that seemed unusual at the time. This is because I felt called to give my whole life, or nothing. I did not feel called, or inclined, that is, to try out first what God wanted me for. Instead, I wished to commit myself for life, or not at all. That seems to be relatively unusual even today. I do not know why. Except, that is, it can put one at loggerheads with organizations. Organizations, such as mission agencies, have their own vision. They want people to fit with their vision. If you do not fit, then they put you aside. The organization wants to own the mission. The individual should fit-in with what the organisation is doing."

"The need for that one hundred percent life commitment seemed irrefutably clear to me. It seemed to me that it was the only logical course to follow. How could I be sure that God wanted me to have a happy first year, had I intended first to test my call? That is: what right has a slave of Christ to demand that he have a good time? Before God, I committed myself—to serve for life.

"What I found in Zambia was a surprise, if not a shock. From the information I had received prior to going there, I had the impression that missionaries and Third World nationals had a hand-in-glove relationship. Going to Zambia, as a teacher at a mission secondary school, I found out that things were different. There were deep differences and misunderstandings separating European missionaries, and development workers, from nationals. Levels of mutual understanding seemed to be very low. This meant that co-operation was low. Zambians seemed to co-operate mostly to get money from foreigners. That seemed to be far from an ideal situation.

"I am sure I was not the only one to have realized this. Nevertheless, it seemed God was giving me a singular task—that of facilitating communication and understanding between African people and Europeans. I was to do that while serving in Africa. That is the role that I continue to endeavor to fulfil today. So then, maybe I have two roles. One, to serve the African people according to the word of God. Two, to communicate back to my own people and help them to understand how they might serve more effectively. It is this latter that has brought me here.

"In my younger years, I used to be advised frequently and sometimes passionately, that I should listen carefully to what is being said and done amongst the people with whom I was working in the majority world, as it is commonly nowadays known. I have done that now for over twenty-eight years, with considerable dedication. That dedication has included my remaining single, and my learning to speak three African languages fluently. In the course of twenty-eight years, I can recount two occasions in which missionary bodies I was working with *put me aside*. Thus, I have had to continue alone, without any mission-organization support. I am grateful to my supporters for remaining faithful despite this.

"I was led to believe in those days that should I devote myself to faithfully listen to majority-world nationals, then I would find listening ears ready to receive what I had to share, back in the West. I am grateful today that part of that anticipation is coming to fruition," Philo paused. I was amazed at the attentiveness of the whole crowd.

"You will appreciate," Philo went on, "that I am obliged to be honest in what I communicate and faithful in how I communicate it. I feel incredibly privileged to be in the position that I am. It seems to be a very rare position. Very few Europeans have done what I have. Very few even have a close working knowledge of non-European languages. That does seem incredible given the rate of globalization in today's world. Frankly, it is shameful for the West. It shows how inbred we are. It seems then that by God's grace, I have uniquely privileged eyes and ears. It would be a travesty if I were to fail at this point to communicate the truth to people like yourselves at this conference. I consider myself obliged to share truth from experience of what God has laid on my heart. Truth-telling is to me more important than man-pleasing, especially when the ones to be pleased are the wealthy and powerful. I will endeavor to share the truth as God has made it known to me."

At that point, an amazing thing happened. I think it caught Philo unaware. It certainly did me. People started applauding. I think Philo had never experienced such before. He had to stop. I saw tears well up again in his eyes. The atmosphere of the conference was electric. It was unbelievable!

"Powerful people seem to want to shut me up on this," Philo went on. "I guess that arises from 'vested interests.' The older people who want to shut me up are those who, let me say, had vested interests, portraying themselves as successful without following any vulnerable mission principles. They are the people who have come back from the majority world with grand stories. They consider themselves to have done a fantastic job in mission, beyond criticism, on the back of foreign money, and with little or no use of an indigenous language. How can they now respond to people who point to the limitations of those two things—outside languages and foreign money?

"I do not stand in judgment on the ministry of other people. God can choose to use people in different ways—including using English with one's pockets loaded, if he so wishes. There are, however, some very good biblical reasons and logical reasons why that kind of ministry has limits. These are the reasons we want people to understand. Then those who have begun to grasp them can also begin to invest in vulnerable mission. I do not want to go into these reasons in detail now. We have been doing that over the last couple of days. It is simply a fact: that an in-depth grasp of what someone is saying requires hearing them in their own language.

Also—that people bought by your money are tempted to be dishonest to protect their livelihoods."

Applause for Philo's presentation was loud. When the applause died down, a murmuring remained. What was the murmuring? It seemed to indicate less than 100% support for Philo.

CHAPTER 30: ON THE STANDARDS OF EDUCATION

Philo finished short on time. Deborah was the next speaker. Within two minutes she was on stage and beginning her presentation.

"As you may have caught, Philo believes in vulnerable mission. No, allow me to re-phrase that ... he *practices* vulnerable mission in villages in Holima. If you were to visit the area where Philo lives, you would see him riding a bicycle or using local transportation. If you rode with him, you would hear him speak the most intimate language of the people, Striden. For sure, you would not see him hand money to a local pastor for an upcoming project. He does have a household of orphans, in case you think he doesn't believe in integral mission. However, he does not artificially raise the kids' status in the village. In other words, the kids go to the same school as their neighbors, drink the same water, and don't live off gifts from foreign visitors coming and going. You won't see them in better or more clothes than the kids around them."

"Does this seem backwards or harsh to you? Do you think he should wear two hats—the gospel hat and the social action hat in order to lift the people in his village into a better economic standing? If he does, he will need to become a donor, which will make him powerful in their context. It is highly possible, in this case, that Philo will be sought after for his power rather than the power of the gospel. Remember Romans 1:16, 'For I am not ashamed of the gospel, because it is the power of God that brings salvation to everyone who believes: first to the Jew, then to the Gentile.' Philo may never tell you, but local Christian leaders have asked him to leave, unless he was willing to serve as a conduit of money. What they meant was that the gospel part of his ministry was not desirable or needed, but the material provision part was highly appreciated. I think Philo has concluded that he would rather be pursued for his faith, even if that means being persecuted, because he refuses to be a source of funding. Perhaps now the concept of vulnerable mission is clearing up for you. The word 'vulnerable' is not a descriptive word for those receiving mission workers, but rather defines the posture and approach in which the missionary serves."

As Deborah spoke, I glanced at my watch. I had not heard anything from Julie. I was concerned for Mum. When Philo saw me looking at my watch, he leaned over. "Any news on Mum?" he asked. I shook my head.

"What Philo wants you to know, and I can certainly validate its benefits, is that missions should be done in a vulnerable way. How does he define 'vulnerable?' Philo talks about 'vulnerable' in this way: a Christian mission's work carried out by Europeans using the languages and resources of the local communities. Now, if I were to be dogmatic and say you need to learn the heart languages and use local assets, you may want to push back. But, if I ask you to identify all the communicational, relational, and strategic benefits of using the people's heart languages and using their local assets, I have no doubt you would identify many benefits. Based on an activity I did with one of the sessions in this conference, they identified fifteen critical benefits. So, why would anybody in their right mind refuse to make a full-hearted effort to use the heart language and utilize local resources? What might we be compromising if we don't make the effort? What is it about today that makes us choose short-cuts? That is a conversation for another time."

"Allow me a few minutes to make my plug for an increased movement of people from the West who are willing to NOT do missions on the back of their money and their own beloved languages. God commanded people to love him with all their heart, soul, and might. Does it not make sense that people should get to know this God, and thus love him, in a language that both relates to and derives from their heart and their worldview? When I have been in the homes of people who use a trade language or second language for business or for a more global platform, I have never heard them argue in that second language in their homes. As we all know, arguing for a viewpoint takes a certain amount of passion and commitment to that viewpoint ... that is why family members switch to their heart language when in a heated dialogue. The same happens when they have a heartfelt, joyful conversation around a meal. The point is that their heart language is their passion language. This sounds like the perfect language to both learn about God and love God with all their heart, soul, and mind. Based on Philo's definition of vulnerable missions, it will take vulnerable missionaries who are willing to learn and use the heart language to make disciples of Jesus. If we desire this outcome, maybe you will need to be someone like that!"

"What about using local resources? Philo doesn't have a ministry that is growing in leaps and bounds due to driving it on the back of foreign money and foreign languages, but the fruit that he does have will last until eternity, because people around him choose or will choose Jesus for the sake of Jesus, for the sake of the scars on Jesus's back, rather than the money in Philo's pack."

"Now that ought to make people think," I said to myself as Deborah was speaking. Deborah had a gift for connecting with people.

"Philo has been accused of being over confident. But maybe he knows something we don't because he knows the heart language of the people, and has to build relationships on mutuality, rather than sponsorship."

"I challenge you this week to open the Scriptures and discover for yourself if Jesus and the disciples approached their apostolic work through vulnerability, or through positions of economic power and linguistic superiority? Maybe you first have to decide if Jesus even knew what he was doing, or if we have found better ways? Maybe, maybe not."

* * *

Applause was even more raucous for Deborah's speech than it had been for Philo's. Philo was invited back on to the platform. Deborah and Philo sat on the platform facing the audience, as Ryan took the microphone. We would have expected, in a conference, that Ryan would have immediately discussed what was said, then to have asked for questions. Instead he said, "Let us pray."

We all joined together in saying the Lord's Prayer. Then Ryan prayed for us. He gave thanks for the messages. Then he prayed that God would continue to guide us as we went forward. The TV crew continued to actively capture proceedings.

One of Nancy's group, a man called Ian, had been designated to respond to the presentations given by Philo and by Deborah. Ian, a slight man with wispy hair around a balding head, was heading up a charitable foundation working mostly in Nepal. Before walking to the front, I noticed him consulting with other members of Nancy's group. It seemed that whatever he was going to say, was going, to some extent, to represent the whole group. I thought to myself—that quite likely they had talked already in advance of the evening. From what Nancy had already said, it appeared that they had been very much moved by events as they had already unravelled before the grand finale, showdown, or battle of Armageddon, as Philo had called it.

People who opposed vulnerability in mission did so by ignoring or refusing contextual and linguistic factors. This conference was organized to be cognizant of things that some conventional mission efforts were ignoring.

I realized that such ignorance could not simply be overcome at such a conference. No matter what we said at the conference, a conference could not get people to the point of having an in-depth experience of a foreign reality. This was a depressing thought—but nonetheless true.

Issues needed to be considered at a level that conventional thinkers were conveniently ignoring. But how to do that, when "conventional thinkers" were all very convinced of the wisdom of what they were doing?

Ian struggled a little with a stammer. Generally, the stammer did not last long, but it could hinder him as he began a presentation. "De- de- de- dear ladies -s -s and -d -d gentlemen," Ian spoke, apart from his stutter, loudly and clearly. I had to admire people like that, who refused to allow their disability to get them down. "All -ll -ll of us -s -s here have had the privilege of partaking in this conference. It has been an outstanding experience. I- I- I- I can certainly say that on behalf of the twenty-one of us who came together as a group. We came out o- o- of concern that we put an end to a movement that was threatening to mislead and destroy. To -o -o destroy, that is, much mission and development work; but w- w- w- we have come to be better informed. We might not agree with them, but we applaud advocates of vulnerable mission. Many of you w- w- w- w- will have heard lively d- d- d- d- discussions. I at this point want to …."

As Ian spoke, my phone rang. I had left it on in case Mum's condition should deteriorate, requiring me to travel quickly to Washington State. It was Julie. "Dave," she said, "Mum is deteriorating. She wants to see you tonight. It might be your last time with her." Five minutes later I was in a taxi, on the phone doing my utmost to book a flight to get me to Washington State that very evening. I found Julie and baby Philo there with Mum. Thank God, Mum was stabilising.

* * *

About two months later I was travelling, trying to chase down a project in Holima. I found I had free time near Philo's home.

I sent him a message. "Meet tomorrow if you are free?"

He sent, "What time, where?"

Instead of sending him an SMS, I decided to call him. I am glad I did, as the call revealed something to me about Philo that I would not otherwise have known.

It was about 8.30 p.m. when I called Philo. It was raining even in Deja where I was. It was quite likely raining much more at Philo's home—that being at a higher altitude. "Hey, what if we meet at the Rosy Hotel at 11 a.m. tomorrow, English time?" I suggested.

"Sounds good. Let's do that," he responded.

Talking to Philo, I noticed that he was puffing. "You're puffing," I said to him. "I'm walking," he answered. "What!" I exclaimed, "8.30 p.m. in the dark, and it's raining!"

The only good reason for walking round at night in Philo's home area was to go to a funeral. Other nights, there was a serious risk of being mugged and robbed, or being mistaken for a cattle rustler and attacked. So why was Philo walking around in the dark at that time of night? I was asking myself. "Where are you?" I asked him.

"Going to meet a girl." he responded. "She's not yet back from a school trip. I can't leave her to walk home in the dark, so I and one of my lads have gone to meet her where the bus drops them—at the school gate."

"Hope you'll be alright," I said.

"We'll be fine," he answered. I was often amazed at Philo's dedication to the children he looked after at his home.

The term "hotel" may be misleading for native English speakers. In Holiman English, what in the UK might be called a rough shack, can be called a hotel. A few banana leaves for shade and a bench cobbled up under it, with a woman making a cup of tea, equals "hotel." The place Philo and I were to meet at was not quite such a shack, but certainly neither was it a hotel in the UK sense.

It was good to see Philo again. We sat, and chatted. Philo had some letters in front of him that he had picked up from the post office.

"Good letters?" I asked him.

"Yes," he said. "One from my parents. Just general home news. They write every week. They might miss me," Philo added, "but they tell me that they know more of what is happening in my life than that of both my brother and my sister!"

"How come?" I asked.

"I write them every week."

"You mean, you've kept that up all these years?"

"Yes. They may not have grandchildren through me, I may not be nearby, but what I can do out of gratitude to my parents, is to keep them informed. A parent-child bond is important!"

"That helps me to understand why you don't get any opposition from your family for what you are doing here, because your actions clearly show that you love and are concerned for them."

"How was your walk last night?" I asked Philo, remembering the previous evening's phone call.

"All's well that ends well," he responded.

"What's that supposed to mean?"

"After getting rained on and plastered in mud," he said, "well, that's all quite an experience."

"So, why?"

"I love those kids," Philo replied. "And I love loving them! When you have kids who have been orphaned, they know how to look at you and ask, 'Do you really care about me? Or are you in this for money or something?' One way to show you care is to go out on a wet night in the mud and rain, at risk of being mugged for your money, to wait for them after a school trip—even if other parents don't do that." We sat quietly as I thought about that.

"The other letter," Philo said, "is from a couple in my home town in the UK. I was with them before I ever came to Africa. That is, an evening when I was telling people about my calling, on a rainy night. They were once linked to Mali. They have evidently been following my news all those years. They are now both retired. He has multiple sclerosis. They have felt led to make a financial contribution to my work, so they have written a letter to inform me of it!"

"So, you were walking around late last night," I continued, bringing us back to our previous night's phone conversation.

"Yes, doesn't happen too often, fortunately." I was always intrigued by Philo's relationship with his adopted children. So, I paused to let him speak some more. "You know, Dave," he said "if you take in children—you've first got to love them 200%! That doesn't mean to love them like you would a British child. They are very different. Hugs, presents, and playing with them won't work. But you have to show you are constantly concerned for them. Orphan children especially don't tell you, but in their heads they are thinking, 'if he was my *real* dad he would—x, y, z.' You can't always please children. But you can show you are committed to them. I am."

Philo's words made me think of the discussion that often goes on in Western missionary circles about how to help orphans. Here was an answer from Philo. Relate to them as far as you can as would their own people. Then commit yourself totally. That's not short-term mission or a handout, but a life given in commitment, living with them in an African village. Children are not a short-term project.

As we chatted, some men walked over from the adjoining table. They started engaging Philo using the Striden language. Philo rattled along with them. I picked up some of what he was saying. It was about girls and women. It seemed to be also about universities, at this time spreading like wild fire around Holima. The discussion was about morality. I guess you could say it was about gender issues.

"Welcome, Dave," one of them said to me in English.

"*Erokamano, amor*," I said in return, airing my best Striden.

"*Warwaki kendo*," which could be translated as "welcome again," he said in return. Both men said "*oritiuru*," that could be translated as goodbye, said to more than one person, as they left. More literally Philo had explained to me before, the origins of "*oriti*" are similar to those of "bye" in English. The latter, "God be with you," for the Striden *oriti* should be taken as meaning "God (i.e., *Nyasaye*) to keep you."

"Where are they going?" I asked Philo.

"They are going to campaign. Campaigning for the next election is in full swing, and they are promoting a local candidate," Philo told me. That was, to me, another slightly ominous warning about the oncoming election. All did not seem to be well this time around.

"Can I tell you what happened last month?" Philo asked me, being apparently less concerned at that time about the election than I was.

"Go for it!"

"Schools are on vacation, so the children are at home," Philo told me. "In the vacations, what we do is to have the younger children read a book. I provide the book. They read in Striden or in Swahili. Unless I am going to do it myself, I need an older child to read with the younger children. Two of the older children were around. Both girls. They were doing other things. I called one and told her 'go and read with the children.'"

"I'm busy sweeping up leaves," she responded.

I saw the other one. "Help the younger children reading," I told her.

"You know, Dave," Philo added, "that politeness in African languages does not need wordiness as it does in English. For example, in British English one says, 'would you mind, please, passing me the salt,' to be polite. In Swahili, one can just say '*nipe chumvi*', and it is just as polite. Or even '*nipe*', while pointing at the salt. Anyway, the latter said, 'I am busy right now.' Indeed, I could tell that she was busy. She was doing this and that, in and out of the kitchen. I reiterated to her; 'I want you to read with the children, and now!' She said yes, she would. Five minutes later, she wasn't doing it."

"What was she doing?" I asked.

"I don't know, but she was busy," Philo said. "Suddenly I was in a very dodgy situation," he added.

"What?" I said. "How come?"

Philo laughed a little "You don't get it, do you?" he said. "It was about my authority."

"But they were both busy and doing necessary things?"

"Right—as a Brit. As a Brit, I should have been satisfied with that answer. Then either I read with the children, or they disperse and come together again later, whenever one of the girls is ready."

"Right!"

"But that's not good enough for an African household. The situation reminds me of that of King Xerxes and Queen Vashti. I don't know what you'd do in the US, but that was too strong an affront to my authority."

"Oh!" I said.

"Now I need to be careful," Philo added, "because the children I keep are, if you like, typical village children. Quite simply, I need to prepare them for life in their own community. In other words, in that sense, I need to be the African father, preparing them to meet their African husbands. If I train them not to pay attention when a man tells them what to do, I will not be doing them any favors. If I act like this, then ten years later, I will see a load of divorce cases. Then also, younger children will realize that they don't need to do what they are told, and so it will go on."

Philo was telling me something about his domestic situation at home, where he was living with twelve local orphan children.

"Okay, Philo," I said, "I think I am following you. In European terms, the girls very politely gave very good reasons for not doing what you asked them to do. What you are saying though, is that because they did not jump, so to speak, at your word, if you don't respond to that in an appropriately harsh way, you would in effect be spoiling the children? Spoiling the children would mean that you would mess up their lives in the days ahead, especially girls with their husbands to be?"

"You've got it, Dave. In fact, I didn't really care. I could easily have let the children off from their reading or postponed it. Both girls responded to me very politely and were genuinely busy. The last thing in my heart was that I should punish them. Both are at the end of their teens." I waited to hear what Philo was going to add to that statement. "It felt clear to me that my British me was condemning my African me for being so harsh," Philo said. "That means also, that if Europeans were to know in detail how I looked after children here in Africa, they might well condemn me for it," he added, "which is why when Europeans come with their big ideas and big money to boot, things can get difficult. In fact, after thinking for a moment, I know of cases where Europeans getting involved with young people around here has ruined the young people's lives."

"You've pointed to some kind of wrong there, Philo," I said. "I am aware that one of the favorite exploits of European young people in Africa is coming to visit orphanages. Young girls from European countries, for I think obvious reasons, especially like doing this. They come full of what they call love for the children. They'll dote on them, cuddle them, give them money, food, and other gifts. Of course, while they are around they'll be looking out for horrible men like you who punish children unnecessarily! If they find them, then they'll condemn them, and quite likely tell the donors about them, and the donors are almost certainly their fellow Europeans." I paused, then went on, "It seems like a circus! The orphanages must be able to take that kind of thing in their stride in order to get money. The children must get to know that the rules change when there are foreign visitors around. Then they have to change back once they have left, so as not to ruin or spoil all the children! The visitors are most likely trying to insist that *their* standards be kept, which they see as trying to improve the care at the orphanages. Meanwhile, Africans will be warning the children not to listen to the foreigners."

"The terrible thing in Holima," I added, thinking that this was probably what Philo was thinking, "is that the educational system trains children to listen to white foreigners more than they do to their own people. This happens in many ways—not least because the whole educational system is in English."

"You know, the West thinks it is so clever," Philo said. I nodded, wondering what else was coming. "Some people seem to think that if we Europeans get responsibility for children in Africa, like in Holima, then we should give them better European values. But," he added, "how is that going to help them to function in their own communities? The West thinks it is so clever and so ahead on gender issues, that everyone else should also be liberating women. I don't see it. I mean—yes, that discourse is here in Holima. The media, government and even churches are, in theory, all for liberation of women. But at the same time—people here really like their women. They like them the way they are. And the women like to be liked! Am I here to liberate their women so as to give them problems with their husbands and families?"

Philo was obviously working through some things. "Take the children I have at home. One girl is a tomboy. She doesn't mind taking on the boys. A boy beats her up at school. What kind of reward is that? I end up telling her, 'Fear the boys or you'll get into trouble!' A boy is not going to accept being bullied by a girl in school after all. Not in front of his mates!" Philo added. "Then at home, I would really like to treat some of the children who stay with me as if they were white children. You know—to respect them as respect would be considered appropriate in the West. But I must not! I could easily end up destroying them. Neighbors and visitors will, in finding them too familiar with me, consider them to be disrespectful. I have to be like an African father, like it or not, and even at times be, I suppose, what we sometimes in England might call 'bossy'! I mean, in simple terms, I don't say 'please'! Bossy would in European English be a derogatory term. So, then I have to live in a way that to the West is derogatory!"

"Hmm," I said, and made other empathic noises.

"Why don't people in the West see that?" Philo presented his question.

When Philo talked like that, it really made me think there should be no alternative in serious mission work to living with the people one is reaching, and doing so in a vulnerable way. The way Philo lived constantly had him hit up against issues that the rest of us would otherwise never even think about. We might not even imagine that such issues might exist!

"So, tell me more?" I asked Philo. Philo was quiet for a while. In fact, it was a particularly long pause!

"I trust you a lot, and you are a very good friend to me, Dave," Philo said. "You have been in Africa for a long time. Almost as long as I have." (Philo didn't like me to forget that he arrived a few months before I did!) "But you live like a white man. That's okay. I don't condemn you for doing so. But it means that there are things you will not understand. Why should I try to explain what I know you won't understand?"

"Okay," I agreed.

"But," Philo added, "the more I have to make adjustments to the culture, the easier it becomes for western people to not understand and even to condemn me. And that hurts."

CHAPTER 31: ELECTION VIOLENCE

"There are some things," Philo said, "that people who are in the West simply know it is their job to condemn. Those no-brainers. Those things that people say when they are laughing. Those that deserve condemnation-by-default. Things that are so obviously wrong that one simply knows that one is on sure foundations when one condemns them."

"Like what?" I asked Philo. He paused again.

"Like oppression of women," Philo said. "The West is so certain that it is important to stand up for women's rights. I'm not saying Africa has got it right and the West has got it wrong, or the other way around. I happen to think that Africa has got it more right. Reality is though, that issues will not just disappear. Men and women living together is not easy. You shouldn't mock people who do it differently. You should respect them for it. Like the Bible does, but modern man sometimes doesn't."

"You left the conference before it ended," Philo said to me, changing the subject to discuss our recent time in the US.

"I know," I said.

"Sorry to hear of your mother. She later made a very unexpected recovery, I hear?"

"Yes, a miracle!" I said. "A miracle, that is, in the African sense of something amazing, not a miracle in the sense of something that broke the laws of science." I knew that the term "miracle" was used very differently in European English than it was in African English.

"So how is she now?" Philo asked.

"I guess she is living by grace, even more than the rest of us," I said. "She said to me the other day—she's of the age at which she could die any time, and no one will be shocked at all if she should suddenly go. She has a strong faith, and is, of course, always glad to get news of little Philo, Julie's baby.

"How did the rest of the conference go?" I asked.

"Very well!" he said. "One thing really intrigued me. It not only intrigued me, it made me laugh out loud! You know, we were a lot of Europeans at the conference ...."

"Yes, that's true," I agreed.

"Someone from Nancy's group wanted us to ask the opinion of the two people who came there, one from Holima, and one friend of Deborah's from Cambodia, who did not speak English. They asked me and Deborah to translate questions they asked of them. When they did so, I looked Deborah in the eye. I think she was thinking what I was thinking. We both translated, her into Cambodian, and me into Striden. Then we translated the answers given back into English for the rest of the conference to understand. Both of us, Deborah and I, gave answers that agreed with what we had been saying, and not with those who were disagreeing with us. Then someone shouted out; 'For all we know, you are just translating the way that you want to!' I laughed! People didn't seem to get why I laughed. I had to explain to them: 'You are right. Whenever you hear anything from outside of the native English world, there is always a translator. Even if the translator is a national—someone is making decisions on how to get local discourse into English. That person is the one determining the agenda. Until you learn the language fluently, and with respect to that culture, you will never know how the person is translating.' Dave, I felt that little discourse made such a good point. But, to be honest, I am not sure how many people got it."

After thinking about it, I responded; "Quite likely, not many. If any did, your point is valid though. We tend to treat translators like machines engaging in mechanical processes. In reality, they are inevitably extremely creative."

"So, so much about my Mum," I said to Philo. "How about your family?"

"They're doing great," Philo responded.

"I'm hoping my mother or sister will soon come out on a visit."

"Do you miss them?" I asked him.

"You can't beat family," Philo responded. "When someone from one's own family gets in touch it is always special. Like a letter from one of my siblings really makes my day. It is painful to have them go through difficulties, while here I am thousands of miles away, not able to help out. In addition—worse than that—because I have become so used to this way of life, communication can go askew, in a way that I end up not understanding. That's a problem. I greatly love family back in the UK, but when I try to express that love—it doesn't always work."

* * *

"Dave, I must go," Philo told me.

"What's up?"

"Baby dedication!"

"Doesn't sound so thrilling," I thought to myself. I told him as much.

"Guess you've never experienced a really African baby dedication then?"

"Didn't know Africans dedicated their babies," I responded, a little naively.

"All could be revealed," Philo added. "Why don't you come along?" I looked at my watch. We had time available. I agreed. Before long, we had paid our bill and started walking off.

"It would be fun if Julie's baby could be here," Philo suggested.

"So that he could also be dedicated?" I asked.

"Yes," Philo said. "Let's call her!" Moments later, there was Julie on the end of the phone. "We're going for a baby dedication, so we thought of you," said Philo.

"Who's we?" she asked.

"Dave's here too," Philo said. "How's little Philo?" he added.

"He's better and I'm better," Julie said. "We took him for a routine check-up yesterday. You can allay any fears you had about him being handicapped due to the stressful circumstances leading up to his birth. He is fine."

"Hi there." That was Derek's voice.

"Hi Derek," Philo said. "Hey—thanks for calling your baby Philo—I feel really important—dad!"

"That's alright, my son," Derek said, chuckling. "For years we never knew we would have a child, but now, we have a very special little boy. I tell you what else," Derek added, "aside from the baby—Julie has found her vocation. She used to try her hand in business, but never got on very well. Her visiting you was like a pilgrimage, through which she found her gifting—helping other women in their walk with God."

At that point Dave took the phone from me. "I tell you one thing Philo was wrong about," I said to Julie and Derek (they had two phone lines). "Philo might have been right to say that short-term visitors shouldn't pretend they understand everything through talking to nationals using English. And, they shouldn't be coming to learn how to use their money. But he was very wrong on another score. Philo reckoned that a short visit to Africa wouldn't change people. But both Richard and you, Julie, were changed by your visits."

"You're right," Philo said to me, "I was wrong on that one — certainly in Richard's and Julie's case."

Before the end of our conversation, Julie gave us news on Richard. "Funny that you should call today," she said, "because Richard and his wife were here yesterday."

"Really?" I said. Philo was close enough to hear what was being said.

"He's still all out for his business, but you might not believe what I am about to tell you," she added.

"What?" I said.

"Richard is providing a lot of the funds for the work that I am doing with the women. And he's the chair to our board."

I couldn't imagine what would be so exciting about a baby dedication. We walked up the hill. Moments later there I was, perched on the back of Philo's bicycle. The comments by people we passed seemed to be more incredulous than ever; "A white man riding a bicycle," was bad enough. Here now was a white man riding a bicycle, carrying another white man on the back of his bicycle! From the voices of the children on the side of the road, one would have thought it should simply never have happened. "There is a white man riding a bicycle carrying another white man on the back!" children on the side of the road announced noisily all along our route.

A few miles and a few hills on, we began to hear the sound of drums and cymbals. That sounded a little familiar. I had heard those sounds before. In the distance, I noticed a large crowd of brightly-dressed people dancing and singing, parading up the road, moving away from the direction we had come.

"What's going on, Philo?"

"That's the baby dedication."

"What!" I had lived in Africa for so long, you would have thought I might have realized that a baby dedication would be other than one might expect in the USA. Still, it was not easy for the connection to sink in. One does not associate a baby dedication with such a brightly-colored and raucous crowd parading up the road to the beat of drums and cymbals! When we caught up with the crowd, Philo brought his bike to a halt. We walked behind. I can't say that we "danced" with them exactly, but it was hard not to have one's body jig a little to the rhythmic beat of the drums.

"Any excuse for a party," I thought to myself as we followed the crowd. Many of our colleagues were sweating profusely, totally engaged in their expressive bodily moves, following every beat of those drums. We must have walked a mile with them. Before long we were snaking along village paths, before arriving at what seemed to be just a "typical" homestead. Only the canvas shelter from the sun, set up outside the house, marked it apart from other homesteads in the area. The canvas offered us some welcome shade. Philo parked his bicycle. We were directed to sit at the front. It was as if we had instantly become some of the star guests. "Had we been at a more European-oriented church, they might even have changed the program on our behalf," I thought to myself. Less likely here though. This indigenous church was following ancient rituals. They didn't need our help. They weren't even looking for our money. They knew what they were doing. I was amazed to discover, with some explanations from Philo, that they were basing what they were doing on the Old Testament! "Had I just been driving down the road," I thought to myself, "I wouldn't have had a clue as to why on earth these people were dancing crazily in front of me. When with Philo, though, all is revealed!"

Philo commented: "If you were to invite these people to engage in some development project, then quite likely they would seem the slowest and most uneducated in the whole bunch. To get them to move would require generous foreign donations. Yet, when they are doing their own thing, they are not only active, but proactive, and very capable of organizing and running a complex event."

I looked at Philo. He seemed to have given his all. There he was. His home of origin was thousands of miles away. He was single. He had launched himself into identifying with that community of Striden people. What even to me remained the strangest of things, to him had become normal.

Now, he wasn't dancing with them. Too much of a British upper lip for that. But he was accepting them, and they were very accepting of him.

* * *

"Dave—it is amazing!" Julie stated, seeming to shout down the phone.

"What is amazing?" I asked her, hoping that she would tone down a bit. "I have just seen a documentary broadcast by the BBC, a half-hour long report on the conference! Philo and you are on it. It has come out very positively. It is challenging people to be vulnerable to the majority world!" I immediately sent an email to Philo. An hour later he watched the same program. He wrote back, telling me that it was mind-blowing. Later that day, I was able to watch it myself. I could see why Julie was so excited. There were some very good accounts of some of the issues we had raised at the conference. I was able to read various reviews of the same on Facebook, and at different places on the internet.

I phoned Richard. "I've done something meaningful to help you," Richard said, very cheerfully.

* * *

A few weeks later I had an unexpected phone-call. It came just as I had emerged from the bathroom. My mind was miles away. I picked up the phone.

"Good morning, Dave," said the voice at the other end. That was a giveaway. It was 7 p.m. in East Africa. Why was I being greeted with "good morning?" This was evidently someone calling from a distance, presumably the US. I did not recognize the voice, although it was evidently Holiman.

"Who am I speaking to?" I asked.

"My name is Ralph Ochieng," said the voice.

"Aha," I thought, "probably a Striden judging by the name." Although—a good number of Striden names are also used by adjoining non-Striden tribes, especially when they have married Striden ladies, so I could not be sure.

"Are you the David Candomble who was taking part in the recent conference at PATS, the Pennsylvania Theological Seminary, that is?"

"Yes, that's me!"

"Look, Dave, I am planning to travel to Holima shortly. I would like to sit down with you and talk with you if that is possible? Do you have any time available in the next four weeks?"

I had to think quickly on this one. Holiman people usually want meetings with white people for money. I wasn't interested in such a meeting, just to be told about their needs.

"What's on the agenda?" I asked. "I don't have any money to give out!"

"I want to discuss the conference," the voice said. "I was really challenged by it. Could you make the time?"

"When do you have in mind?" I asked. "Be more specific."

"Would in around ten days' work for you?"

"You are coming to Holima?"

"Yes, in a week."

I looked at my calendar. We made a date. We were to meet at 10 a.m. in Deja.

I reflected on the conversation. I had agreed to have the meeting. That was contrary to some extent to my better judgment. Holiman people, as it seems many around the world and not only Holima, have been landed in the very difficult position whereby they always seem to be looking to the West for money. They have adopted European languages and education, yet for Africans at least, these don't work for them without contributions from European donors. So, they are constantly hamstrung by their need for money to do what they are told by their own governments and school teachers, i.e., agents of the West.

I recalled someone telling me that European languages being imposed onto European people was basically no different to ways in which European languages are imposed onto Africa. Ironically—Europeans themselves can end up thinking that way. We link other people's experiences to our own, after all. No European country, however, has ever appropriated someone else's distant language while rooted in a very different culture, in order to try to make it their own, as was happening in much of Africa. Now, I was asking myself, how was I going to be able to engage with the Striden person who was coming to see me? If he wasn't looking for links to the West, help, finance, scholarship, opportunity to study, then what did he want? What was the point of agreeing to have a meeting that would commit me to sitting with someone like that for an extended period, just to be asked to do what I could not agree to do? I was not about to add to the disastrous contemporary situation by becoming yet another European charitably reaching out to the poor African ... digging the African deeper and deeper into a dependency hole. Even I, although much more Philo, was trying to bring some light into this situation. In short, I was concerned about the likely outcome arising from my meeting with Ralph.

While I was contemplating all those issues sitting at home, I had another surprise phone call. It was also from the USA. "Hi, you must be Dave?" said a male voice with an American accent.

"Yes, speaking."

"I am a friend of Professor Nancy's," said the voice. "She advised that I contact you."

"It is great to hear from you," I responded.

"Look," said the voice, "I am due to visit Holima in two days' time. Professor Nancy has advised me to talk to you, and a fellow called Philo. I believe you are in Holima? Do you think it might be possible for us to meet?"

"What would you like to talk about?" I asked.

"I understand you can help missionaries do better projects," the voice replied, "so I'll be looking for advice."

"When will you be free to come?" I asked. After I had said that, my computer started making a noise. It was a Skype call, coming in as I was on the phone. I turned off the volume so that it would not disturb my phone call with America. My American correspondent mentioned two possible days for us to meet, and one of those was the very day when I was due to meet with Ralph! The other day I was not going to be free. Now there was a thought; should I have him join Ralph and me? I could hardly invite him to come and then spend all my time with Ralph. But, that conversation had just so many unknowns for me. Ralph was the one with the agenda. What if Ralph was mostly intent on looking for money? Would it be good for this visitor to hear him explain why he needed money? I could be giving Ralph privileged access to an American, which he could turn into a "donor-friend." … I had to make a quick decision. "Look, the second day you mention I am not available, but Philo might be. I can give you his number if you don't already have it, so that you can contact him. The first day you mention, I am available. In fact, I already have a meeting arranged. It will be with a Holiman who is living in the USA. I am sure he won't mind if you join us. You are welcome. Do you want to do that?"

"Sounds good to me," was the response.

"Look, plan your travel, tell me where to pick you up. You need to arrive in Deja at 9.30 a.m. at the latest, then we'll go and wait for my colleague Ralph, so that we can meet with and discuss with him together."

Having completed that call, I initially forgot all about the person who had called me on Skype. It was a couple of hours later before I remembered. I put down my pen and looked at Skype on the computer. The surprise call was from Rickson, none other than Philo's one-time headmaster in Zambia at Mubantu mission! I knew Philo had some contact with him, but he had never got back in touch with me. Try as I might, I couldn't get him on Skype. Fortunately, he had left me a message: "I've been watching the documentary made of your conference. Philo and yourself have done an impressive job at that conference. Glad someone is speaking up. You may not even remember me? I was Philo's headmaster at Mubantu. I have talked to Philo, and encouraged him. Sorry we couldn't connect. Best wishes and keep up the good work."

I never did manage to communicate further with Rickson.

Ten days later, the day arrived for Nancy's friend to come. He flew into Deja. I was there to pick him up at the airport. "Hi, my name's Steve," he said as we met. He was short and, well, round. "Steve seemed to be the wrong name for him!" I thought to myself. It did not fit with his appearance. That was a strange thing to think, but those were the thoughts that came to mind as I met with him. "He ought to be called something like 'Rolly,'" I thought to myself. As that thought was going through my head, following a brief pause after announcing his name, he added, "but people call me Rolly, so you are free to call me Rolly!" That was just amazing! I had never met the man before, and I am sure no one had ever told me that he ought to be called Rolly; I guessed that ought to be his name, and I got it right! I didn't tell him what I had just been thinking. It would seem wrong to say that he looked like a 'Rolly,' when it would be implying that he was short and tubby and kind of spherical in shape, as indeed he was.

"My name is Dave," I introduced myself, although certainly he already knew that.

Rolly was a talkative kind of fellow, jovial, to say the least. He talked about Professor Nancy: "Professor Nancy told me about you folks," he said, "that you know how to do mission. You can help other people do it better. I doubt it though. No-one tells me what to do! I've been doing this work for decades. I accepted to meet with you. Don't expect to convince me of anything," he emphasized.

"Well," I thought, "that was a good conversation opener." Engaging with Rolly didn't really require conversation openers however. He was one rolling conversation; a conversationalist in the best sense of the word.

I thought about telling him about the sensitivity of the engagement we were entering. Then I thought better of it. Let him take it as it comes. If it's a typical conversation with a Holiman, then certainly no way will I convince Rolly of anything that he hasn't already known after decades of project work, presumably in Africa.

"How is Nancy getting on?" I asked.

"A whirlwind," he said, "blowing people in multiple directions. You won't convince me easily, but whatever it was you said and did, it made her think."

I almost coughed and spluttered after hearing that. "Well, we did something!" I thought to myself. It seems that our recent trip to the USA was having ongoing consequences.

"What's your take on the security situation?" Rolly asked me. "The US government is warning tourists to avoid Holima," he added.

"I'm not sure," I responded, "but I have word that my bosses are thinking they may soon be pulling us out of the country. There is something that I heard," I added. "A widespread comment in this area is that if we don't win, it'll be war. 'Why has no one from this tribe ever been president of Holima, and it's been over fifty years since independence?' people are asking. Those are provocative comments."

We took a *tuk tuk* (motorized rickshaw) to our meeting place with Ralph. It might have been Rolly's first time in a *tuk tuk*. I don't know. He seemed to enjoy the ride. We reached the café, and sat down. Five minutes later, Ralph turned up.

"*Oyawore*," he said to me. That Striden word could be translated into English as "good morning."

I responded "*oyawore*." That much Striden I could deal with.

"You must be Dave?" he said.

"That's right," I said. "And this is Steve, otherwise known as Rolly."

"Good to meet you also, Rolly," Ralph said. Ralph, in his forties, was very black, as was typical of Striden people. He was of medium build, and had a remarkably friendly and amicable face. This contributed to his general amicability, appearing to be always serious, and simultaneously always friendly.

"We're very glad to meet you, Ralph," I said, after we had sat around a table and completed talk on the weather and Holiman politics. "Please fire away. Tell us what's on your mind."

"You are aware that I am to talk to Dave about Philo?" Ralph said, looking at Rolly. He didn't want to dominate the conversation for nothing, and he hadn't been expecting the two of us.

"Yes, I am aware. Carry on, I'm looking forward to hearing you," Rolly added. That was a diplomatic response from Rolly; I had not told him what was on the agenda, as I hadn't even known myself. I did have to think myself at that point—what more genuine an introduction can someone get than to have a third party tell you about them? Rolly was indeed privileged. I only hoped that he would be able to understand, and that Ralph had sufficiently positive things to say, as he evidently knew Philo very well. Unlike the rest of us, Ralph knew Philo as an African, through having related to him on and off in Holima for many years. Ralph told me that Philo is a long-term friend of his. His conscience convicted him that he ought to look for an opportunity to speak with me. He started telling me his own story.

"As a young man, after finishing secondary school, I felt led to serve God," Ralph told me. "I was searching for opportunities to do so. My mother was a strong believer. She worshipped in an indigenous *Roho* church. One day,

Philo visited that church. He was accompanied by a group of students. They were theological students. This was a part of Philo's efforts to help the students understand and value their own heritage. He took the students to learn from this very indigenous, African-led congregation. My mother was obviously impressed. It isn't every day that a white man visits an indigenous church. This white man was also speaking the Striden language. That Sunday she came home very enthused."

"My mother told me that the same white man, who of course was Philo, was also teaching a Bible class. The class was held just about five miles from home. It was at a place that I could reach by bicycle. The following week I went along to that class. Philo was true to his word. He was there at the church. He arrived very early. On the dot at 2 p.m. the class started. We were about four students. Philo guided us in a discussion about the Bible for about two hours. Our discussion terminated in a short test. Just multiple choice, not that difficult. The idea was that it should test whether we were paying attention in class. For the class, we sat on simple benches in that bare church building. Philo didn't seem to mind.

"That was the beginning of what turned out to be a long relationship that continues to today. It has been to me a very challenging relationship. Also in a sense, a very frustrating relationship." Rolly and I sat listening attentively.

"In due course, Philo and others in the leadership of the school made me aware that they were looking for teachers. I was very interested in filling such a role. That was when I began to realize something of the difference between God and *Nyasaye*. You know, *Nyasaye* is the name we Striden people give to God. My mother was very much a follower of *Nyasaye*. Her interest in *Nyasaye* took her in the direction of Striden traditions. Now I was to discover, at least in so far as that college was concerned, that believing in God required doing things in a European way. One could even say—in an American way. I was to be sent to an American-run college to be taught in English, on how to share God's word with Striden people in the middle of Africa! I should not sound too shocked though. That is the system in Africa. Africa imitates America. My interest in *Nyasaye*, now translated as God, that took my mother to devoting herself to service in an indigenous church, was now taking me towards America! I think the day that I visited that college was my first day ever to see a computer. It is quite something, when it is one's interest in God that proves to be one's introduction to computing."

"Anyway, that aside, there is a reason I want to tell you about my experiences. Philo was, if you like, pulling me in one direction. That is, like that I should be preparing myself to serve local churches. But there always seemed to be more powerful forces pulling me in another direction. That is, of doing things in such a way as to please Americans. Philo's way seemed to lead to a life of poverty. The other way led to prospects of wealth, prosperity, and even fame."

"Hang on," I responded to Ralph at that point. "Didn't Philo introduce you to these American people?"

"Yes, he did. Whether that was an error I do not know. In a way, though, he had little choice. That is to say—in Holima all roads of theological education lead to America. Had Philo not had a cake to offer, a scholarship to study at an American college, he might soon have had no followers at all. I doubt if I would have stayed on. Philo was trying to help us to function in the Striden church. But he himself was not a Striden. His language skills were then more limited than they are now. How could he teach us how to function in Striden churches? What Philo was doing was however very challenging to me. That's really why I have come to talk with you. I want to encourage you, Dave, to keep doing what you are doing! I am telling you because Philo would not tell anyone else, if I was to tell him just how much many, many, of us appreciate what he is doing. Philo challenged me, more than any other white man I know. He continues to do so today. Then, you may ask, why I have not responded to his challenge? Why am I living in America? Why have I chosen to follow God instead of *Nyasaye*? The answer is, because my family and friends would not allow me to do otherwise. Was I right to allow my family and friends to so influence me? Who knows? I am not sure. Many of us are in such a position. Our people need money. Everyone else, it seems, except for Philo, encourages me to follow money. That pressure is hard to stand up to."

"That came to me very quickly at the theological college. I would have had to be super-human not to be influenced by my colleagues there. I mean— we all respected Philo enormously for what he was doing. I think he was probably the only white staff member at the college ever to have been very fluent in an African language. And, Philo was fluent in three! He lived more and more like we do. So, we really respected him for doing that. But at the same time, we despised him for it. He could not hope to understand us, so why try? By bringing things to an African level, he was interfering with our own aim. We students wanted to learn English and to get an education that would be recognized in the USA. Philo was interfering in and endangering that process. That is why at the end, he was asked to leave the college; because he valued what was African."

"While at the college, I was seduced. I don't mean by a girl, although around that time I married. I mean: I was seduced by a church. By some friends, that is, who were also students, to join their church. They encouraged me to give up on my affiliation with Philo. They told me it wasn't going to take me anywhere. They didn't believe that Philo would be around much longer. I mean—his project, teaching African pastors theology in their own languages without using foreign money, could not work! He was going to leave me high and dry, they told me. I allowed my colleagues to take me away from Philo. What I am saying to you again now though is—*actually Philo was right*. I was wrong to abandon him. But I had no choice. Family pressure to follow the American route to prosperity was just too enormous."

Rolly interrupted at that point. "Ralph. It is really good to hear you say these things," he said. Rolly was, like many Americans, good at affirming people. "That does explain something. When folks come to America from Africa, they are often very intent on making money. You are helping me to realize that we don't need to blame them—they can be under enormous pressure from their extended families."

"There was a break-in at a shop in my street," Rolly added. "We have one African family in the street. Some people suspected them. You can see why—that desperate search for money. It wasn't them though. It turned out it was the son of a school teacher who broke in. His dad was also his teacher, and it was driving him crazy. He's the one who started the rumors about the family from Africa." Rolly paused. "Sorry. Carry on Ralph," he said. "I do talk too much."

"That's okay, Rolly," Ralph said. "Philo was gracious. He valued me as a person. Even after I had resigned from the program. Philo valued me and our friendship. You could say that he valued me as a son. He continued to visit me. Because I resigned from the Bible teaching program that Philo was involved in, of course, I lost the scholarship. I had only completed one year out of four of my studies. The church I had linked up to was American. They eventually got around to giving me another scholarship to study. I went back to the same college, but this time full-time, and not formally linked to Philo. He still allowed me to live in his house at the college for the first six months. You could say that students walked all over Philo—appreciating him while undermining him. He didn't seem to mind. He carried on doing what he was doing. He carried on speaking the truth and he carried on caring for us, especially me. I feel I still have a very special relationship with Philo."

"Are you here to tell us that Philo is a wonderful fellow, or are you telling us that he has important things to say?" Rolly interrupted at that point. That American abruptness would have thrown many East Africans. A good period of living in the US presumably helped Ralph to know how to respond to it.

"Both," he said. Rolly had meant his question well, although of course he was open to misinterpretation. Ralph went on. "From thereon, I was a friend, who was no longer dependent on Philo's charity, or his lack of charity." I laughed a little. I guess Philo isn't known for his generosity. "I had abandoned him, but he kept on building bridges of friendship."

"How did he build bridges of friendship?" Rolly asked, in his cutting but jolly way. Rolly was trying to get at the heart of the question that had brought him: was Philo providing privileges for Ralph arising from his connections with the West? That is standard practice for many Europeans. Philo claims that some European people should be relating to African people other than on the back of incentives arising from their connections to the West. Was he himself doing this?

"He would visit me. Even when I was far away in Tanzania, Philo would make occasional long trips to come and spend some days with me. Once I was back home, still over an hour's cycling from his home, Philo would keep appearing on his bicycle."

"How often?" Rolly asked.

"Maybe every six months, maybe once a year," Ralph said.

"So, did he give you anything?" Rolly asked Ralph. I wondered if I ought to be embarrassed at having invited Rolly join our conversation, something of which Ralph, of course, did not have any advance notice. In response to this question, Ralph laughed. He understood something at least of what Rolly was driving at.

"His time," Ralph replied, "and that's all," he added. "And," he added a few seconds later, "if you think that Philo never used English with me, you would be right. Philo does not talk with Africans in English. He uses their languages."

"How come, then, that you got to live in the US?" Rolly asked.

"Not due to Philo," Ralph answered, "like I have said. I bypassed Philo. I was seduced by other churches. I was seduced, in other words, by their money. Their offers were irresistible. That's why I have made the effort to come here now and talk to you and Dave, and I ask you to treat what I say with sensitivity; Philo is right, but we Africans can't afford to be seen to agree with him. Even now that applies to me. We're in a fix. A fix, as a result of which in public we have to agree with the things that in the long run will kill us. Hence, I say: please listen to Philo, and take what he says seriously."

At that point, Rolly leaned back in his chair. Had he a pipe, I imagine he would at that point have lit it. It seems the gravity of what Ralph was saying was still sinking in. If Ralph was right ... then a lot of changes were needed in ways in which Europeans worked with Africans. Rolly had told me he would not easily be convinced of what we were saying. Could he be convinced at all? Would our conversation with Ralph convince him that "development" and "mission" were best done using African languages and resources? That was asking a lot.

As I was thinking about that, Rolly asked another question. "What should we do with our money?"

"Who are you asking," I responded.

"Both of you," he said.

"I don't know," Ralph said, "but your Western money is killing us." When he had said that, and I was trying to think what to add, Ralph's phone rang. He spoke to someone using Striden. He cut the phone. He stood and said, "Must go."

He shook our hands. No amount of pleading on our part could convince him to stay any longer. "*Oritiuru, nyaka adhi,*" he said. That could be translated into English as *good bye (plural), I must go.*

Ralph walked off. I was left with Rolly. "There you have it," I said, "From a local! Make of it what you will …." We sat in silence for a long time, before we picked up conversation again, on different, albeit related, topics.

* * *

I am forced to bring this account to a rather abrupt ending.

Shortly after my meeting with Rolly, I had a phone call from Philo. We talked about the security situation in Holima. Philo was concerned for me! "Living in town could be dangerous," he told me.

"What about you?" I asked him.

"I'll be okay," he said, "God willing. People know me around here. Towns and cities are the hot-spots in election times," he emphasized. "Remember, my home is far from any big towns."

Various provocative statements by opposing parties in the run up to the election were to have many international bodies withdraw their personnel. My own organization was one such. A few weeks later, I was given twenty-four hours to pack my bags, get to Imbigen, and take a flight to the USA.

In the USA, I have had three months during which I have had very few other assignments. With the approval of my organization's director, I have used some of that time to complete this account. The idea of writing it is one I had already discussed with Philo in some depth, hence I had Philo's part of the story in hand. This ending is abrupt, because Philo is not around for me to discuss with him how better to bring the story to a close.

Philo's village is located in the area of the strongholds of opposition to the ruling government. He has stayed behind in his village home to do his best for the children in his care. Since leaving Holima, to date three months later when this book is going to the publishers, there has been limited communication, as the tension associated with the election has severely reduced internet availability. I am not even sure if Philo is dead or alive.

* * *

The following, mostly more academic books, have also been written by the author of this novel. Readers interested in the issues raised in this novel are encouraged to acquire copies to further explore its key themes:

Harries, Jim. 2011. Vulnerable Mission: Insights into Christian Mission to Africa from a Position of Vulnerability. Pasadena: William Carey Library. Paperback. ISBN-10: 0878085246; ISBN-13: 978-0878085248

Harries, Jim. 2011. Three Days in the Life of an African Christian Villager. Sandy, Bedfordshire; Authors online. Paperback. ISBN 978-07552-1383-2

Harries, Jim. 2012. From Theory to Practice in Vulnerable Mission: an academic appraisal. Oregon: Wipf and Stock. Paperback. Kindle edition. ISBN-10: 1610979443; ISBN-13: 978-1610979443

Harries, Jim. 2013. Communication in Mission and Development; relating to the church in Africa. Oregon: Wipf and Stock. Paperback. Kindle edition. ISBN-10: 162032878; ISBN-13: 978-1620328781

Harries, Jim. 2015, Secularism and Africa: in the light of the Intercultural Christ. Oregon: Wipf and Stock. Paperback. Kindle edition. ISBN-10: 1625647700; ISBN-13: 978-1625647702

Harries, Jim, 2016, New Foundations for Appreciating Africa: beyond religious and secular deceptions. World of Theology Series 9, World Evangelical Alliance. Bonn: Verlag für Kultur und Wissenschaft. Paperback. Kindle edition. ISBN-10: 1498294456; ISBN-13: 978-1498294454

Harries, Jim, 2017, The Godless Delusion: Europe and Africa. Oregon: Wipf and Stock. Hardback. Paperback. Kindle edition. ISBN-10: 1532614985; ISBN-**13:** 978-1532614989

www.ingramcontent.com/pod-product-compliance
Lightning Source LLC
Chambersburg PA
CBHW071231230426
43668CB00011B/1388